LOCKE ON PERSONAL IDENTITY

¶MP

PRINCETON MONOGRAPHS IN PHILOSOPHY

Harry G. Frankfurt, Editor

————————————ꟼMP————————————

The Princeton Monographs in Philosophy series offers short
historical and systematic studies on a wide variety
of philosophical topics.

LOCKE ON
PERSONAL IDENTITY
Consciousness and Concernment

Galen Strawson

PRINCETON UNIVERSITY PRESS

PRINCETON AND OXFORD

Copyright © 2011 by Princeton University Press
Published by Princeton University Press, 41 William Street,
Princeton, New Jersey 08540
In the United Kingdom: Princeton University Press, 6 Oxford
Street, Woodstock, Oxfordshire OX20 1TW

press.princeton.edu

Revised edition, and first paperback printing, 2014
Paperback ISBN 978-0-691-16100-6

Library of Congress Control Number 2013957469

British Library Cataloging-in-Publication Data is available

This book has been composed in Janson

Printed on acid-free paper. ∞

Printed in the United States of America

1   3   5   7   9   10   8   6   4   2

I DO NOT KNOW HOW WE MAY EVER KNOW, IN RETRACING THE RECORD OF THE PAST, WHERE OUR RESPONSIBILITY LIES, AND WHERE WE HAVE MERELY UNDERGONE RATHER THAN ENACTED, LIVED THROUGH RATHER THAN LIVED, AN EVENT, UNLESS BY THE SENSE WE HAVE OF ABIDING IDENTITY WITH THAT PAST SELF, OR EVENT, OR ACTION PERFORMED, FOR BETTER OR FOR WORSE. I FIND, FOR MYSELF, THAT THIS SENSE OF IDENTITY WITH PAST SELVES IS BY NO MEANS CONTINUOUS. IT IS RATHER AS IF AT TIMES I WAS PRESENT IN MY LIFE, AT OTHER TIMES ABSENT FROM IT ALTOGETHER; ESPECIALLY AFTER MY CHILDHOOD. THE MIND WHICH WANDERED AMONG THE STRUCTURES OF MOSSES AND LYCOPODIA IN THE LABORATORIES OF DOWNING STREET WAS CERTAINLY MINE; BUT NOT THE GIRTON UNDERGRADUATE WHOM MANY OF MY CONTEMPORARIES SEEM TO REMEMBER BETTER THAN I REMEMBER MYSELF; NOR THE NEUROTIC BOHEMIAN WHO SO DISHONOURABLY PROLONGED HER RESIDENCE IN CAMBRIDGE, WHICH SHE DARED NOT LEAVE BECAUSE SHE DID NOT KNOW WHERE ELSE TO GO, BY THE TRAVESTY OF A MARRIAGE.

—KATHLEEN RAINE[1]

N'ATTENDEZ PAS LE JUDGMENT DERNIER. IL A LIEU TOUS LES JOURS.

—ALBERT CAMUS[2]

---

[1] 1975: 74. Raine is referring to Downing St. in Cambridge. As far as I know, she knew nothing of Locke's views on personal identity.

[2] 1956: 111.

Contents

Preface

THIS BOOK BEGAN as a paper in the autumn of 1994, when I reread Locke's discussion of personal identity in book 2, chapter 27 (2.27) of his *Essay concerning Human Understanding*, three hundred years after its first publication in 1694, and realized that I'd been misrepresenting him in tutorials at Oxford for fifteen years. I should have inferred this from the fact that Michael Ayers's chapter on personal identity in volume 2 of his book *Locke* (1991) had a year earlier seemed bizarrely peripheral to the subject I thought I knew and in any case taught. Reading Ayers is one of the things that sent me back to Locke's text—for better or for worse.

I set out to correct my errors in writing (with some enthusiasm, because I knew many held the same false views as I had), but was sidetracked early in 1995 by an invitation to give a lecture on the notion of the self in the 1996 Wolfson College lecture series "From Soul to Self."[1] This led to an attempt to work out the necessary conditions of self-consciousness[2] and, eventually, to a book called *Selves:*

---

[1] This resulted in "'The Self'" (1997) and "The Self and the Sesmet" (1999b).

[2] This appeared in abridged form in "Self, Body and Experience" (1999c) and forms part 3 of *Selves* (2009).

An Essay in Revisionary Metaphysics. In the meantime, Marya
Schechtman's important brief observations about Locke in
her book *The Constitution of Selves* (1996: 105–9) and Udo
Thiel's outstanding article "Personal Identity" (1998) were
published, and I came to feel that the paper would be largely
superfluous. Don Garrett's paper "Locke on Personal Identity, Consciousness, and 'Fatal' Errors" (2003) later took
some further steps in the right direction.

Appointment to a professorship at the City University
of New York Graduate Center in 2003, and the faith of those
who appointed me that I was a historian of philosophy, in
addition to being a philosopher of mind, together with their
expectation that this would be manifested in some way in my
teaching, brought me back to Locke's account of personal
identity. It also prompted me to prepare a modern English
version of 2.27 of the *Essay* for pupils on both sides of the Atlantic (see appendix 1). When I first read Locke, I sometimes
found him hard to understand, even though I was a classi-
cally educated native speaker familiar with English literature
from the fourteenth century on.[3] Few who read Locke today
have such a background, and many are not native speakers.

The Day of Judgment plays an important part in Locke's
discussion of personal identity, but those who—like myself—
don't believe in God or the Day of Judgment shouldn't think
that their place in Locke's theory makes it less interesting.
All questions about the Day of Judgment can be converted
into wholly earthly questions about one's overall moral status or being as one stands here now, firmly on the ground,
with no prospect of going anywhere else. The idea of the

[3] I came to Locke late in the day—some time after sitting the Oxford
BPhil examination in 1977. One of the three exam papers I sat for that
degree contained a question about the difference between *man* and *person*
that I answered without knowing that it contained an implicit reference
to Locke's theory of personal identity.

Day of Judgment is, no doubt, a fantasy, but the fundamental idea behind Locke's discussion of personal identity doesn't depend on it in any way, although he was bound to pose the question of personal identity in eschatological terms in the intellectual context of his time. In particular, the respect in which his conception of personal identity (or moral identity) is intuitively natural is independent of the story of the Day of Judgment. It's helpful, when reading Locke, to bear in mind Camus's advice: "Don't wait for the Last Judgment. It takes place every day."[4]

This book, though short, may be judged to be too long. One reason for its length is that I restate points in different ways. Some ways seem more helpful to some readers, others to others. It may not help to note that it can be said of Locke's chapter, as "it can be said of many a book, *that it would be much shorter if it were not so short*" (Kant 1781/7:A xix); nor is it any justification that this book is a trifle next to the tens of thousands of pages that have been written on Locke on personal identity. If it were to lead to a reduction in the number of false things that are written about Locke on personal identity, that would be another matter; but also, no doubt, a vain hope.

This book may also be judged to be more difficult than it is, because of the respects in which it departs from patterns of interpretation of Locke's views on personal identity that have become entrenched. There are of course many points of connection with other recent writings on personal identity—by Johnston, J. L. Mackie, Parfit, Shoemaker, Snowdon, Wiggins, and Williams, to mention some I know—but I have concentrated on Locke's text.

I'd like to thank Max de Gaynesford for providing the book's epigraph. I'm most grateful to Michael Ayers, Kathy

---

[4] 1956: 111. Camus had no religious beliefs.

Behrendt, Ruth Boeker, Aaron Garrett, Don Garrett, John Greenwood, Stephen MacLeod, Rae Langton, David Rosenthal, David Wiggins, Gideon Yaffe, and, particularly, Michelle Montague and Udo Thiel, for their reactions to larger or smaller pieces of this material, their reading recommendations, and other suggestions. Among my students on both sides of the Atlantic in the years 2004–2006, I would particularly like to thank Joe Krohn, Peter Langland-Hassan, William Tone, and Rosemary Twomey. I'm further grateful to Udo Thiel for directing me, late in the day, to Edmund Law's *Defence of Mr. Locke's Opinion Concerning Personal Identity*, which I've transcribed from the original 1769 edition and included as appendix 2; and to Mark Johnston (and more distally Dan Garber), for alerting me, even later in the day, to the relevance of the doctrine of mortalism, or more particularly *thnetopsychism*, the view that the mind or soul dies when we die. This doctrine was held by many Christians at the time, including John Milton. It's also endorsed by Locke, or so I will assume in this book, and is one of the underpinnings of his radical claim about personal identity.[5] One reason why Law understood Locke, no doubt, was that he (Law) too was a convinced mortalist or thnetopsychist.[6]

---

[5] The crucial underpinning remains in place even if Locke is not a mortalist. See p. 102 below.

[6] To get an idea of the case for Locke's thnetopsychism, read the opening of his book *The Reasonableness of Christianity* (1695). See also Nuovo 2002 and Ball's very useful summary (2008: 119–26). The mortalist doctrine was perhaps most vigorously expounded by Richard Overton in his book *Mans Mortalitie* (1644; republished in an expanded version as *Man wholly Mortal*, 1655), whose title page announced it as "A Treatise Wherein 'tis proved, both Theologically and Philosophically, that whole Man (as a rationall Creature) is a Compound wholly mortall, contrary to that common distinction of Soule and Body: And that the present [i.e. immediate] going of the Soule into Heaven or Hell is a meer Fiction:

I would also like to record a philosophical debt to J. L. Mackie, in whose company I first encountered Locke. Although Mackie never supervised me, we were colleagues at University College, Oxford, for a year in 1979–1980, and I'm very grateful to him both for the example he set as a philosopher and for equipping me, almost single-handedly, through his writings (especially his *Problems from Locke*, 1976), to teach the wide range of subjects I was called upon to teach at Oxford after a mere six months as an undergraduate in philosophy and three years of a very narrowly focused graduate career.

Finally, I would like to thank Ian Malcolm of Princeton University Press, for his patience when it seemed that this book would never be finished, Leslie Grundfest, also of Princeton University Press, for her expert production, and Joan Gieseke, for saving me from a number of errors at the copyediting stage. I'm also most grateful to the British Academy and the Leverhulme Trust for awarding me a Senior Research Fellowship for the academic year 2009–10. I wasn't awarded the fellowship specifically to finish this book, but it turned out to be a necessary part of the work I had applied to do.

When I cite a work, I give the first publication date or estimated date of composition, while the page reference is

---

And that at the Resurrection is the beginning of our immortality, and then Actuall Condemnation, and Salvation, and not before" (1644: title page). As Ball remarks (2008: 100), Overton wasn't attacking religion in rejecting what one of his supporters called "the Hell-hatch'd doctrine of th'immortall soule"; he was agreeing with the mortalist Milton in *Paradise Regained* (1671: 4.313): "Much of the soul they talk, but all awry." There is a rich discussion of some of the issues raised by mortalism in Johnston 2010: chap. 1.

to the edition listed in the bibliography. I mark individual paragraphs of 2.27 of Locke's *An Essay concerning Human Understanding*, "Of Identity and Diversity," with "§." When I quote, I mark the author's emphases in **bold italics** and my own in plain *italics*.

Preface to the Paperback Edition

In this paperback edition, which supersedes the hardback edition, I've corrected a number of typographical errors and made a number of other changes in an attempt to increase clarity. I've also made a few substantive revisions. On p. 44, n. 5, for example, I've deleted a quotation from Descartes that doesn't support the claim I make there about him, replacing it with one which (I believe) does.

There is a more significant revision on p. 122, prompted by a insightful review of the first edition by William Uzgalis (*Notre Dame Philosophy Reviews*: http://ndpr.nd.edu/news/28700-locke-on-personal-identity-consciousness-and-concernment/). In the first edition I wanted to emphasize the point that Locke's main focus, in giving a theory of a person's 'forensic identity,' was on the actual human case. My phrasing led some readers to think that I held two views I certainly don't hold (see e.g. page 37 note and page 82): [1] the view that Locke's theory of personal identity, correctly interpreted, needn't—and doesn't—accommodate imaginary cases like the case in which cobbler and prince swap bodies; [2] the view that it doesn't really matter to Locke that his account of personal identity should be able to accommodate imaginary cases like the cobbler/prince case.

LOCKE ON PERSONAL IDENTITY

—————————————————ꟼMP———————————————————

Chapter One

Introduction

It's widely held that Locke's account of personal identity, first published in 1694, is circular and inconsistent, and blatantly so. Locke, however, thought long and hard about the matter.[1] He discussed it extensively with friends and colleagues, and was a profoundly intelligent, generally very careful, and exceptionally sensible philosopher. He made no foolish error.

Why has he been so misunderstood? I blame certain influential commentators, in whose vanguard one finds one of the worst readers of other philosophers in the history of philosophy: the good Bishop Berkeley. Thomas Reid is also to blame, for although he is a great (and often funny) philosopher, and sometimes accurate enough in his renderings of the views of his predecessors, he enjoys mockery too much to be reliable, he's too free with the word "absurd," and his misreading of Locke's views on personal identity, which follows Berkeley's, is spectacular.[2] Bishop Butler is the other

[1] His central thought on the question was in place by 1683; see Ayers 1990: 2.255.

[2] Berkeley 1732: 304–5, Reid 1785: §3.6. Reid also follows Berkeley in mistakenly attributing to Locke the view that secondary qualities are in the mind (1764: §6.6). He makes many other such errors.

main reprobate, although the objection to Locke for which he is well known is not his, having been put by John Sergeant in 1697 and by Henry Lee in 1702, among others.[3]

History has designated Butler and Reid as the main representatives of the circularity and inconsistency objections, and their influence has been such that few since then have had a chance to read what Locke wrote without prejudice. The tide of misunderstanding was already high in 1769, when Edmund Law provided an essentially correct account of Locke's position in his *Defence of Mr. Locke's Opinion Concerning Personal Identity*. His intervention was, however, little noticed.

The extent of the misreading of Locke is remarkable. Edmund Law judged it an "endless" task to "unravel all the futile sophisms and false suppositions, that have been introduced into the present question"; he "endeavoured [only] to obviate such as appeared most material, and account for them" (1769: 36). If, however, one embarks on Locke's discussion confident that his view will not contain any glaring error, it becomes hard to understand how he can have been so misread for so long. For he makes his central point extremely plain, and he does so, it must be said, over and over and over again. To read the wonderfully fluent and imaginative text of 2.27 of *An Essay concerning Human Understanding* is to see how familiar Locke is with his material, how easy in exposition he is, how he has thought through the objections, and how much he's enjoying himself. Locke likes to vary his terms, and is sometimes loose of expression by modern lights, but not in a way that makes it possible for a moder-

---

[3] Butler 1736: 441. Sergeant picked up the objection for which Butler is known from a debate in which Robert South (1693) made it validly against a proposal by William Sherlock (1690). See Ayers 1990: 2.257, 269; Thiel 1998: 875–77, 898. Leibniz does not make it in his *Nouveaux Essais*, contrary to the initial appearance (c. 1704: 236 [2.27.9]).

ately careful reader to misread him in the manner of Butler, Berkeley, Reid, and many who have followed them.[4]

The following essay records my line of thought as I read and reread, and sometimes struggled with, Locke's chapter. I spend the next several sections introducing a number of distinctions that I believe to be useful, extracting some central notions for inspection—notably *person, consciousness, concernment*—before returning them to context. The discussion lacks a standard expository structure, and it's not meant to be introductory. I assume basic familiarity with Locke's text, and criticize other accounts of it only indirectly. I think that almost all the elements of a correct view of his theory of personal identity are now to be found in the writings of a few Locke scholars, among whom Udo Thiel stands out,[5] but misunderstanding is still widespread in the philosophical community as a whole.

The interpretative situation was hardly better in the eighteenth century, as just observed.[6] Law was honestly amazed that Locke had been so "miserably misunderstood"—that so many "ingenious writers" had been "so marvellously mistaken" about Locke's views on personal identity, and had engaged in so much irrelevant and "egregious trifling" on the matter (1769: 23, 21). Law cites, as an "extraordinary instance" (p. 22) of this trifling, the inconsistency argument that Berkeley gave in his *Alciphron* (1732), and for a version of which Reid later became famous (see p. 53 below).[7]

---

[4] Mackie sufficiently answers the Butler objection in *Problems from Locke* (1976: 186–87).

[5] See e.g. Thiel 1998, 2011.

[6] See Thiel 2011, chap. 4.

[7] "Many historians of philosophy, with all their intended praise, . . . attribute mere nonsense . . . to past philosophers. They are incapable of recognizing, beyond what the philosophers actually said, what they really meant to say" (Kant 1790: 160). "If we take single passages, torn from

The root cause of the misunderstanding, perhaps, is the tendency of most of Locke's readers to take the term "person" as if it were only a sortal term of a standard kind, i.e. a term for a standard temporal continuant, like "human being" or "thinking thing," without paying sufficient attention to the fact that Locke is focusing on the use of "person" as a "forensic" term (§26), i.e. a term that finds its principal use in contexts in which questions about the attribution of responsibility (praise and blame, punishment and reward) are foremost. No doubt it's natural enough to take "person" only in the first way, but this doesn't excuse the perversity of doing so when reading what Locke says, and says again and again. (The common mistake of thinking that Locke means memory by "consciousness" is, relatively speaking, a smaller mistake.) That said, Locke must also bear some of the responsibility for the misreading—a point addressed by Law in the brief appendix to his *Defence*.

---

their context, and compare them with one another, contradictions are not likely to be lacking, especially in a work that is written with any freedom of expression . . . ; but they are easily resolved by those who have mastered the idea of the whole" (Kant 1787: Bxliv).

Chapter Two

"Person"

THE WORD "PERSON" has a double use, both now and in the seventeenth century. In its most common everyday use, today as in the seventeenth century, it simply denotes a human being considered as a whole, a *person₁*, as I will say. Its next most common everyday use, which I will call the *person₂* use, is the one that allows us to say, of a single human being, "She's not the same person anymore," or "He's become a completely different person." When Henry James writes, of one of his early novels, "I think of ... the masterpiece in question ... as the work of quite another person than myself ... a rich ... relation, say, who ... suffers me still to claim a shy fourth cousinship,"[1] he knows perfectly well that he's the same human being (person₁) as the author of that book, but he doesn't feel he's the same person₂ as the author of that book, and we all know what he means, even though the notion of a person₂ is not a precise one. James is using the word "person" in the familiar way that allows one to distinguish

---

[1] 1915: 562–63. Typing "I am (I'm) not the same person" into an Internet search engine produces thousands of examples of this usage.

the person or self that one is from the human being that one is considered as a whole. His claim is that he no longer relates to his early novel in such a way as to feel that he—he who is here now in the person$_2$ sense—is its author.

The current everyday person$_2$ use of "person" is closely connected to the notion of personality, but we ordinarily think of personality as a property of a creature, a property that can change, and not as itself a thing of any sort; whereas when we use "person" to mean a person$_2$, we naturally take it to denote a thing or entity that isn't just a property. We take it to denote a persisting subject of experience, a self; we don't feel we're using the word just as a way of talking about personality, where personality is a mere property of a person$_1$. When people say, "She isn't the same person anymore," using "person" in the person$_2$ sense, they tend to feel that they're saying something more than merely that a person$_1$'s personality has changed, although they may also allow a sense in which this is all that has happened.

At the same time, we don't feel obliged to come up with clear identity conditions for these supposed entities, these persons in the person$_2$ sense. For while people sometimes look back to a past time and say categorically, "I'm not the same person any more," i.e. not the same person$_2$, they don't usually think there's some sharp dividing line between the person$_2$ in the past and the person$_2$ present now (except, perhaps, in rare cases, e.g. those that involve a radical conversion).

I think that the person$_2$ use of "person" gives us some useful insight into Locke's use of "person," because it's related, although it's not the same. A Lockean person, a *Person*, as I'll say, marking my employment of the term in his sense with a capital letter, is certainly not a person$_1$, because a Person doesn't have the same identity conditions as a person₁. A person₁ is simply a human being (a *man*, in Locke's terminology, in which "man" refers equally to male and female). It's a human being considered as a thing of such a kind that *same human being* doesn't immediately entail *same Person*. In §15, Locke famously and explicitly considers imaginary cases in which Persons switch human bodies: cases in which one has to do with the same *man* (human being) even though one doesn't have to do with the same *Person*, and, conversely, cases in which one has to do with the same *Person* even though one doesn't have to do with the same *man*.²

There is, moreover, a respect in which the identity conditions of Persons may be said to allow a kind of partial, piecemeal gappiness that is ruled out by the identity conditions of persons₁. Consider yourself both as a human being and as a Person, and consider the set of actions done by you throughout a single day a year ago. All those actions were and are actions of the *human being* that you are today. It may be, though, that only a few of them, or even only one, or none, are actions of the *Person* that you are today—on Locke's view.

---

² Although Locke says at one point that "the idea in our minds, of which the sound *man* in our mouths is the sign, is nothing else but of an animal of such a certain form" (§8), he doesn't hold that a man, i.e. a human being, is just a human body or animal. If we do indeed have immaterial souls, as well as bodies, as Locke standardly assumes, then a man or human being is made up of both an animal body and an immaterial soul. It is "not the idea of a thinking or rational being alone, that makes the idea of a *man* in most people's sense; but [also] of a body so and so shaped joined to it." See also §15: "*the body, as well as the soul, goes to the making of a man*," and §28: "there can ... be no absurdity ... to suppose, that the same soul may, at different times be united to different bodies, and with them make up, for that time, one man." See also §16.

If this seems peculiar, then it's useful as an expression of the special character of Locke's notion of a Person. It's difficult to grasp, at first, and I'll consider it further in chapters 9, 11, and 12. For now, note that even if (even though) there's a respect in which the identity conditions of Persons allow a kind of gappiness, there's also a fundamental respect in which they don't. For there is on Locke's (and most people's) view, for any thing x of any kind whatever, a fundamental respect in which x's existence must involve some sort of causal continuity over time, if x is going to persist over time. This is so as much in the case of Persons as in the case of anything else.

We have, then, a conflict. We have a respect in which Personal identity over time may be said to be a gappy thing, and a sense in which Personal identity over time must be a matter of genuine continuity. One way to put this is to say that although a Person must exhibit causal continuity over time considered as a *subject of experience*, there is a sense in which it need not do so considered as a *Person*.[3]

This may sound very puzzling indeed; I hope it will eventually become clear. There is, in any case, a *sense* in which the identity conditions of Persons permit gappiness, as compared with the identity conditions of persons$_1$. The same goes when we compare Persons with persons$_2$. For although the identity conditions of persons$_2$ are no doubt imprecise, they too—at least as they're ordinarily understood—rule out a kind of partial gappiness that the identity conditions of Persons seem on the face of it to permit.[4]

---

[3] Locke lays out the fundamental conditions of diachronic identity in §§1–3 of 2.27. He is perhaps not sufficiently clear on what is required to preserve Personal identity between death and resurrection. See chapter 20 below.

[4] In the case of people with dissociative identity disorder (once called "multiple personality disorder"), people in whom "different personalities"

Nor can a Person be assimilated to a person₂ if there's any suggestion that a person₂ is some sort of special "inner mental entity." For let [**P**] stand for a Person, i.e. an ordinary Lockean person such as you or me, considered at a particular time. We may then say that [**P**] consists, literally consists, ontologically speaking, of the following three components:

[**M**] a whole human *material* body

plus

[**I**] an *immaterial* soul,

if, that is, we have immaterial souls, a matter on which Locke is at bottom agnostic,[5] and (a more difficult idea)

[**A**] a set of *actions* (including thoughts and perhaps other experiences) both present and past.

We may say that this is what constitutes—literally constitutes—a Lockean person, a Person, in so far as a Person is rightly understood in a straightforwardly ontological way as a *thing* or *object* of some sort.

It is of course odd to include [**A**] as part of what literally constitutes a Person. This oddity is linked to the gappiness just mentioned. It's part of a persisting tension in Locke's use that one simply has to get used to. (This chapter, which introduces it, is likely to seem particularly difficult.)

A Person also has certain capacity properties, of course, capacity properties of the sort specified by Locke in his famous definition of *Person* in §9, which I'll consider in chap-

---

control the body at different times, it's assumed that the different personalities do not have a gappy existence, but continue to exist even when they're not in control.

[5] Locke agrees that "the more probable opinion is, that this consciousness is annexed to, and the affection of, one individual immaterial substance" (§25), but we should not rest too much on this.

ter 8. For the moment, we may say simply that a Person [P] considered as an ontological unit is [M] ± [I] + [A]:

$$[P] = [M] ± [I] + [A].$$

A Person is also and essentially

[S] a *subject of experience* of a certain sophisticated kind

—the kind described in detail in the definition of *Person* in §9. But the concrete reality of [P]'s subject-of-experience-hood, considered at any given time, will not amount to anything more than the concrete reality of its [M] component at that time, if materialism is true, or the concrete reality of its [I] component at that time, if we have immaterial souls (if "that which thinks in" us [§14] is in fact immaterial).

It will be necessary, later, to focus sharply on the [S] component of [P]. For the moment I'll say only that Locke takes the diachronic continuity of [S] as given, when he's trying to establish what Personal identity is.[6] It ought to be possible to note this point in passing, but the history of Locke scholarship makes it of crucial importance. For one way to characterize the central error in the interpretation of Locke's discussion of personal identity is to say that it rests on a failure to recognize this point, a failure to realize that Locke simply *assumes* the continuity of the [S] component of [P], the continuity of a subject of experience, the continuity of "*a* consciousness," in his count-noun use of the term "consciousness" (§23), even as he engages in dramatic thought-experiments, involving soul-jumping and body-hopping, when considering what might underwrite this continuity (what might

---

[6] In other work, I consider the proposal that subjects of experience are very short-lived things (see e.g. Strawson 1997, 2009). Here I assume throughout, in a Lockean spirit, that they are long-lived things.

"carry" it, what it might "reside" in).[7] The error consists in taking Locke's account of Personal identity to be an attempt to give an account of something he takes as given: the diachronic identity of [S], the continuing existence of the subject of experience, which can survive radical change of substantial realization. [M], [I], and [A] can all change, while [P] remains and continues, but [S] must continue the same, if [P] is to remain and continue.[8]

Locke, then, simply takes a continuing subject of experience [S] as given, and asks two questions. First, what does a subject of experience [S] have to be like to be a Person [P]? He answers this question with his definition of *Person*. Second, given an [S] who is a [P], how do we work out the Personal *identity* of [S]? He answers this second question, which is a "forensic" question about [S]'s responsibility and concern, by reference to his account of what he calls "consciousness."

Neither of these two questions has much to do with the traditional reading of Locke's discussion, according to which his difficulty arises from his attempt to give an account of Personal continuity in terms of "consciousness." Nor (therefore) do they have much to do with the "neo-Lockean" project of giving an account of personal identity/continuity in psychological terms. For Locke, working out the Personal identity of [P] is *not* a matter of working out the continuity conditions of [P]s

---

[7] ". . . should the soul of a prince, *carrying* with it the consciousness of the prince's past life ... " (§14); ". . . a vital union with that, wherein this consciousness then *resided* ... " (§25).

[8] In §7 Locke famously distinguishes "substance," "man," and "person," declaring that it is "one thing to be the same *substance*, another the same *man*, and a third the same *person*." But we need another term—subject of experience (= [S])—in addition to *substance*, and Person (= [P]), and *man* (= [M] ± [I]), if we are to lay out Locke's position clearly.

—i.e. of [S]s that qualify as [P]s according to the definition of *Person*. Rather, one starts from an [S] that qualifies as a [P] given its capacities, an [S] whose continuity is given and unanalyzed, although it is argued to be such that it can survive radical change of substantial realization, and one works out the Personal identity of that [S] by looking at the "consciousness" of that [S].

Again I fear this will seem unclear. I hope it will become clearer in what follows. Here let me repeat the point that it seems odd to line up [A] as a literal constituent of [P] on an equal footing with [M] and [I]. For one thing, it's far more natural to think of the actions that constitute [A] as *properties* of [P] rather than *constituents* of [P]. For another, if we consider [P] as present now, then [M] and [I] are also present now, whereas almost all the actions in [A] are in the past.[9] I think, nevertheless, that it's very helpful to line up [A] with [M] and [I] in this way, when trying to articulate Locke's position.[10]

Although a Person can't be identified with a person$_2$ understood simply as an inner mental entity of some sort, Locke's use of "person" (which I'm rendering with "Person") does share with the person$_2$ use of "person" its connection with the admittedly unclear notion of "the self," and Locke himself uses the words "self" and "person" fully interchange-

[9] They are for all that concrete entities with material ± immaterial being, just as [M] and [I] are; and [M] and [I] also exist in the past.

[10] Whatever the ultimate status of [A], as a component of a Person, a disembodied soul—i.e. [I] alone—is certainly not a Person, on Locke's view. He endorses the then widely accepted definition of "person" according to which a human person (a thing for whom the forensic question of Personal identity arises) consists essentially of "soul and body, not soul and body separately" (Boethius, c. 510: 11).

ably. Locke's use of "person" also shares with the person$_2$ use the odd property of being naturally used to denote a thing or object of some sort, and not merely a property of a thing (you and I are Persons, and we're not, we suppose, just properties or sets of properties), even while at the same time operating in effect as a term for something that we do take to be a property or aspect of that most paradigmatic of things or objects, a person$_1$ (a human being). Many terms have this kind of doubleness; consider "seamstress" and "carpenter." But the doubleness isn't so clear in the case "person$_2$" and "Person." In the case of "person$_2$," the property in question is personality, while in the case of "Person," the property in question is one's moral nature or identity, one's overall moral being; as I will try to make clear.

This flexibility or doubleness in Locke's use of the word "person" is relatively easy to grasp in historical context. It has, however, caused a great deal of confusion. This is unsurprising. It is confusing, inasmuch as it seems to move cross-categorially between a thing and a property of a thing, in a way whose coherence can be questioned.

More needs to be said. For the moment, the inclusion of component [A] among the ontological components of a person is enough to indicate the fundamental respect in which a Lockean person considered as a whole, i.e. a Person, isn't *simply* a normal temporal continuant, unlike a person$_1$ (and indeed unlike a person$_2$ as ordinarily understood). One might put the point dramatically, if in the end unacceptably, by saying that when it comes to your Personal identity or Personhood—when it comes to your being the particular Person you are, at any given time—there is a respect in which you are a different Person every day, and indeed every moment, in Locke's view. This is plainly not so given either the primary person$_1$ use or the less common but still everyday person$_2$ use.[11]

One way to put this, given the present symbolism, is to say that [S] represents the normal-temporal-continuant component of a Lockean Person [P], while [A] represents the component that can change from day to day. Thus,

$$[P] = [S] + [A].$$

We may add that

$$[S] = [M] \pm [I],$$

understanding by this that the subject of experience [S] is at any given time concretely identical with, i.e. wholly substantially realized by, some [M] ± [I], although the [M] ± [I] in question may change from moment to moment.
From

$$[S] = [M] \pm [I]$$

and

$$[P] = [S] + [A]$$

we can infer

$$[P] = [M] \pm [I] + [A]$$

—which we already have. And the tension in Locke's use of the term "person" can be expressed by saying that he defines "person" in such a way that [P] = [S] + [A] is true. The fact

---

[11] The notion of a person$_2$ is employed in many ways, and doesn't strictly rule out the constant-change view. There's also a use that allows for gappiness, as when someone says, "You had become a completely different person. Now (thank God—or unfortunately) you're back again, the old you is back again."

that some sort of concrete continuity is a necessary condition of Personal identity is contained in the [S] component; the [A] component introduces the element of gappiness. It remains to explain why there isn't a conflict between these two conditions.

I take it that Locke makes exactly these claims—so that I'm not being anachronistic, or playing with his text in some irresponsible way, or not really doing history of philosophy. Locke famously says that "consciousness makes personal identity" (§10); so if I can show that what he takes us to be conscious of, in his special sense of "conscious," at any given time, is our [M] ± [I] + [A] at that time, then the case should be made.

When Locke speaks of actions he is (as remarked) often concerned with conscious mental occurrences as well as larger-scale bodily actions. We could accordingly take the word "action," in his broadest use of it, to refer to any conscious mental going-on at all, or at least any conscious mental going-on for which one may be held to be responsible, as well as to more paradigmatic cases of action. We could do this although Locke does at one point distinguish action and thought (in §9, for example, he speaks of "action or thought"), and although he also regularly uses "thought" (along with "perception") in the familiar wide Cartesian sense to denote all conscious mental occurrences whatever (e.g. in §9). We could in other words use the single word "action" in an essentially Lockean fashion to refer to *all those things that are forensically relevant when it comes to considering a Person.* I think, though, that things like lusting after one's neighbor's spouse, or feeling a great impulse of love or pity, or hoping that someone will fall on his face, or wishing that one could remove someone else's pain and bear it oneself, must be numbered among the mental occurrences that are forensically relevant to one's Personhood, even when such things are completely involuntary; and although Locke's notion of an action seems able to extend to such unintentional things (because its basic meaning is "forensically relevant occurrence"), our ordinary notion of an action doesn't. So I'm going to introduce the count noun "experience" to cover all conscious mental occurrences, and speak of our *actions and experiences* as being what are forensically relevant when it comes to our Personhood.[12] Thus, [A] above becomes

[A] a set of actions and experiences both present and past,

and the outright ontological claim is that a Lockean person, a Person, consists of a whole material human body [M], ± an immaterial soul [I], + a set of actions and experiences present and past [A], where members of [A] are open to being thought of as properties, in the fundamental ontological order of things, in a way that [M] and [I] aren't.[13]

---

[12] Are conscious thoughts in our narrower sense of "thought" rightly called experiences? Certainly. All conscious mental goings-on are experiences, and conscious thoughts involve (among other things) cognitive-phenomenological goings-on, understanding-experience. See e.g. Strawson 1994: 5–13 and Bayne and Montague 2011.

[13] I'm putting aside doubts about the distinction between objects and properties, which I've expressed elsewhere (e.g. Strawson 2008).

Chapter Three

"Person ... is a forensic term"

THE WORD "PERSON" contains considerable opportunities for confusion, as we have seen. But help is not far to seek. Udo Thiel makes a crucial point when he notes the sense in which "person" is indeed a property term, a term for a *moral quality*, in Locke's text. Throughout the seventeenth century, he says,

> "person" most commonly referred to an individual human being: it was simply a term for the individual human self. But in some philosophical discussions "person" referred to a particular aspect, quality, or function of the individual human being.

This use of the word derived from Roman law, in which "'persona' simply referred to the individual human being in so far as he or she stands in a relationship to legal matters," and was therefore what Locke calls a "forensic" term.[1]

J. L. Mackie often reads Locke well, and he's right when he says that Locke's theory "is ... hardly a theory of per-

---

[1] 1998: 868–69. To be a person is to be an entity that is legally liable. That is why impersonal entities like commercial companies are, legally speaking, persons. For a flawed but highly suggestive historical account of various different uses of the notion of a person, see Mauss 1938.

sonal identity at all, but might be better described as a theory of action appropriation" (1976: 183). This, after all, is exactly what Locke says himself. Mackie is not completely right, though, when he goes on to claim that "Locke seems to be forgetting that 'person' is not only 'a forensic term,' appropriating actions and their merit, but also the noun corresponding to all the personal pronouns," for Locke is not forgetting this. He has chosen to use the word "person" in a less common but time-honored way, which, for all that it is forensic, can still be supposed to "correspond ... to all the personal pronouns." One might say that he blends the thing use and the property use as follows. He takes human subjects of experience; he then considers them specifically in respect of their moral being or "identity." He then takes this way of thinking of them—as *subjects-of-experience-considered-specifically-in-respect-of-their-moral-being*—as delivering a special kind of object or entity: a person, i.e. a Person, in the current terminology.

As before, it's worth comparing this thing-and-property-blending use of "person" with thing-and-property-blending words like "programmer," carpenter," "actress." In effect, the thing-and-property-blending use of "person" compresses our ordinary notion of a person into the much more specific notion of a person's moral identity, while at the same time insisting on maintaining the idea that the resulting thing is indeed a thing, a person. I'll return to this idea in chapter 10. Anyone who finds it too confusing would do best to give up studying Locke on personal identity, because this is Locke on personal identity "101."

Locke is well aware that he needs to draw attention to the particular way in which he's using "person," although the usage is fully available at the time he is writing, and he duly does so. "Person, *as I take it*," he says, i.e. "person" as I am taking the word "person," "is ... a forensic term, appropriating actions and their merit" (§26). He's also aware of the confusion that can be caused by pronouns. He writes in response to one imagined objection that

> we must here take notice what the word *I* is applied to; which in this case is the man only. And the same man being presumed to be the same person, *I* is easily [but mistakenly] here supposed to stand also for the same person. (§20)

Some may think that his move here is illegitimate, on the ground that "I" can't be supposed to shift its reference in this way. But the idea that the pronoun "I" isn't always univocal in its reference (even as used by a single subject of experience) isn't a special provision introduced by Locke to brush over some implausibility in his theory of personal identity. The non-univocity of "I" is a feature of our everyday use of "I." Usually "I" is used to refer to a human being considered as a whole, a person₁ in the present terms. Sometimes, though, people use it to refer to themselves conceived as an inner mental entity of some sort, and sometimes its use or reference is simply indeterminate between these two possibilities—or refers indifferently to both.[2]

"Person," then, "is a forensic term, appropriating actions and their merit" (remember that Locke includes thoughts under actions). One finds the same thing in Hobbes, as Thiel observes:

---

[2] There is resistance to this idea in analytic philosophy, although it is quite harmless. One mistake is to think that it follows from the public nature of language that "I" must refer to the human being considered as a whole, and only to the human being considered as a whole. See e.g. Strawson 2009: 20–23, 331–35, Strawson 2011.

when we consider an individual human being under the notion of **person**, we do not consider it with respect to its metaphysical make-up, but with regard to the actions attributed to that being, that is, under moral and legal aspects. Hobbes seems to take up the old legal usage of "persona." He reminds the reader of the history of the term "persona" and appeals to Cicero's use of "persona" as rôle. (1998: 882)

Hobbes's critic Pufendorf does the same, taking the word "person" to "relate ... to the individual human being *in so far as* he owns actions and is held to be responsible for them."[3] Edmund Law, moved by a friend to add a clarificatory appendix to his *Defence* at the last moment, when the rest of the text had already been typeset, makes the point as follows:

> Mr. Locke says, that *Person* stands for a *thinking intelligent Being, that has reason and reflection* ... the expression would have been more just, had he said that the word person stands for an attribute, or quality, or character of a thinking intelligent Being. ... The word person ... , according to the received sense in all classical authors, [stands] for a certain guise, character, quality, i.e. being in fact a mixed mode, or relation, and not a substance.

---

[3] Thiel 1998: 882, referring to Pufendorf 1672: 1.1.12–13. Velleman captures part of this when he writes (2006: 1) that "Locke ... described a person's consciousness of his past as making him 'self to himself' across spans of time. Implicit in this phrase is the view that the word 'self' does not denote any one entity but rather expresses a reflexive guise under which parts or aspects of a person are presented to his own mind." One shouldn't, however, think that Locke gives up the idea that a self or Person is a single entity.

This being so, Law says,

> we must next enquire, what particular character or quality it stands for in this place, as the same man may bear many characters and relations at the same, or different times. The answer is, that here it stands for that particular quality or character, under which a man is considered, when he is treated as an intelligent Being subject to government and laws, and accountable for his actions: i.e. not the man himself, but an abstract consideration of him, for such and such particular ends: and to enquire after its identity, is to enquire, not after the identity of a conscious Being, but after the identity of a quality or attribute of such a conscious Being.[4]

Rephrasing slightly: to inquire about Personal identity, to inquire about the diachronic identity of subjects of experience who are Persons, is to ask which parts of their lives up to now are relevant to, and in fact constitutive of, their overall moral and legal standing.

---

[4] See p. 251 below. Law remarks that this point "perhaps is not sufficiently explained by Mr. Locke in any one place of his admirable essay, although it occurs pretty often," and that "he has been pleased to set it forth in a manner somewhat paradoxical" (p. 244). See also Uzgalis (1990), who argues that Lockean Persons are not substances but "mixed modes."

Chapter Four

Concernment

If we look for a thing-denoting term that corresponds to "Person," it looks as if we need something like "unit of accountability." A Person is a unit of accountability. A unit of accountability is always a subject of experience, and we naturally think of the subject of experience alone as the thing that is accountable. Strictly speaking, though, the subject of experience [S] consists only of [M] ± [I], at any given time, and we don't have a full, actual unit of accountability, a Person, until we add on [A].

The fact remains that we naturally think of [S] alone as the unit of accountability, taking it for granted that it comes with a set of actions and experiences, [A], for which it is morally accountable. And if we ask the question "What entity is Locke is concerned with, when he raises the question of its Personal identity?", the best answer, for almost all purposes, is the simplest: he's concerned with an ordinary human subject of experience, something with a particular character or personality and history. He takes the diachronic identity or continuity of this subject of experience as given, as already remarked. He's not trying to construct an account of the diachronic identity or continuity of this subject of experience that is a Person in terms of something else, in a "neo-Lockean" fashion. He is uninhibited in his metaphysical speculations, when analyzing the notion of Personal identity, and in speculating about what could substantially realize the diachronic continuity of a subject of experience, but his actual philosophical concern is entirely with ourselves, complex subjects of experience like ourselves whose diachronic identity he takes as given (although he aims to deny that it depends on the continuity of any particular substances). This is where he starts from—the fact of enduring and continuously existing, personalitied, human subjects of experience who are born, live, and die, who are—he assumes—eventually resurrected, who can feel pleasure and pain, happiness and misery, and who are, quite crucially, "capable of a law" (§26), i.e. capable of grasping the import of a law *in such a way that they can understand themselves to be subject to it, and can thereby be subject to it*. From this perspective, the question of which, or what, Person a given subject of experience is, considered at some particular time—the question of what such a subject of experience's Personhood or Personal identity consists in, at that time—is simply a question about what that subject of experience is (morally and legally) responsible for, at that time. In this respect, Locke's account of Personal identity begins where neo-Lockean accounts of personal identity end. It begins with the assumption of what they seek to give an account of: a diachronically continuous subject of experience that qualifies as a Person by the definition in §9 and §26 (see chapter 8 below), and whose diachronic psychological continuity and identity doesn't necessarily depend on the continuity of any particular substances.

One could put this by saying that the question of which or what Person a given subject of experience is, at a given time, is a question about that subject of experience's overall

field of responsibility

at that time. This isn't quite right, though, for there's a sense in which the notion of *concernment* is for Locke more fundamental than the notion of responsibility, when it comes to the question of Personal identity. It's better to say that the question of which or what Person a given subject of experience is, at a given time, is a question about that subject of experience's overall

field of concernment

at that time. A sufficient reason for making the adjustment stems from the fact that a subject of experience's field of concernment (whose extent defines the extent of the subject of experience's Personhood) is wider than its field of responsibility. One's field of responsibility falls wholly within one's field of concernment, but the latter also comprises (among other things) one's concern with one's own pleasure and pain considered entirely independently of moral and legal matters.

But this isn't quite right either. The being or extent of a subject of experience's Personhood or Personal identity isn't simply identical with the being or extent of its field of responsibility, because the notion of a Person isn't an *exclusively* moral or forensic term, as it might be if it concerned only [A]. One's Personhood or Personal identity also comprises one's substantial constitution, i.e. [M] ± [I]. The move from field of responsibility to field of concernment captures this, by bringing in [M] ± [I], one's substantial realization, but the being or extent of a subject of experience's Personhood or Personal identity isn't identical to the being or extent of its field of concernment either. For while the move from

the field of responsibility to the field of concernment brings
in [**M**] ± [**I**], in addition to [**A**], it also brings in things that
aren't part of one's Personhood or Personal identity, as I will
soon point out, and the further notion we need, because of
this, in addition to the notions of the field of responsibility
and the field of concernment, is the notion of the subject of
experience's

field of consciousness

in Locke's special sense of "consciousness," which I'll mark
from now on with a capital letter: *Consciousness*. The being or
extent of a subject of experience's Personhood or Personal
identity is, as Locke says, identical, strictly identical, to the
being or extent of its field of Consciousness—it's identical to
what falls in its field of Consciousness.[1]

What does this amount to? Before I explain what Locke
means by "Consciousness," I need to say more about what
he means by "concernment."

Locke characterizes concernment by reference to pleasure and pain, happiness and misery, as when he speaks of
"our pleasure or pain; i.e. happiness or misery; beyond which
we have no concernment, either of knowing or being."[2]
Concernment is a matter of having interests. Locke's use
of "concernment," which I'll mark from now on with an
initial capital letter—*Concernment*—is in fact synonymous
with our use of "concern"; and just as both terms have a

---

[1] Here as in the case of "person," the initial capital letter marks my
use of the term in its Lockean sense, and so doesn't occur in quotations
from Locke. When I'm not using these terms only in their distinctively
Lockean sense, I stick to lowercase.

[2] 4.11.8; see also 4.2.14, where he speaks of "our happiness, or misery,
beyond which, we have no concernment to know, or to be."

psychological application, in which they mean a certain sort
of feeling or attitude, so too, no less importantly, they both
have a nonpsychological or "objective" application, given
which one can have concerns or concernments one knows
nothing about.[3]

All sentient creatures have concerns or Concernments, on
Locke's view, simply insofar as they're capable of pleasure or
pain and therefore have interests. They're Concerned for
their bodies and their experiences, if for nothing else. And
just as a capacity for pleasure and pain entails Concernment,
in Locke's view, so too Concernment entails a capacity for
pleasure and pain:

[Concernment ↔ capacity for pleasure and pain].

We, however, are not only sentient creatures. We are also,
crucially, moral beings, creatures "capable of a law," and this
adds a vast extra dimension to our Concernment. Many
kinds of sentient creatures act and have experiences, good
and bad, but our actions and experiences have moral qualities, and are therefore things for which we may be praised
and blamed, punished and rewarded; and praise and blame,
punishment and reward, are of course a matter of pleasure
and pain, happiness and misery. So there's a dimension to
our Concernment in our actions and experiences that is
completely absent in the case of nonmoral animals. By far
the most important part of our Concernment in our actions
derives from the fact that we're morally assessable with respect to them, in fact, because our fate on the Day of Judgment—than which nothing can be more important, given

---

[3] "This concerns all left-handers"; "I'm looking after her concerns
while she's away / because she's in a coma."

only that eternity is in question—will depend entirely on the moral quality of our actions.

But we'll be morally assessable only with respect to those of our actions and experiences of which we're then Conscious—i.e. those actions and experiences of which we're "conscious" in Locke's special sense of the term. Rephrased (because there's a sense in which this way of putting it is misleading in the Lockean context), we will indeed be responsible for *all* our actions—that is, we will *considered as Persons* be responsible for all our actions, i.e. all the actions that are actions *of the Persons we are*. But there are likely to be many, many actions that we *considered as human beings* have performed which we won't be Conscious of any more, and which therefore won't be actions on our part *considered as Persons*—so that we won't be responsible for them.

This may not be clear yet; again I hope it will become so. It brings us, in any case, back to the notion of Consciousness, which is even more fundamental than the notion of Concernment, when it comes to Locke's theory of personal identity, for a reason already given.

It's true, given Locke's notion of Concernment, that

for any *x*, if *x* is you, the sentient creature you are, or if *x* is part of the sentient creature you are, then you're *Concerned* in or for *x*.

It's also true, more particularly, that

[1] for any *x*, if *x* is you, the Person you are, or if *x* is a part of the Person you are (whether an action or a limb), then you are *Concerned* in or for *x*.

But the converse of claim [1], i.e.

for any *x*, if you are *Concerned* in *x* then *x* is you, or is a part
of you, the *Person* (sentient creature) you are

is not true. This is because the field of Concernment of a
Person—you, say—extends way beyond whatever one could
reasonably suppose a Person to be. Your field of Concernment includes members of your family, for example, not to
mention your "business concerns,"[4] whereas the only objects
of your concern that are at issue when it comes to the matter of what constitutes you as a Person are those to which
you have a certain kind of direct or immediate access—the
access of *Consciousness*—which you neither do nor can have
to members of your family, any more than you can or do
to your business concerns. The question of which or what
Person one is, at any given time—now, or in ten years' time,
or on the Day of Judgment—is, as remarked, and most fundamentally and exactly, a question about one's

field of Consciousness

at that time. The being or extent of one's Person—or equivalently one's Personhood—or equivalently one's Personal
identity—is strictly identical to the being or extent of one's
field of Consciousness. For "consciousness makes personal identity" (§10), or so Locke famously claims; "***personal
identity*** depends on ... same consciousness" (§10).

If this is right—if it's right to understand "consciousness
makes personal identity" and "personal identity depends on
same consciousness" in this straightforward way—then if we
can work out what Locke thinks Consciousness is, then we

---

[4] A parallel remark can be made about sentient creatures that are not
Persons; Locke considers the way in which fox parents are Concerned
about (in or for) their cubs in 2.11.7. For our human case, see e.g. 2.25.7.

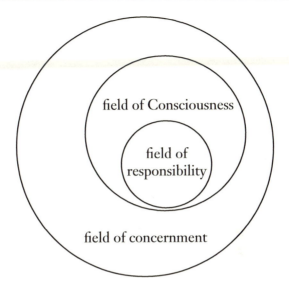

can work out what Locke thinks a Person is, or at least—should this be something different (and there is a sense in which it is something different)—what Locke thinks Personal identity is.

For the moment, we have it that the field of responsibility lies wholly inside the field of Consciousness and the field of Consciousness lies wholly inside the field of Concernment.

Chapter Five

Consciousness

THE ONLY THINGS of which one can be Conscious are

[**M**] one's own body,

[**I**] one's immaterial soul (if any), and

[**A**] one's actions and experiences (including one's thoughts in the narrower cognitive sense).

So these, presumably, are what wholly constitute one as a Person, in Locke's view, at any given time, as remarked on pages 14–15: [**P**] = [**M**] ± [**I**] + [**A**]. If the notion of a Person were a wholly or merely moral notion, one would expect the being or extent of oneself as Person to be identical to the being or extent of one's field of responsibility. In fact, though, the notion of oneself as Person also includes one's substantial makeup, material and/or immaterial.

—How can Consciousness extend to these three things, given that Locke defines Consciousness as "the perception of what passes in a man's own mind" (2.1.19)?

Take [**I**] first. [**I**] just is one's own mind, given that one has an immaterial soul at all. In this case [**I**] "partakes in" one's Consciousness (§10), and one is Conscious of it in being

Conscious of its activity—of what's going on in it. Put otherwise: one is, as a Person, Conscious of oneself as subject of experience, as [S]. So if "that which thinks in" one (§14), i.e. that which constitutes one as [S], is indeed one's immaterial soul [I], and not just one's brain, i.e. part of [M], then in being Conscious of oneself as subject of experience, one is Conscious of [I].[1]

So much for [I]. What about [A]? We normally think of actions as in large part nonmental things, not in the mind. But, first, many actions are mental; secondly, physical actions do of course have a crucial mental component that is essentially constitutive not only of their moral status, but also of their counting as actions at all. So we may be said to be Conscious of [A] even when Consciousness is defined as "the perception of what passes in a man's own mind" (2.1.19). Thirdly, Locke explicitly increases the reach of Consciousness in 2.27. He explicitly extends the notion of Consciousness to cover not only our actions and experiences, [A], but also our material bodies, [M]. He speaks, for example, of our

> bodies, all whose particles, whilst vitally united to this same thinking conscious self, so that we feel when they are touched, and are affected by, and conscious of good or harm that happens to them, are a part of our *selves*: i.e. of our thinking conscious *self*. Thus the limbs of his body are to every one a part of *himself*: he sympathizes and is concerned for them. Cut off a hand, and thereby separate it from that consciousness, we had of its heat, cold, and other affections; and it is then no longer a part of that which is *himself*. ... (§11)[2]

---

[1] I noted on p. 10 that we may add [S] to [M], [I], and [A], when saying what a Person is, although [S] is not something ontologically extra.

[2] Thus [M] is covered as a whole, i.e. independently of the respect in which the brain is covered if "that which thinks in" one is one's brain.

It may still seem best to say that Lockean Consciousness extends to one's material substance (and perhaps also to one's immaterial substance) only indirectly, given that Locke's fundamental definition of Consciousness is in terms of a certain kind of reflexivity of mind, a reflexivity of mind that inevitably accompanies what we ordinarily think of as conscious goings-on—

> it is altogether as intelligible to say that a body is extended without parts, as that anything *thinks without being conscious of it*, or perceiving, that it does so (2.1.19)

—and is indeed an essential part of what *constitutes* them as conscious:

> thinking *consists* in being conscious that one thinks (2.1.19).

At the same time, we should take account of his claim that "consciousness … unites *existences* and actions … into the same person" (§16), and his claim that "every one finds that, whilst comprehended under [his] consciousness, the little finger is as much a part of himself as what is most so" (§17). When such passages are taken together with the passage just quoted from §11, it becomes clear that the extended understanding of Consciousness is the correct one to work with, when considering Locke's discussion of personal identity. It's the one he works with himself.[3]

Suppose it granted that one can be said to be Conscious of [M] and [I], in addition to [A]. Why are they the only things of which one can be Conscious (remember that they already

---

[3] I'll return to this issue in the next chapter, and in chapter 8, when I consider the reference to Consciousness in Locke's famous definition of Personhood in §9.

include [S])? We need to look further at Locke's use of the notion of "consciousness" in 2.27.

One might first characterize it as follows:

> to be Conscious of *x* is *to experience x in a certain immediate kind of way.*

Which way is this? It can be sufficiently indicated, in a familiar manner, by saying that it's the way in which we (and all sentient creatures) experience our own pains, and indeed all our own experiences considered just as such, i.e. as occurrences with a certain experiential qualitative (phenomenological) character. There is, clearly, also a sense in which we can experience or be conscious of other creatures' experiences. Nobody, though, thinks that we can be conscious of others' experiences in the immediate kind of way in which we can be conscious of our own.

This is the basic *occurrent* use of Locke's term "Consciousness," the use of it to refer to experience that is actually occurring. But the term also, and crucially, has a wider and equally basic *dispositional* use: according to which to be Conscious of *x* is to be *able* to experience *x* in the special immediate way just indicated. Locke makes this clear in §16, when he writes that "consciousness, as far as ever it *can* be extended, should it be to ages past, unites existences, and actions, very remote in time, into the same person," and again in §17: "that with which the **consciousness** of this present thinking thing *can* join it self, makes the same **person**, and is one *self* with it" (see also §9 and §10).

Putting the occurrent and dispositional uses together, we have the following claim:

> [2] to be Conscious of *x* is *to experience or to be able to experience x in a certain immediate kind of way.*

This, I propose, is precisely Locke's notion of Consciousness. It's not any sort of elaboration of his notion—it doesn't add anything extra. To be Conscious of a body, or body part, or mind, or soul, or subject of experience, or action, or experience, is to experience it, or to be able to experience it, in a way in which one can as a matter of metaphysical fact experience it only if it is in fact one's own, or oneself. It is, as philosophers say, to experience it, or to be able to experience it, *from the inside*.[4]

It is of course very important that Locke's understanding of the notion of consciousness has this dispositional aspect. To be Conscious of *x* at a given time is for *x* to be *accessible* to one's experience at that time, not necessarily for one to be actually experiencing *x* at that time. I'm tempted to signal this dispositional aspect by adding an asterisk at the end of "Conscious," to give "Conscious*." On second thought, though, the capital "C" seems enough to mark Locke's special use of "conscious," so I won't do this. Instead, from time to time, I'll insert "(be able to be)" in front of "Conscious" (and "be able to" in front of "experience") as a reminder of the dispositional aspect of the notion of Consciousness.

The vivid if slightly unstable phrase "from the inside," which I'll consider further in the next chapter, allows us to rewrite [2] as

[3] to be Conscious of *x* is to (be able to) experience *x from the inside*:

to be Conscious of *x* is to (be able to) experience *x* in a way in which I can't possibly experience your joy or pain, or your past action, or body, only my own.

---

[4] Shoemaker introduced the term (Shoemaker 1970: 273); see also Mackie 1976: 174ff., 187.

I think it takes some time, when one studies Locke, to spread out and appreciate the connections between Concernment, Consciousness, immediacy of experience, and Personhood. An air of circularity may seem to hang about the matter. Isn't the notion of something's *being one's own*, or *being part of the Person one is*, being defined in terms of being accessible to one's Consciousness, only for Consciousness to be defined in such a way that one can be Conscious only of things that are in fact one's own?

There is no circularity; the notion of Consciousness is sufficiently independently characterized in terms of immediacy. One can in fact illuminatingly rewrite claim [2] as

to be Conscious of *x* is to (be able to) experience *x* *as one's own* in a certain immediate kind of way.

If one does this, though, one risks being misunderstood by analytic philosophers, although not, I think, by Phenomenologists.[5] To avoid misunderstanding by analytic philosophers, one needs to stress the point that this kind of experiencing something as one's own is found in all sentient beings, however lowly, and doesn't require or involve any sort of express or explicit or "full" self-consciousness of the sort with which we ourselves are familiar. Put otherwise, the "as one's own" in the rewriting of [3] doesn't imply any explicit conceptual representation of *x as* one's own, of the sort that is characteristic—definitive—of genuinely conceptually articulated full self-consciousness.[6]

---

[5] I use "Phenomenologist" with a capital "P" to denote members of the Phenomenological school of philosophy associated with Husserl.

[6] Note that the "in a certain immediate kind of way" is still needed, because I can experience things as my own in other ways (I can for example think of my arm as my own).

I'll consider this further in the next chapter. For the moment, I'm going to take it that the notion of Consciousness can be sufficiently defined in independent terms like those used in claims [2] and [3], as well as in other terms that I'll consider in chapter 7.

Locke is perhaps insufficiently clear about the difference between the epistemological claim that being (able to be) Conscious of *x* is conclusive *proof* that *x* is one's own, or part of the Person one is, and the metaphysical claim that being (able to be) Conscious of something is part of what *makes* or *constitutes* it as one's own, or part of the Person one is.[7] One way to get a sense of what is going on is to imagine starting out with a vast initial pool of things—actions, experiences, material or immaterial entities, what have you—that are *candidates* for being parts or properties of the Person I now am, simply in being associated with the person₁ or human being

---

[7] It's a small point, but one might think it necessary to qualify "being (able to be) Conscious of something is part of what *makes* or *constitutes* it as one's own" by "at least in the case of actions and experiences," on the ground that one's body ± immaterial soul are going to be part of the Person one is whether or not one can be Conscious of them. Whether or not Locke needs to add this qualification depends on what he says about parts of one's body (or soul) that one can no longer feel or contact in any way (because of some irreversible mental or physical paralysis, say). He can say that one is no longer Concerned for them by being Conscious of them, and that they're (therefore) no longer strictly speaking part of the Person one is, although one is still Concerned for them in the larger sense that doesn't require Consciousness of them ([1] above, p. 27). Alternatively, he can say that they're still part of the Person one is, and add the "at least in the case of actions and experiences" qualification to his account of Person-constitution proposed above. (Note that it's natural to think that there are many parts of one's body that one can't possibly be Conscious of. See the discussion of [6] in the main text following.)

I am.[8] The task is then to work out which of these candidate components really are part of the Person I am.

To do this, one looks at the Concernment and Consciousness relations. Thus, suppose the initial pool of candidates for being part of the Person that I am now includes all the actions and experiences and material particles and immaterial entities (if any) that have ever been part of the total spatio-temporal career of the human being known as GS. Only a few of them will pass the test of being part of the Person that I now am, for only a few of them will pass the accessibility-to-present-Consciousness test. None of the material particles that composed me in the past will pass the test, given that they no longer compose me; nor will any of the actions and experiences of which I am now no longer Conscious.

This doesn't settle the question of whether Locke's stress is epistemological or metaphysical, when he considers the connection between Consciousness and Personal identity. For the moment, though, we can allow that his stress may vary, for, either way, his claim is that

[4] for any x, if you are Conscious of x then x is you, the Person you are, or is a part (e.g. an action or a limb) of the Person you are.

This is a claim Locke makes in many places, most succinctly (too succinctly, it has turned out) when he says in §10 that "consciousness makes personal identity." And to claim [4] we may now add Locke's crucial claim that

[8] More strictly (given the feasibility of the prince-cobbler swap Locke discusses in §15), we need to consider those associated with the subject of experience or [S] that I am, where the subject of experience is understood to be something that can possibly survive body-swaps. See p. 122 below.

[5] Consciousness of x entails Concernment in or for x.[9]

Concernment is, as Locke says in §26, "the unavoidable concomitant" of Consciousness (see also §17).

What about the converse of claim [5], i.e.

[6] Concernment in or for x entails Consciousness of x?

We can't add claim [6] in this unrestricted form, because we may as remarked have Concernments for things we're not only not Conscious of but know nothing about (p. 26), including things in the future. Locke does nevertheless claim, of a self considered at some particular time in its career, that

> whatever past actions it cannot reconcile or appropriate to that present self [i.e. to itself in the present] by consciousness, it can be no more concerned in, than if they had never been done (§26)

and this claim has the form "Concernment entails Consciousness" (in its contrapositive version, "no Consciousness, no Concernment"). So he does here seem to endorse a version of [6], albeit a version restricted to actions (in particular, actions that are in the vast set of prima facie candidates for being actions of the Person you are, because they were performed by the human being you are).

One could rewrite [6] in a restricted version as follows:

[6*] for all actions that are prima facie candidates for being actions of the Person you are, Concernment in or for x entails Consciousness of x.

This would mean that if there are actions that have some

___

[9] This claim can in fact be interestingly challenged within a broadly speaking Lockean scheme: see chapter 19.

prima facie claim to be actions on the part of the Person you are, we can find out whether or not they really are actions on the part of the Person you are by seeing if you're still Conscious of them. If you're not, then they're no concern of the Person you are, moral, legal, or otherwise—despite any initial appearances.[10]

[10] Does Locke endorse a restricted version of [6] with respect to anything else that is a prima facie candidate for being part of the Person or self one is? Surely not, one might think, for one can presumably be said to be *Concerned* for any particle that is currently part of one's body, in being Concerned for one's body, without being (able to be) *Conscious* of that particle in any way at all. At one point, though, Locke seems to claim (in a passage already quoted) that our Consciousness does indeed extend to every one of our constituent particles, suggesting that Concernment entails Consciousness in this case too (given that one is Concerned for any particle that is currently part of one's body). He is speaking of our "bodies, all whose particles, whilst vitally united to this same thinking conscious self, so that we feel when they are touched, and are affected by, and conscious of good or harm that happens to them, are a part of our *selves*: i.e. of our thinking conscious *self*" (§11).

The passage is ambiguous, however. One natural reading takes the words "so that" to mean "in such a way that" and to interact with the words "vitally united" to yield, not the claim that (i) we feel or are Conscious of absolutely all the particles of our bodies, but the claim that (ii) we feel or are Conscious only of some of those particles—those, precisely, that are, in being part of our bodies, vitally united to our "thinking conscious self" *in such a way that* we feel or are Conscious of them. Claim [4] above seems to sit best with (i), but a Lockean could consistently endorse claim [4] while allowing, in accordance with (ii), that there are or may be particles in one's body that aren't part of the Person one is.

It's "vital union," in any case, that is the key requirement on being part of a Person in the case of substances like particles of matter. In §25 Locke lists vital union and Consciousness as two different ways in which something may be part of a Person: "any substance vitally united to the present thinking being, is a part of that very same self which now is: anything united to it by a consciousness of former actions makes also a part of the same self, which is the same both then and now" (§25). In other words, when it comes to being part of a Person, there are two quite different basic principles of part-membership. There is one for substance(s) (vital

So far, then, Locke holds [1]–[5] and [6*], a version of [6] restricted in the way just described. All this seems clear when one examines his text. I've attempted to isolate his main claims in numbered propositions—at the risk of making things seem (at least initially) considerably more difficult and complicated than they are—because it can take time to get used to his terms.

One thing that becomes plain, once one understands that to be Conscious of something is to experience it as one's own, in the special from-the-inside way, is that

[7] Consciousness is not memory.

Many, many commentators have followed Butler and Reid in supposing that memory and Consciousness are to be identified, when it comes to Locke's discussion of personal identity. There is, however, nothing to support this identification in the text. The primary case of Consciousness isn't a matter of memory at all (see chapter 9).

It's true that Consciousness is an essential feature of from-the-inside autobiographical memory, and it's true that Locke is centrally concerned with such autobiographical memory, but memory generally considered needn't involve Consciousness at all, so far as the thing that is remembered is concerned, any more than Consciousness need involve memory.[11] The point is not just that there's memory

---

union), another for actions (Consciousness). For a *substance* to be part of a person [P] at any given time is for it to be vitally united to whatever substance or substances [P]'s Consciousness then "resides" (§25) in. For an *action or experience* to be part of [P], by contrast, at any given time, is for it to be united to [P] by Consciousness, at that time. The former is covered by the latter insofar as being united by vital union entails being united by Consciousness.

[11] Consciousness and Concernment can also reach into the future, on Locke's view, but I'll restrict attention to present and past.

without Consciousness when I remember that the Second World War began in 1939. It's also true that there can be memory without Consciousness in the case of autobiographical memory—as when my "from-the-inside" memory of *falling* out of the punt has decayed into merely factual or "propositional" memory *that I fell* out of the punt.[12]

I think, in fact, that there can be memory without Consciousness even in the case of autobiographical memory that retains a from-the-inside character. I'll argue for this in chapter 19—I'll argue that this is a natural thing to say, given Locke's notion of Consciousness.[13] It's not clear that Locke would have agreed, but there are some good reasons for thinking that Concernment can lapse, in the case of memories that retain a from-the-inside character, even if Consciousness doesn't or can't. (Some of these reasons have to do with the idea of repentance, and of how repentance can change one's relation to a past action.)

If I could persuade Locke of this, then he'd either have to give up [5], or allow that Consciousness can indeed be absent in the case of memories that retain a from-the-inside character—given that Concernment can be absent. Either way, there'd only be a very minor (in effect merely terminological) adjustment to his theory.

---

[12] See further chapters 8 and 15.
[13] See also Strawson 2004: 194–95.

Chapter Six

"Consciousness ... is inseparable from thinking"

BEING CONSCIOUS of some action or experience, experiencing it as one's own in a certain immediate (i.e. nonmediated) or from-the-inside sort of way, needn't—and standardly doesn't—involve any sort of explicit or express or attentive or "thetic"[1] second-order taking of it as one's own. That the action or experience is one's own needn't be in the focus of conscious attention in any way, and in fact the "experiencing-as-one's-own-ness" of Consciousness is, in the normal case of present awareness of one's body and one's surroundings, wholly "non-thetic," "pre-reflective," "non-egological," in the Phenomenologists' terminology. It is in other words devoid of any express, spelled-out, distinct representation of the subject of experience or self or "ego" considered specifically as such.[2] To experience one's mental goings-on as one's

---

[1] This is a term used by philosophers in the Phenomenological tradition (other similar terms are "thematic," "positional," "reflective"). It means—in Sartre's use, which I follow, rather than Husserl's use—something close to explicit, express, attentive.

[2] See in particular Gurwitsch 1941, who follows Sartre. The claim is not that Consciousness of x can't involve any explicit or thetic awareness that x is oneself or one's own, only that it doesn't normally do so.

own in the requisite way is simply for them to have the character of being immediately given to one; it's simply for one's mental goings-on to have the character that one's experience always and necessarily has just in being one's experience.[3]

Locke makes this plain in §9 when, using the words "thinking" and "perceiving" in the general (Cartesian and Arnauldian) way in which I use the word "experience," i.e. to cover "everything that occurs in us in such a way that we are immediately conscious of it,"[4] he says that Consciousness is

> inseparable from thinking, and, as it seems to me, essential to it: it being impossible for any one to perceive without perceiving that he does perceive. (§9)

This passage settles the point, I think, for if one thing is certain it is that Locke, that most sensible of philosophers, doesn't think that we spend our whole lives having—and indeed principally occupied with—explicitly second-order thoughts or experiences, thoughts or experiences that are explicitly concerned with thoughts or experiences, still less thoughts or experiences that are explicitly about oneself, "egological" "I-me-my" thoughts or experiences. He doesn't think this any more than Descartes does when he says such

---

[3] It's a matter of their "immediate first-personal givenness," in Phenomenological terms; see e.g. Zahavi 2006: chap. 1. (Note that the use of the term "first-personal," widespread in Phenomenological writings, is potentially very misleading, because it's meant to apply as much in the case of chickens and spiders—assuming they have experience—as in the case of creatures like ourselves who have use of the first-person pronoun. I think "first-personal" is best deleted from the phrase "immediate first-personal givenness.")

[4] Descartes 1641: 2.113, cf. also 1.195. This plainly covers things like pangs of hunger. I'm putting aside questions about whether we are (for example) directly conscious of the position of our arms (cf. Yablo 1990: 151, n. 3). Descartes later had some tendency to use "thinking" more for higher cognitive activities.

things as that "when I will or fear something, I simultaneously perceive that I will or fear."[5]

Descartes is following Aristotle, who also makes the point explicitly. When we perceive or think, Aristotle says, "we ... perceive that we perceive, and think that we think"[6]—though "knowledge and perception and opinion and understanding have always something else as their object, and themselves only by the way" or "in the margin," *en passant*.[7] The claim seems plain. All awareness comports awareness of awareness in some sense, but awareness of awareness is in the normal case wholly non-thetic. Note that it would be heavily anachronistic to think that when Aristotle, Locke, and Descartes say that we perceive *that* we perceive, this shows that they must think that this involves some sort of expressly propositional apprehension.[8]

---

[5] 1641: 2.127. As Clarke (2003: 189) points out, *volo* in the above passage should be translated by "will," which refers to an occurrent mental episode, not by "want," which has a natural dispositional reading. "It is certain that we cannot will anything without thereby perceiving that we are willing it. And . . . this perception is really one and the same thing as the volition" (1648: 1.335–6). This is powerful support for the view that Descartes rejects any second-order view of the perception, for he identifies the willing and the perception even as he notes that this is strictly speaking incompatible with his view that perception is passive and willing active.

[6] c. 350 BCE: *Nicomachean Ethics* 9.9.1170a29-b1; see also *De Anima* 3.2. 425b12–17.

[7] c. 350 BCE: *Metaphysics* 12.9.1074b35–36. There are of course many disputes about what Aristotle's views are. See in particular Caston 2002.

[8] Do we ever have conscious experience without in some way or other registering the fact that there is experience going on? The first thought is, "No, never—contradiction in terms to suppose otherwise." The second thought, popular among those who have gone a little way in philosophy, is, "Yes, obviously we do; if you doubt it, think first of the case of watching an exciting film, and then go on to the point that something like this is in fact the normal case." The third thought (when one has gone a little further in philosophy) is that the first thought is in fact correct, although its secure expression requires some delicacy. Aristotle puts it well, as re-

Locke's next sentence confirms the point, for he continues his explanation of the nature of Consciousness by saying that

> when we see, hear, smell, taste, feel, meditate, or will anything, we know that we do so.

This is something that we ordinarily take to be straightforwardly true, and rightly (Locke is only concerned with conscious mental goings-on). But we don't for a moment think (obviously falsely) that all these things necessarily involve some sort of explicit or express or reflective or "full" self-consciousness, i.e. consciousness of oneself *grasped specifically as oneself* (this is the standard definition of self-consciousness in analytic philosophy). Here, Locke is simply talking about the "immediate givenness" of experience, which is in fact nothing other than or more than the "what-it's-likeness" of experience, the experiential qualitative character that experience has for those who have it as they have it.

This last claim may seem to need qualification, because it

---

marked, as does Gurwitsch when, speaking of perception, he says that "consciousness ... is consciousness of an object on the one hand and an inner awareness of itself on the other hand. Being confronted with an object, I am at once conscious of this object and aware of my being conscious of it. This awareness in no way means reflection: to know that I am dealing with the object which, for instance, I am just perceiving, I need not experience a second act bearing upon the perception and making it its object. In simply dealing with the object I am aware of this very dealing" (1941: 330). Note that Gurwitsch's impersonal formulation "aware of this very dealing" is better—because less open to misinterpretation—than his "aware of my being conscious of [the object]," since the phenomenon in question does not require any thought of oneself as such. This is indeed Gurwitsch's main point, which he has already made three pages earlier: "the subject in his dealing with the object, aware as he is of this dealing, is nevertheless in no way aware of his ego, much less of his ego's involvement in his dealing" (327).

entails that any creature that has experience at all has Consciousness, simply because all experience has, by definition, the character of immediate givenness that is in question:

[8] all experience involves Consciousness (of itself).

But this, I take it, is precisely Locke's view of Consciousness—following Aristotle, Descartes, and many others.[9] He puts the point strongly, earlier in the *Essay*, in a passage already quoted: "thinking consists in being conscious that one thinks"—just as "hunger consists in that very sensation."[10] Nonmediated or from-the-inside givenness is the core of the notion of Consciousness, and Locke, who takes himself to disagree with Descartes in holding robustly that nonhuman animals have conscious experience,[11] has no difficulty with the idea that a nonhuman animal, too, is necessarily

---

[9] There is, I think, a fundamental sense in which it is correct. For some discussion, see Gallagher and Zahavi 2008: chap. 3.

[10] It is "as intelligible to say, that a body is extended without parts, as that anything **thinks without being conscious of it**, or perceiving, that it does so. They who talk thus may, with as much reason … say, that a man is always hungry, but that he does not always feel it; whereas hunger consists in that very sensation, as thinking consists in being conscious that one thinks" (2.1.19).

[11] "Perception, I believe, is, in some degree, in all sorts of animals" although it is in some "so obscure and dull, that it comes extremely short of the quickness and variety of sensation which is in other animals" (2.9.12); "dogs or elephants" give "every demonstration of [thinking] imaginable, except only telling us that they do so" (2.1.19). It is in fact the fundamental difference between plants and animals, for Locke. Many plants, he says, have "some degrees of motion, and upon the different application of other bodies to them, do very briskly alter their figures and motions, and so have obtained the name of sensitive plants, from a motion which has some resemblance to that which in animals follows upon sensation: yet I suppose it is all *bare mechanism*; and no otherwise produced than the turning of a wild oat-beard, by the insinuation of the particles of moisture, or the short'ning of a rope, by the affusion of water. All which is done without any sensation in the subject, or the having or receiving any ideas" (2.9.11).

Concerned for its body in being Conscious of it in the way that it is. That said, nonhuman animals aren't in question in the discussion of Personal identity in 2.27 of the *Essay*, because they're not persons—they're not "capable of a law," or of express or full self-consciousness—and Locke in this chapter is concerned only with Consciousness as it is found in Persons.

It may be objected that Locke does talk of Consciousness as if it were something that has some sort of essential internal connection with a capacity for express or full self-consciousness of a sort necessary for moral accountability—at least in 2.27 of the *Essay*. It may be objected, in other words, that he holds that

[9] [Consciousness → full self-consciousness].

I disagree, but we don't have to settle the issue here, because 2.27 is, from §9 onward, explicitly concerned with persons, and whatever the fundamental definition of Consciousness is, we know that a Lockean *person*, i.e. a Person, is something that is fully and expressly self-conscious, i.e. capable of grasping itself specifically *as itself*.

In this sense, Leibniz is exactly right when, commenting on Locke, he equates human Consciousness with "the sense of *I*."[12] Some philosophers (Phenomenologists or not) might be prepared to allow Leibniz's phrase to apply to creatures that aren't capable of full or express self-consciousness, but

[12] 1704: 236. Priestley speaks similarly of "the idea of *self*, or the feeling that corresponds to the pronoun *I*" (1777: 284 [*Disquisitions* X.V]). Frege adds that "everyone is given to himself in a particular and primordial [*ursprünglichen*] way, as he is given to no other" (1918: 25–26). In a manuscript note, Locke writes that "our own existence is known to us by a certainty yet higher than our senses can give us of the existence of other things, and that is internal perception, a self-consciousness or intuition" (MS Locke c. 28, fols. 119r–20v); see King 1830: 2.138.

we can certainly take it in its more restricted sense when considering Locke's views on personal identity, for a Person is of course, as Locke says, something that

> can consider it self as it self (§9)

and this is a definition of what it is to be fully or expressly self-conscious, already mentioned, that can't be bettered.[13]

Consciousness, then, is inseparable from all "thinking" in the wide Cartesian sense, from all "perception" in an equally wide sense, i.e. all experience, and it is according to Locke equally inseparable from Concernment, "the unavoidable concomitant of consciousness" (§26). Locke's misfortune (so it has turned out, in the long history of the discussion of his view) is that he makes the inseparable connection between Consciousness and Concernment explicit only in §11, a page after giving the basic cognitive definition of Consciousness in §9, and arguing that "consciousness makes personal identity" in §10. This small gap, it seems, has been enough for three hundred years of misunderstanding premised on the assumption that Consciousness is simply memory, or is at any rate a cognitive matter that can be understood independently of any notion of immediacy, or affect-engaging "from-the-insideness," of the sort I tried to characterize in chapter 5. This assumption has held sway in spite of the fact that the notions of Consciousness and Concernment are constantly entangled in the rest of the chapter, and in spite of the fact that Locke stresses their mutual involvement ear-

---

[13] The point that thinking of oneself as oneself is a quite distinctive way of being able to think about oneself that is unlike any other (one is not thinking of oneself as, say, *the daughter of x*, or *the thing reflected in the water*, or *the person most troubled by the baggage retrieval system at Heathrow*) has been the subject of a considerable amount of discussion (see e.g. Castañeda 1966; Perry 1979).

lier in book 2 of the *Essay*, in which he anticipates the discussion of personal identity that was not included in the *Essay* until the second edition in 1694:

> if it be possible, that the soul can, whilst the body is sleeping, have its thinking, enjoyments, and concerns, its pleasure or pain apart, which the man is not conscious of nor partakes in: [then] it is certain that Socrates asleep, and Socrates awake, is not the same person; but his soul when he sleeps, and Socrates the man consisting of body and soul, when he is waking, are two persons: since waking Socrates, has no knowledge of, or concernment for that happiness, or misery of his soul, which it enjoys alone by itself whilst he sleeps, without perceiving anything of it; no more than he has for the happiness, or misery of a man in the Indies, whom he knows not. For if we take wholly away all consciousness of our actions and sensations, especially of pleasure and pain, and the concernment that accompanies it, it will be hard to know wherein to place personal identity. (2.1.11)[14]

---

[14] Locke sometimes uses "consciousness" as a count-noun, e.g. when he speaks of "consciousnesses" in the plural in §23. I won't follow this usage, but it fits into the present scheme as follows: a Consciousness, say [C], considered at a given time, is a subject (or locus) of experience [S]. [S]/[C] must always be substantially realized by something at any given time (typically [M] ± [I]) in order to exist, and it typically comes with a set of actions and experiences [A]; so all of [M] ± [I] + [A] typically lie in [S]/[C]'s field of consciousness in such a way as to constitute [S]/[C]'s existence. But [S]/[C] needn't be realized by any particular thing or stuff, and in this crucial sense the diachronic continuity of [S]/[C], which is as remarked simply assumed by Locke, is completely independent of any substantial continuity. [C] may be a non-Personal Consciousness; it may be the Consciousness of a fox. Or it may be a Personal Consciousness, a Person [P]: all it has to do is to qualify as a [P] by the definition of Person as stated in §9 supplemented by §26. Note that if [C] were dreamlessly asleep and suffered loss of all personal memory it would have, at that time, no [A] at all.

Chapter Seven

"From the inside"

In current philosophical discussion, Shoemaker's term "from the inside" is mainly applied to autobiographical memory, although it's also a feature of all one's current experience. The difference between remembering something from the inside and remembering it only from the outside is the difference between remembering *falling out of the boat*, the water rushing up to meet you, and so on, and remembering *that you fell out of the boat*—which may after a time be all that you have left, in the way of memory of the event, and which someone other than you may remember equally well. In these terms, Locke's use of the word "consciousness" can perhaps be fully if somewhat rebarbatively conveyed by saying that a subject of experience's field of Consciousness is identical with its

field of from-the-inside givenness,

where this includes all its present experience, as well as all memories accessible from-the-inside, and also everything somatosensorily available (given the extension of Consciousness from mind to body discussed on p. 31 above).

If someone suggests that "from-the-inside givenness" is in itself something merely cognitive, empty of affect, then it may be more accurate to say that a subject of experience's field of Consciousness is identical with its

field of morally-affectively-concerned from-the-inside givenness

—a barbarous phrase that I'll immediately discard, in spite of its accuracy, because Locke has effectively built moral-affective Concernment into the term "Consciousness." There is, as remarked, a purely cognitive core to Locke's notion of Consciousness, which I'll consider further in the next chapter, but Lockean Consciousness is in fact always accompanied by Concernment, its unavoidable concomitant—

> self [or person] is that conscious thinking thing ... which is sensible or conscious of pleasure and pain, capable of happiness or misery, and so is *concerned* for it *self*, as far as that consciousness extends.[1]

It's worth repeating the point that the field of one's from-the-inside givenness, one's field of Consciousness, isn't just a matter of one's present conscious experience (which may be wholly focused on one's present surroundings or bodily state, or mental mood, or wholly taken up with consciously remembering something), but also, and crucially, has a dispositional aspect, so that it also contains all of those past experiences, and in particular actions, that one (a) *can* remember from the inside and (b) is still Concerned in:[2]

---

[1] §17. It's striking that loss of such Concernment, which is characteristic of clinical depression, is called "depersonalization" in modern clinical psychology. (It would certainly be absurd to punish a person suffering from severe depersonalization.)

[2] I distinguish (a) and (b) because I think—perhaps contrary to Locke—there may be (a) without (b). See below.

as far as this consciousness *can* be extended backwards to
any past action or thought, so far reaches the identity of
that person (§9).

How far into the past does this "can" reach? It certainly
reaches beyond what one can now bring back to mind completely unaided, and perhaps also beyond what one can remember when suitably prompted or shocked. For it reaches
back—in Locke's view—to all of those past actions that one
is Conscious of in one's conscience or "heart" (§22). What
one is Conscious of in one's heart may not be fully known
or accessible to one now, but that doesn't matter, for there
is nevertheless a fact of the matter about what one is Conscious of, and on the Great Day, the Day of Judgment, "the
secrets of all hearts will be laid open" (§§22, 26).

One's Consciousness certainly doesn't reach back to early
childhood, if only because of the universal phenomenon
that psychologists call "infantile amnesia." Nor does it reach
back to most of the actions of childhood. On one natural
but perhaps non-Lockean reading of Locke, it doesn't reach
back to these actions *even if they're remembered*; for one
isn't still Concerned in them in the relevant responsibility-
engaging way.[3] Nor does it reach back to the vast bulk of one's
past life. When Locke imagines a "spirit wholly stripped of
all its memory or consciousness of past actions, as we find
our minds always are of a great part of ours," he seems to
suggest that most of one's (psychological and agentive) past
is not part of the person (the Person) one is now, not part of
one's Personal identity.[4]

---

[3] I return to this idea in chapter 19.

[4] §25; presumably most of this will not come up when the secrets of one's
heart are laid open. (It's not helpful to take this passage simply as a huge
understatement on Locke's part, i.e. as the obviously true claim that we are

Thomas Reid tells the story of a boy who becomes a young army officer and then a general.

> Suppose a brave officer to have been flogged when a boy at school, for robbing an orchard, to have taken a standard from an enemy in his first campaign, and to have been made a general in advanced life: Suppose also ... that when he took the standard, he was conscious of his having been flogged at school [and also, let's say, of the robbery]; and that when made a general, he was conscious of his taking the standard, but had absolutely lost the consciousness of his flogging [and robbery]. These things being supposed, it follows, from Mr. Locke's doctrine, that he who was flogged at school is the same person who took the standard, and that he who took the standard is the same person who was made a general. Whence it follows, if there be any truth in logic, that the general is the same person [as] him who was flogged at school. But the general's consciousness does not reach so far back as his flogging, therefore, according to Mr. Locke's doctrine, he is not the person who was flogged. Therefore the general is, and at the same time is not the same person with him who was flogged at school.[5]

Following Berkeley, Reid objects that on Locke's account of personal identity (i) the general may be the same person as the young officer, because he's Conscious of some experi-

---

not at any given time *occurrently* Conscious of a great part of most of our past actions.)

[5] 1785: 276 (§3.6). One of the oddest (most ungenerous) things about Reid's misreading of Locke to mean "memory" by "consciousness" is that Locke's core definition of "consciousness" is essentially the same as Reid's. Note that although Reid follows Berkeley's objection (see pp. 243–244, n. 12 below), Berkeley does not in fact confuse memory with consciousness.

ence had by the young officer, (ii) the young officer may be the same person as the boy, because he's Conscious of some experience had by the boy, while (iii) the general may not be the same person as the boy, because he's not Conscious of the experience of the boy. The objection is that the conjunction of (i), (ii), and (iii) contradicts the principle of the "transitivity of identity," and that Locke's theory is therefore inconsistent.

The conjunction of (i), (ii), and (iii) does contradict the principle of the transitivity of identity, but this isn't an objection to Locke's view of personal identity. It is, rather, an illustration of its fundamental and forensic point, the commonsense point (it's common sense relative to the story of the Day of Judgment) that human beings won't on the Day of Judgment be responsible for all the things they have done in their lives, but only for those that they're still Conscious of and so still Concerned in.[6] What they'll be responsible for will, in practice, be a bundle of actions dating from many different periods of their lives. Note (to anticipate) that they may be Conscious of one bad action A1 performed on a certain day long ago, and not of another action A2 performed on that same day. In that case, A1 will be part of the Person they now are, while A2 won't. It simply doesn't follow, for Locke, from the fact that the Person I am now performed (was and is the agent of) A1 on January 18, 1977, that the Person I am now performed (was and is the agent of) A2, although A2 is another action GS performed on January 18, 1977.[7]

---

[6] As usual, it's wrong actions that are principally in question. One might hope to continue to be responsible for one's good actions even if one was no longer Conscious of them; but it's hard to see why there should be any such asymmetry. See further chapter 19 below.

[7] When Edmund Law considers the discussion of Locke's views on personal identity, he laments the "want of ... proper application" from which

This is, in fact, the key to understanding Locke on Personal identity. As in chapter 2, one can put the point by saying that the term "Person" isn't simply a sortal term of a standard kind, i.e. a term for a temporal continuant as ordinarily conceived, as Reid and Berkeley assume. We may say that "Person" is a term that initially picks you out as [S], something that is indeed a temporal continuant, although of a special sort (since it may have traveled in and across many different substances), but then crucially qualifies that identification of you as [S] by [A].

I'll say more about this. For the moment, it may help to repeat the point that the Lockean question of Personal identity is often best taken as a question raised about a subject of experience considered at a particular time. The particular time at which the question is raised (now, next year, or on the Day of Judgment) is important, because [A], the action-and-experience-constituted part of a subject of experience's Personhood, which is the forensically relevant part of a subject of experience's Personhood,[8] is differently constituted every day, on Locke's view. This follows immediately from the fact that a subject of experience [S]'s overall field of Consciousness, and, more particularly, the overall field of actions and experiences [S] is responsible for, changes each

---

"men of genius and good sense have fallen into ... egregious trifling," and which "has filled the above celebrated question with a multitude of quibbles, which Mr. Locke's clear and copious answers to his several opponents might, one would have hoped, have most effectually prevented, but which are subsisting to this very day, to the no small mortification of all sincere lovers of truth, and admirers of that able defender of it. ... An extraordinary instance of this kind is to be met with in Bishop *Berkeley*," whom Law cites at length. Speaking as a (I hope only formerly) guilty party, I don't think Law could have guessed how much worse things were going to get.

[8] The other two parts are [M] the material body and [I] the immaterial soul-substance if any—see p. 9.

day, and indeed every minute—for no other reason than that
[S] has done more things a day or a minute later. It may also
be for other reasons, though. [S] may for example have finally ceased to be Conscious of (and so Concerned in) some
morally nonneutral past action that it was still Conscious of
(and so Concerned in) yesterday.[9]

It may well be, then, that a man is still accountable, when
he is a young officer, for stealing plums as a boy. If Arthur
Wellesley, say, had stolen plums as a boy, and had died while
still a young colonel at the battle of Srirangapatna in India
in 1799, the plums might on the Day of Judgment have been
"on his conscience": he might well still have been Conscious
of and Concerned in the theft. He didn't die then, but lived
for another fifty years, and went on to become the Duke of
Wellington, and entirely ceased—we may suppose—to be
Conscious of or Concerned in his juvenile delinquency. So
be it. This means that he, a subject of experience who is a
Person, will not on the Day of Judgment be held accountable for the theft, although he, a subject of experience who
is a Person, would have been held accountable for it if he
had died in 1799. A subject of experience's moral or forensic
Personhood is in this simple sense differently constituted
every day. It would be very odd, given our ordinary understanding of moral being, if one's wrongdoings simply piled
up without any possible remission (although some enthusi-
asts of hellfire would have it so).

Reid's primary mistake is to equate Consciousness with
memory, a mistake I've noted and will say a bit more about
in chapter 9. One could as just remarked express the sense
in which a subject of experience's Personhood is differ-

---

[9] In chapter 19, I consider the question of whether repentance can change
one's field of responsibility.

ently constituted every day by saying that there's a respect in which one is a different person—Person—every day, although one is the same person$_1$ from day to day (as noted on p. 13), and is indeed the same [S] from day to day, even if one has swapped one's material body or one's immaterial soul. One is a different Person from day to day, a different forensic entity, inasmuch as the contents of one's field of Consciousness change from day to day and indeed from minute to minute, and are what wholly constitute one as a Person.

But although this use fits some aspects of Locke's use of "person," it's pretty strained overall. Treating the actions and experiences that make up [A] as straightforward ontological components of a Person is useful for some purposes. It's a useful way of capturing the tension in the term "Person" (the tension that stems—see chapter 3—from the term's operating both as a term for a type of substance and as a term for a particular quality of that substance). But it doesn't fit all aspects of Locke's use, because he also (and of course) conceives of a Person as a continuing thing that remains the same Person over time even while it changes its properties in having new experiences, performing new actions, and ceasing to be Concerned in actions it was previously Concerned in. When one is thinking of a Person in this way, it seems clear enough that the contents of [A] should be thought of simply as properties of the Person. I'll return to this point.

Chapter Eight

"Person"—Locke's Definition

I'M AN INDIVIDUAL AGENT, a thinking being, a persisting human subject of experience—very much as I think I am. All this is clear. But what am I insofar as I am a Person—a person in Locke's sense? This still doesn't seem so clear, and I'm now going to go in more detail over some ground I've already briefly surveyed.

The first answer is terminological: the Person I am is the self that I am:

> Person, as I take it, is the name for this *self*. Wherever a man finds what he calls *himself*, there, I think, another may say is the same *person* (§26).

It's also true by definition, for Locke, and crucially, that Persons are "capable of a law, and happiness, and misery" (§26).

It's a further and nondefinitional matter what Persons are made of, metaphysically speaking. I gave Locke's answer in chapter 2 and will now rehearse it with quotations. The Person or self that I am, the individual morally accountable subject of experience [**P**] that I am, considered at any given particular time *t*, consists of the following things. First

[**M**] my living body at *t*,

for as Locke says, "any part of our bodies, vitally united to that which is conscious in us, makes a part of our *selves*" (§25).[1]

What else? Well, if I have an immaterial soul—which may, as Locke stresses, be doubted—then the Person that I am at *t* consists also of

[**I**] my soul at *t*,

the immaterial soul-substance in which my thinking goes on; for "any substance [now] vitally united to the present thinking being is a part of that very *same self* which now is" (§25), be it material or immaterial. [**M**] and also [**I**] (assuming that materialism is false and that [**I**] is to be included) are literally part of, constitutive of, the Person that I am at *t*. They substantially constitute [**S**], the subject of experience that the Person I am is, at any given time. ([**S**] may be constituted of other substances at other times, but must always be constituted of some substance or substances at any time that it exists.)

---

[1] See also §11. Note that in these passages Locke uses "our selves" in a sense directly related to his use of the word "self," not in some more indeterminate or generic way: "Thus any part of our bodies, vitally united to that which is conscious in us, makes a part of our selves: but upon separation from *the vital union by which that consciousness is communicated*, that which a moment since was part of our selves, is now no more so than a part of another man's self is a part of me: and it is not impossible but in a little time may become a real part of another person" (§25). In a passage already quoted, he asks us to consider our "bodies, all whose particles, whilst vitally united to this same thinking conscious self, so that we feel when they are touched, and are affected by, and conscious of good or harm that happens to them, are a part of our selves; i.e. of our thinking conscious self. Thus the limbs of his body is to everyone a part of himself: he sympathizes and is Concerned for them" (§11).

The most general description of what constitutes me as a Person, however, is: anything of which I am Conscious. This description encompasses [M] and [I] (and so [S]), on the account of Consciousness given above, but there is, vitally, more. The third and most crucial component consists of everything else, everything other than [M] and [I], of which I am Conscious at *t*, i.e.

[A] all the actions and experiences, past and present, of the individual persisting subject of experience that I am of which I am now (occurrently or dispositionally) Conscious at *t*.[2]

If we stick to the full ontological idiom, in which these actions and experiences are literally components of the Person, the addition of [A] has the consequence, already noted, that we are, considered as Persons, very oddly shaped entities. For Consciousness of the past is a very fine-grained matter, in Locke's view. It may as remarked pick up one thing I did on my birthday twenty years ago and completely fail to pick up a thousand other things I did on that day, things I've completely forgotten and am no longer Concerned in in any way.[3] This is because it's only "that with which the consciousness of this present thinking thing can [now] join it self" that "makes the same person, and is one *self* with it" (§17). The present thinking being that I am

[2] Note that when Locke says that "anything united to the ... present thinking being ... by a consciousness of former actions, makes also a part of the *same self*, which is the same both then and now" (§25) the scope of "anything" is only "former actions": it's not as if the material particles that made you up ten years ago, when you performed a certain action of which you are now Conscious, are still part of the person you are now.

[3] It's more fine-grained than Parfitian psychological connectedness, which also picks and chooses. See chapter 12.

attributes to itself, and owns all the actions of that thing, as its own, as far as that consciousness reaches, *and no farther*.[4]

So it is that

if there be any *part* of [an immaterial substance's] existence, which I cannot upon recollection join with that present consciousness, whereby I am now my *self*, it is *in that part of its existence* no more my *self*, than any other immaterial being. For *whatsoever any substance has thought or done, which I cannot recollect, and by my consciousness make my own thought and action*, it will no more belong to me ... than if it had been thought or done by any other immaterial being anywhere existing.[5]

So when Locke famously says that Consciousness of one of Nestor's actions would make one "the same person with Nestor," he certainly doesn't mean that one would be the same person as Nestor with respect to all of Nestor's actions. One's Consciousness doesn't reach any further into Nestor than that one single action, and although one is in this case the same person as Nestor, it's only so far as that action is concerned.[6] What happens in this *per-impossibile* speculation

[4] §17. In full the passage reads "that with which the consciousness of this present thinking thing can join itself, makes the same person, and is one self with it, and with nothing else; and so attributes to itself, and owns all the actions of that thing, as its own, as far as that consciousness reaches, and no farther." It may help understanding to remove the last three commas: the present thinking being owns "all the actions of that thing as its own as far as [its] consciousness reaches and no farther," i.e. *only* as far as its present consciousness reaches.

[5] §24. Locke is here focusing on the notion of an immaterial substance, but the point is quite general.

[6] §14. Here I disagree with Garrett (2003). Many think that the imagined case is one in which one connects with and becomes one with the

is that a piece of Nestor's (forensic) Personhood becomes a piece of one's own Personhood.[7]

This, then, is a Person—a person in Locke's special sense of the word. I've stated his answer in a straightforwardly ontological manner because I think that its peculiarity when stated in this way is illuminating, even if it must in the end be abandoned.

I've left until last the most famous definitional passage in chapter 27, according to which a Person is

> a thinking intelligent being, that has reason and reflection, and can consider it self as it self, the same thinking thing, in different times and places; which it does only by that consciousness which is inseparable from thinking, and, as it seems to me, essential to it ... (§9)

—partly because I think that the passage has often been misread. It's been cited without sufficient attention to the fact

---

whole forensic Person that Nestor is, but I don't think this can be right. (One point is this: even if one is supposed to connect with and become one with the whole forensic Person that Nestor is at the time he performs the action in question, one can't reasonably be supposed to connect forensically with any actions that he hasn't yet performed.)

[7] Nestor remains otherwise his own Person, and the action—the piece of Personhood—you acquire is accordingly no longer any part of Nestor's Personhood, because it's impossible for two People to be Conscious of the same action: "that with which the consciousness of this present thinking thing can join itself, makes the same person, and is one self with it, and with nothing else" (§17). This passage might be thought to provide further support for the reading according to which I become the same Person as Nestor through and through; but that reading depends on misjudging the import of the speculation. One of the nice things about Locke's theory is that original sin is ruled out: for on the Great Day, "no one shall be made to answer for what he knows nothing of" (2.27.22). In order to be guilty of original sin one would have to be Conscious of Adam's or Eve's action. It would have to be one's own action, and one would have to be them in that respect.

that a Lockean person is essentially "capable of a law, and happiness, and misery" (§26), and the fact that "person" is, for Locke, a forensic term. I also think that the word "thinking," which Locke often explicitly uses in the wide Cartesian sense, has sometimes been read too narrowly. So let me now try to display Locke's definition of a Person as a set of singly necessary and jointly sufficient conditions, using only his words.

Certainly a Person is a

(1) thinking
(2) intelligent

being that has

(3) reason

and

(4) reflection.

These four things are ground-floor necessary conditions, essential preconditions, of being a Person, and there is I believe no redundancy in this list. *Thinking*, (1), may be understood in the widest Cartesian sense to cover all conscious mental goings-on, the simplest cases of which are mere sensation.[8] *Intelligent*, (2), further requires a certain level of mental sophistication additional to (1) (at the very least, it requires cognition in addition to sensation). *Reason*, (3), further specifies the required level of sophistication (a creature can cognize that things are the case without being able to reason; it can grasp propositions without any capacity for inference). *Reflection*, (4), is in turn an addition to reason. It's

---

[8] "All the operations of ... the senses are thoughts" (Descartes 1641: 2.113).

not only "that notice which the mind takes of its own operations, and the manner of them, by reason whereof there
come to be ideas of these operations in the understanding"
(2.1.4); it's also a capacity, the capacity for higher-order
thought, the capacity to think explicitly about one's thinking
(*reflexio*), which we possess and nonhuman animals do not.

(1)–(4) are necessary sensory-cognitive-capacity conditions of Personhood, but they're not sufficient. Nor are they
the focus of the definition: the passage has yet to tell us what
it is about such a sophisticated subject of experience that
makes it a Person. The crucial addition, when it comes to
Personhood, so far as cognitive-capacity conditions are concerned, is that the thing in question

(5) can consider itself as itself

and, more particularly,

(6) can consider itself as itself, the same thinking thing, in
different times and places.

(5) goes beyond (4) in stating that a Person is fully or expressly self-conscious in the way defined on p. 45.

It's a familiar point that a being could fulfill condition (4),
and be able to take its own thoughts as objects of thought,
without being fully self-conscious, without being capable
of thinking of itself specifically as itself. The full self-consciousness of (5), however, is still not enough for Personhood. For a creature that entirely lacked memory and fore-
sight could possibly be fully self-conscious, but it would fail
to qualify as a Person in Locke's scheme, because a Person's
self-consciousness must have genuine temporal reach.[9] A

---

[9] Clive Wearing, whose memory was destroyed by a herpetic infec-
tion of the brain, and whose constant experience is that he has only just

Person must, as (6) specifies, be able to think of itself as itself as existing at places and times other than the present. This is essential if it is to be a proper subject of punishment and reward.[10]

Locke then states that a Person's fulfillment of conditions (5) and (6) depends essentially on the fact that it possesses

(7) Consciousness.

A being can consider itself as itself in the required way, he says, "only by that consciousness which is inseparable from thinking, and, as it seems to me, essential to it."

It may be said that this is obvious. Of course (5) requires (7): of course self-consciousness requires Consciousness. In fact Consciousness (7) is already entailed by (1), thinking, as Locke has just said. So why does he mention it only now? Why does explicit reference to Consciousness occur only at this point in the definition? One reason, I think, is that Consciousness is essentially a kind of *reflexivity*, and thus has a special foundational connection with (5), which is itself a special case of reflexivity. But, this noted, it should be said again that all thinking/experiencing animals have (7) the basic reflexivity of Consciousness that is essentially constitutive of any (1) thinking/experiencing at all, even mere sentience. So although (7) is necessary for (5), the capacity for full self-consciousness, it's certainly not sufficient. What is

---

become conscious, is a tragic and extraordinary actual case of (5) without (6); see Wearing 2005. He is clearly a person in our sense.

[10] Leibniz is among those who stress this point. The inappropriateness of holding Clive Wearing accountable for his misdemeanors on the Day of Judgment is strikingly apparent. Although he is a person in our ordinary understanding of the term, he's not a Person, a Lockean person, because he's not a genuine locus of moral accountability. (Locke considers a case of total memory loss in §25.)

also necessary for (5), by way of reflexivity, is no doubt (4), the more sophisticated capacity for reflection which we have and other animals lack.

(4) as defined is not on its own sufficient to turn Consciousness into full self-consciousness, for a creature could be able to think about its thinking without thinking (or being able to think) of its thinking as its own. True enough, but so be it. In including a requirement of full self-consciousness among the conditions of Personhood, Locke is not trying to produce a statement of the sufficient conditions of full self-consciousness.[11]

So far we have a statement of the basic mental cognitive capacities that must be possessed by anything that is to count as a Person. But this is not all. For Consciousness, as we have seen, is inseparable from Concernment. It follows that a Person is, by definition, necessarily

(8) Concerned for itself.

This requirement, however, doesn't distinguish a Person from any other sentient creature, for all sentient creatures are Conscious, on Locke's view, and so Concerned for them-

---

[11] It's possible to read the "only" in "only by that consciousness which is inseparable from thinking" as indicating a statement of a sufficient condition, but this seems wrong, since all sentient creatures have Consciousness, on Locke's view, but not full self-consciousness. "But there is a *sense* in which all sentient creatures have full self-consciousness, a sense recognized in Phenomenological accounts of the respect in which all sentience involves some sort of self-awareness: 'to be a subject [of any sort at all] is to be in the mode of being aware of oneself' (Husserl 1921–1928: 151)". Yes, but such self-consciousness isn't full self-consciousness, on the terms of the standard definition of self-consciousness in analytic philosophy, and it may also lack the explicit autobiographical temporal dimension that Locke takes to be constitutive of Personhood.

selves, and the final and fundamental remaining condition on being a Person is that a Person

(9) is capable of a law, and happiness, and misery.

When it's found in a Person, Concernment has an essentially moral dimension, and it's (9) and (6) that state what is most truly distinctive about being a Person. (9) depends on (6), the capacity to consider oneself as oneself at different times and places, because (6) is necessary for being a moral being, as already remarked, and (9) and (6) together confer on Persons their central defining property, considered as Persons: their property of being proper objects of reward and punishment with respect to what they do and equally with respect to what they have done in the past. If Consciousness weren't accompanied by Concernment, and in particular by *moral* Concernment (which depends both on (6), temporally extended self-consciousness, and on (9), being "capable of a law"), it wouldn't have this effect. If there were fully explicitly self-conscious, cognitively sophisticated, fully memory-equipped subjects of experience that had no self-Concernment—not only no capacity for pleasure and pain, but also more particularly, no grasp of a law, no capacity for happiness or misery based in morality—they wouldn't be *Persons*, genuine moral Persons, although they fulfilled all the clauses of the definition in §9.[12]

In §9, then, Locke first offers a wholly functional definition of "person," a definition given wholly in terms of the possession of certain capacities.[13] The functional-capacity

---

[12] It is important to bear in mind that happiness and misery, as opposed to mere pleasure and pain, have a special connection with our eternal fate. For a good discussion of this, see Garrett 2003.

[13] Having given such a purely functional definition, Locke would be

part of his definition of "person" is then supplemented by one further definitional element that is not a matter of a general functional capacity. This is the claim, at the end of §9, that everything that lies in the field of Consciousness of a Person, a field that is greatly enlarged by temporally extended self-consciousness, is part of that Person—or at least part of that Person's Personal identity.

It may be said that Locke is not in §9 concerned with the essential link between Consciousness and Concernment. He's concerned, first, with the sensory-cognitive core of Consciousness, according to which to be Conscious of something is to (be able to) experience it in a certain direct or immediate way, "to experience it as one's own" in a sense of this phrase that does not imply full self-consciousness, and, secondly, (5) and (6), the no less purely cognitive capacity for temporally extended full self-consciousness. And it's true that he doesn't explicitly mention Concernment until the next page. It's also clear that Consciousness and temporally extended full self-consciousness don't in and of themselves necessarily involve Concernment: there's no conceptual incoherence in the idea that there could be sentient, fully cognitively self-conscious, autobiographical-memory-equipped, utterly Concernment-free creatures (although their experience could not include pleasure and pain). It doesn't, however, follow that Consciousness (+ temporally

---

unimpressed with any definition that proposed to restrict the class of Persons to a particular species, say human beings, ± angels and God. To be a Person is simply to be a moral being, and to be a moral being is simply to have certain capacities and sensitivities. What good reason could anyone have, in "this vast and stupendious universe" (2.2.3), for thinking that membership of the species *homo sapiens sapiens* was somehow essential to morality?

extended self-consciousness) as we have it in Locke's text—
Consciousness by which "every one is to himself that which
he calls *self*," Consciousness "which makes every one to be,
what he calls *self*"—can exist without Concernment. Nor
can it, if it's sufficient for Lockean Personal identity, as it is
by definition in Locke's text.[14] Locke's official and correct
position is that Concernment merely "accompanies" Consciousness (*Essay* 2.1.11). It "extends as far as" it (§17). It is, if
you like, a mere "concomitant" (§26) of Consciousness. But
it is at the same time an "unavoidable concomitant" (§26) of
Consciousness in any creature capable of pleasure and pain,
as Locke supposes all sentient creatures to be.

I'll end by repeating the point that one mustn't assume
that Locke means something merely cognitive by "thinking"
in §9, because he regularly uses "thinking" in the wide Cartesian sense to cover experience in general, sensing, feeling,
perceiving, meditating, and willing as well as cognition. This
is shown by the immediate continuation of the famous definition of a person, in a passage already discussed in chapter 4:

> . . . can consider it self as it self, the same thinking thing,
> in different times and places, which it does only by that
> consciousness which is inseparable from thinking, and, as
> it seems to me, essential to it: it being impossible for any
> one to perceive, without perceiving, that he does perceive.
> When we see, hear, smell, taste, feel, meditate, or will any-
> thing, we know that we do so. Thus it is always as to our
> present sensations and perceptions: and by this every one

---

[14] One might express Locke's position by saying that if there were
no Concernment in a creature that was, cognitively speaking, fully self-
conscious, fully capable of considering itself as itself, then there would be
no self and no person; a point arguably well made in the Buddhist tradition.

is to himself that which he calls *self* ... consciousness always accompanies thinking, and 'tis that, that makes every one to be, what he calls *self*.

One of the problems in the discussion of Locke's theory of personal identity is that many encounter the famous passage only in a truncated form, without this passage, and are led to think that by "thinking" Locke means only something cognitive.

Locke's account of these things is imperfect inasmuch as he takes it (on the one hand) that Consciousness is found in all creatures that have any sort of experience at all, but sometimes seems to suggest (on the other hand) that it is Consciousness by itself that gives us temporally extended self-consciousness of the distinctively human kind, rather than just being a necessary foundation of such self-consciousness. This isn't important, in practice, because his discussion is focused on human beings. It does, however, mean that his famous remark, in the next paragraph, that "consciousness makes personal identity" (§10), is strictly speaking incorrect, even on his own terms. What he means, more strictly speaking, is that it is Consciousness *as it is found in creatures like us*, i.e. Persons, creatures possessing temporally extended self-consciousness and capable of a law, that makes personal identity. It's only "as far as any intelligent being can *repeat* the idea of any past action with the same consciousness it had of it at first [by means of its temporally extended self-consciousness], and with the same consciousness it has of any present action" that it is now "the same *personal self*" (§10) as the agent of that action.

One might put the point by saying that the Consciousness referred to in this passage may be thought of first as (i) the basic Concernment-entailing Consciousness we share with animals like foxes (see p. 28, n. 4). What must then be added is the point that Consciousness is in our case infused with (ii) awareness of moral considerations. But (ii) is not enough for Personal identity either. What must also be added is (iii) is a creature's capacity to "repeat the idea of [a] past action with the same consciousness it had of it at first" (§10), a capacity which depends, of course, on "the capacity to consider [one] self as [one]self, the same thinking being at different times and places" (§9). This is also necessary for Personal identity, for (pleonastically) Personal identity *over time*.

Chapter Nine

Consciousness Is Not Memory

IT'S CLEAR THAT Consciousness—Lockean consciousness—
isn't the same as memory, contrary to what many have
supposed. The primary and paradigm case of Consciousness
involves no memory at all: it's the Consciousness one has
of one's own experience and action in the present, the
Consciousness that's "inseparable from thinking" (i.e.
experience), "essential to it" (§9), essentially constitutive
of it. One can be fully Conscious in this fundamental way
and have no memory at all, or only a few seconds' worth.[1]
Consciousness of past actions and experiences, which
does of course involve memory, is just one special case of
Consciousness. It's a case of Consciousness that is explained

---

[1] "David cannot learn any new fact at all. ... He knows very little about
himself except his name. He talks to you very charmingly, even intelli-
gently. ... Left to his own devices, he sustains purposeful behavior relative
to the context he is in for many minutes or hours, provided that what he
is doing is engaging. ... He can play a whole set of checkers—and win!—
although he does not even know the name of the game and would not be
able to articulate a single rule for it , ... and ... the affective modulation of
his voice as the game approaches its decision point is a primer of human
emotion. ... He's a very happy person, jovial, delighted to talk to people.
... But he doesn't know the date, why he is talking to you or who you are.
He doesn't know who he is in the proper sense of the term. He is a consciousness without an identity" (Damasio 1999: 43–47, 113–21; 2000: 48).

and characterized by reference to the basic case, which is Consciousness of one's experience in the present moment. The identity of a person "extends it *self* beyond present [conscious] existence," Locke says,

> only by consciousness,—whereby it becomes concerned and accountable; owns and imputes to it *self* past actions, *just upon the same ground and for the same reason as it does the present* [actions]. (§26)[2]

Consciousness, as far as ever it can be extended—should it be to ages past—unites existences, and actions, very remote in time, into the same person, as well as it does the existences and actions of *the immediately preceding moment.* (§16)

As far as any intelligent being can repeat the idea of any past action with the same consciousness it had of it at first, and with *the same consciousness it has of any present action*; so far it is the same *personal self.* For it is by the consciousness it has of *its present thoughts and actions*, that it is *self* to it *self* now, and so will be the same *self*, as far as the same consciousness can extend to actions past or to come.[3]

---

[2] Reid (1785: 24) takes it to be true by definition that "consciousness is only of things present. To apply consciousness to things past . . . is to confound consciousness with memory." Locke's proposal is precisely to extend the notion of consciousness from its primary use, in a highly suggestive way. Compare Kierkegaard in the next note.

[3] §10. Note how the point made in the last paragraph of the previous chapter applies here. It seems that Locke is saying that it is simply Consciousness that is getting one back into the past. And this is right insofar as Consciousness is the foundation of the capacity to consider oneself as oneself in different times and places. But one does nevertheless need to distinguish between (i) the capacity for temporally extended self-consciousness that gets one to the past action, and (ii) the basic Consciousness that consists in experiencing the past action as one's own in the immediate kind of way in which one experiences one's present actions as

In each case the basic reference point for attributions of Consciousness is the subject of experience considered in the present moment. Consciousness can't be identified with memory.

---

one's own—which is presumably the Consciousness that is constitutive of all "thinking" or "perception" (conscious mentation) whatever.

Note also that the third formulation, from §10, may seem hopelessly demanding, at first, and entirely unrealistic. But it can be read in such a way that it doesn't require that one possess the capacity to relive the past experience just as it was originally experienced. It simply requires that one be able to experience the past action, A, say, as one's own with the same immediacy as that with which one experienced it at first, where this (obviously) doesn't require that one achieve total recall of A, but only that one experience it *as one's own* with the same sort of immediacy as that with which one experiences one's present actions or experiences as one's own. The fundamental requirement is simply that one experience A as something that Concerns oneself, so far as its moral quality is concerned, just as fully and immediately as one experiences the moral quality of an action one has just performed as something that Concerns oneself. So long as that is in place, one's memory of the details of the episode may have dramatically faded.

It's worth comparing Kierkegaard's idea that it's important to moral life that one be able to "relive" one's past actions in some way. (I'd like to thank Patrick Stokes for alerting me to this.) Writing as "Anti-Climacus," Kierkegaard states that "the past is not actuality—for me. Only the contemporary is actuality for me. That with which you are living simultaneously is actuality—for you" (1850: 64). Accordingly, he thinks that accurate moral grasp of one's past actions requires being able to apprehend them in the mode of "contemporaneity," i.e. as if they were occurring now—an idea close to Locke's idea that one needs to be able to be Conscious of them in the way in which one is Conscious of present experiences. At the same time, Kierkegaard seems clear on the point that "really coming to grips with" past actions by reliving them in the way that is morally important doesn't require that one's reliving be vivid in all details. (One of the things that can have happened, in the time that has passed since one did A, is that one can have come to see that what one felt at the time of action was wrong. One may have been wrong at the time to think that A was right, or at least not wrong, or wrong to think that A was wrong.)

It may be said that Consciousness *of the past*, at least, is the same as memory, on Locke's view. But this isn't true, as remarked in chapter 5, unless one restricts one's attention to from-the-inside memory (my memory of the date of the Battle of Hastings is not an instance of concernment-involving Consciousness). Would Locke have accepted the identification of Consciousness of the past with memory once he'd confined his attention to from-the-inside memory? Not if he'd thought that there can be from-the-inside memory without Concernment. Could there be? It seems to me eminently possible. One can think quite unconcernedly not only about supremely boring episodes in one's past, but also, in certain cases, about one's former pains and emotions (see p. 139 below).

The problem with most commentators, as Marya Schechtman says, is that they have thought of Consciousness as merely

> a faculty of *knowing*, and this makes the interpretation of consciousness of the past as memory almost irresist-ible. This is not, however, the aspect of consciousness that Locke most emphasizes in his discussion of personal iden-tity. Instead he stresses the *affective* side of consciousness. (1996: 108)

She asks a very good question: if Locke means memory when he talks of Consciousness, why doesn't he say so? Why doesn't he simply talk of memory? Why does he "*never say* . . . that memory connections constitute personal identity if this is what he means"? There's an extended discussion of memory in 2.10 of the *Essay*, and Locke uses the word many times in his discussion of personal identity, but "when he tells us what personal identity consists in," Schechtman says, "which he does many times throughout the chapter, he *always* talks about extension of consciousness and *never* about memory connections" (1996: 107).

The principal reason for this is that most Consciousness isn't a matter of memory at all, but the point Schechtman stresses is no less important—the point that she expresses (albeit in a not strictly Lockean way) by saying that "we extend consciousness back in time to some past action or experience by caring about it in the appropriate way."[4] I'll return to this in chapter 19, where I'll say something about the importantly connected matter of repentance.

[4] 1996: 109. In Lockean terms, the caring is strictly speaking a matter of the Concernment that invariably accompanies the Consciousness; it's not essentially constitutive of the Consciousness itself. But Charles Taylor gets things exactly wrong when he writes that Locke "has no inkling of the self as a being which essentially is constituted by a certain mode of self-concern" (1989: 49). So does Velleman, when he writes that "Locke thinks that the psychological relation making for a person's survival is exclusively a relation of memory…Locke's theory implies that one may share virtually no motivational characteristics with one's past or future selves. One may in the past have possessed vastly different attitudes and traits of character, so long as one remembers being the person who possessed them" (1996: 336-337).

Chapter Ten

Personal Identity

I'VE ATTEMPTED to clarify Locke's notions—definitions—of consciousness (Consciousness), concernment (Concernment), and person (Person). It seems high time to put the canonical personal identity question:

> What are the necessary and sufficient conditions of the truth of the claim that a person considered now at time t_2, whom we may call [**P**], is the same person as a person considered at a different past time t_1, whom we may call [**P**$_x$]? What has to be true if it is to be true that [**P**$_x$] is the same person as [**P**]?

There is, certainly, a sense in which Locke is interested in this question in his discussion of personal identity. It is, however, hard to get the word "person" to behave properly if one takes the canonical question to be his question. This is because the canonical question assumes that "person" denotes a thing or object or substance that is a standard temporal continuant in the way that a human being or person$_1$ is (or an immaterial soul, on most conceptions of what an immaterial soul is). But while Lockean persons (Persons) are certainly temporal continuants of some sort, considered as subjects of experience, they're not standard temporal continuants insofar as they're partly constituted by actions and experiences.

A *human being* (a *man*, in Locke's terms, a person$_1$) is a standard temporal continuant, a diachronically continuous entity, and Locke gives a statement of the nature of the diachronic continuity of living things like human beings and plants that has yet to be bettered. It's "a participation of the same continued life, by constantly fleeting particles of matter, in succession vitally united to the same organized body" (§6). He is, as remarked in chapter 2, clear in his view that anything that is a *thing* or *substance* has to be diachronically continuous over time in order to remain the same thing (§§1–3), whether the thing in question is material (a material particle, say, or an animal, with its own special "organic" conditions of diachronically continuous existence) or immaterial (a soul or soul-substance, say). But he also explicitly and famously distinguishes *person* both from *human being* (*man*), as something that has quite different identity conditions, and from (*individual*) *substance*, material or immaterial, on the same ground; and there's a sense in which he's not concerned to show that a person (a Person) is a continuous thing in the same sort of way that a human being or a particle or a soul-substance is.

One might say, as in chapter 3, that in Locke's use, "person" is sometimes better taken as a term for a fundamental property or aspect of a kind of thing. One might say that for Locke, "person" functions more like "baker" or "rogue" than "human being." For "baker" and "rogue" function smoothly as names for things in spite of the fact that they highlight properties of things. On this account, and in the ordinary, actual case (i.e. putting aside all strange thought-experiments), a Person, say [$\mathbf{P}_{GS}$], is a human being, say GS, *considered specifically in respect of his moral identity.*[1] And the moral identity of [$\mathbf{P}_{GS}$], at any given time (say now), is a function of the totality of those actions of the human being GS from birth until now of which GS is now still Conscious. It is, equivalently, a function of all the actions of GS in (or with) which GS is now still *Concerned*, in such a way that he feels that those actions to be his own, where this is a matter of his heart, about which—as we will see—he may not be fully authoritative. This "considered specifically in respect of his moral identity" qualification brings us very close to the Hobbesian-Pufendorfian notion of a person (chapter 3), and prevents "Person" from being a standard sortal term for a standard temporal continuant.[2]

I think this is one good way to say what a Lockean person is. It won't, however, stop the standard-temporal-continuant-presupposing use of the word "person" from continuing to tug at our intuitions. Nor should it. For although there is a sense in which Locke isn't concerned to provide an answer to the question of Personal identity that has the consequence that a Person, in being a thing with a past, is a diachronically continuous entity in the presumably unproblematic way in which a perfectly preserved stone is, or in the unproblematic way in which a living organism like a human being is, there is nonetheless another key sense in which he does require that there be continuity. He requires mental continuity, continuity of a locus of consciousness. He requires—or rather takes for granted—the continuity of a subject of experience [**S**].

---

[1] Just as he can be considered specifically in respect of his *professional specialization*, e.g. carpenter, so too he can be considered specifically in respect of his *moral identity*.

[2] As remarked, Law (1769) and Thiel (1998) are clear on the point.

Let me characterize Locke's notion of a person once again, in the straightforwardly ontological terms first introduced in chapter 2.

What are you, as a Person, considered at *t*—now, say? You consist, first, of the material—and perhaps also immaterial—substance that now at this moment actually makes you up, i.e. [**M**] and [**I**] in chapter 2, to which I'm now going to give the joint neutral name "[**X**]."[3]

Why is [**X**] literally part of what constitutes you specifically as a Person? Because it's situated in the field of one's Concernment, or—more particularly—one's field of Consciousness.[4] Its being so situated is a sufficient (as well as necessary) condition of its being part of the person one is, for one is constituted as a Person, at any given time, by whatever lies (by everything that lies) in one's field of Consciousness.[5] Given a subject of experience [**S**] at a particular time *t*, it's the reach of [**S**]'s Consciousness at *t* that determines and wholly settles the question of which or what Person [**S**] is, at *t*, where this reach extends not only to (morally assessable) actions and experiences but also to whatever (else) constitutes [**S**] substantially speaking at *t*, whether materially or immaterially: i.e. [**X**]. Everything that one's Consciousness touches or "can join it self … with" (§17), everything that is "comprehended under" one's Consciousness in this sense, is part of the Person one is. This and only this settles the question of [**S**]'s Personal identity or Personhood, at *t*, which

---

[3] I use "[**X**]" rather than "[**IM**]" or [**I/M**] because there may be no [**I**].

[4] One may also say that it is [**X**]'s being "vitally united" to you that is fundamental, and that its being situated in one's field of Consciousness follows from that vital union.

[5] It's not the Consciousness itself, but the objects of that Consciousness, that are in question. Note that nothing can lie in the field of Consciousness of more than one person. See note p. 62, n.7.

is also the question of its forensic identity, at t.[6] One's [**X**], one's material ± immaterial substance, is literally part of what constitutes one as a Person, now in the present.

Given the standard conception of the immaterial-substance component, there's a difference between the contribution of the immaterial stuff and the contribution of the material stuff. This is because the immaterial stuff that lies in one's field of Consciousness now, and is therefore part of what constitutes one as a Person, is, according to the standard conception, numerically the very same substantial stuff that constituted one as a Person (by lying in one's field of Consciousness) ten years ago. By contrast, the material stuff that lies in one's field of Consciousness now, and is therefore part of what constitutes one as a Person, isn't the same stuff that constituted one as a Person by lying in one's field of Consciousness ten years ago.[7] That said, it's central to Locke's overall argument that the standard conception of the contribution of the immaterial-substance component may not and need not be correct. He holds, famously, in §13, that the Person one is now can be said to exist ten years ago even if one has not only acquired 100 percent new [**X**] on the mate-

---

[6] Consciousness is all that matters, because it is "the same consciousness that makes a man be himself to himself" (§10). Consciousness is all that matters, because "consciousness ... is that, that makes every one to be what he calls *self*, and thereby distinguishes himself from all other thinking things, in this alone consists *personal identity*, i.e. the sameness of a rational being" (§9).

[7] If one thinks of the material substance that constitutes one as a Person now as one's living animal body, then one can say that there's a sense in which one is as a Person constituted by numerically the same material substance as one was constituted by ten years ago, by appealing to the special diachronic identity conditions of living things; but this remark may be 100 percent false at the level of individual particles. There may also be particles that have in that time arrived and belonged, departed, and then returned and belonged again.

rial side, but also 100 percent new [**X**] on the *immaterial* side. On Locke's truly radical view, the Person or subject of experience one is can be said to exist ten years ago even if one has in the last ten minutes acquired 100 percent new body constituents and a 100 percent new soul constituent. This is in fact his most dramatic proposal, in the context of his time. It's the combination of the well-known prince/cobbler body-swap thought-experiment in §15, which needs no special comment here, with the soul-substitution thought-experiment in §13, which will need six chapters to itself.[8]

Certainly one must have some [**X**] or other, but—roughly speaking—one's diachronic identity as a Person or subject of experience doesn't depend on the diachronic identity of one's [**X**]. One's being as a subject of experience, [**S**], is and must be constituted by one's [**X**], at any given time, or at least part of one's [**X**], e.g. one's brain, or one's immaterial soul, or one's brain plus one's immaterial soul (but not, say, one's foot); but it can, as far as we know, survive complete replacement of one's [**X**]. In these terms, Locke's key thought (or a very important part of it) consists in the idea that one's [**S**] can migrate relative to one's [**X**], although one must always have some [**X**] or other at any given time.

So much for [**X**]. The remaining component of one's Personhood is [**A**], on the terms introduced in chapter 2: all the actions and experiences, present and past, that lie in the field of Consciousness of a subject of experience at a given time. We may say, then, that a Person considered at a given time, say now, consists of [**X**] + [**A**] and nothing else:

$$[\mathbf{P}] = [\mathbf{X}] + [\mathbf{A}].$$

---

[8] Here we find a forerunner of Parfit's argument to the conclusion that a certain sort of psychological continuity "with any cause" whatever, between t_1 and t_2, may be sufficient for personal survival between t_1 and t_2.

The way the field of Consciousness extends into the past in the case of [A] is different from the way in which it does so in the case of [X], for in the case of [X] we can say that the field of Consciousness now contains an entity—a soul-substance [I], say, or a living organism [M]—which has criteria of diachronic identity that allow us to say that it is a thing that exists now and that existed in the past; whereas in the case of any action or experience, we cannot say that it is a thing that exists now at all, although it existed in the past. We may accordingly say that in the case of the [X] component(s), the field of Consciousness normally extends into the past by containing diachronically continuous things—[I] and [M], one's body and/or soul—that are properly held to exist both now in the present, and in the past, wholly independently of any considerations relating to Personhood or the field of Consciousness.[9] When it comes to the [A] components, by contrast, this isn't so. As far as all past actions and experiences go, they existed in the past but do not exist now at all, although I am now still Conscious of them.

Once again it may feel ontologically odd to place [X] and [A] side by side like this, as if they were equally and literally components of a Person; they seem to be such different sorts of things. Again I think the uneasiness can be revealing—revealing of the special notion of Personhood that is in play. The fundamental notion for Locke, when it comes to Personhood, is the notion of the field of Consciousness, and relative to that notion, [X] and [A] naturally and tellingly line up side by side.[10]

[9] "Normally," because in §13 and §15 Locke considers cases in which this breaks down: [S] can survive instantaneous complete replacement of both [M] and [I] (=[X]). See also the quotation from §24 on p. 61.

[10] The actions and experiences that are part of what constitute the Person are of course concretely existing entities, occurrences in the world that have as such substantial being, both material and/or immaterial.

At one point in his book on Locke, Michael Ayers proposes that Locke holds that life in an organism is "a nonsubstantial principle of substantial unity, and that consciousness is just like life" (1991: 2.263). I think this is a very good remark (note that one might say that its first use of "substantial" is straightforwardly Lockean, while its second use is Aristotelian), and it seems directly transferrable to the notion of Personhood, to give: Personhood is a *nonsubstantial principle of substantial unity*. Or one might say that for Locke, Personhood is a *fundamental but ultimately nonsubstantial principle of unity* (given that the second use of "substantial" is indeed non-Lockean, and indeed frowned on by Locke), while being for all that our most fundamental principle of unity, given our status as moral beings, i.e. given what we most fundamentally are—Persons. It's a fundamental principle of *forensic unity* that is not strictly speaking a principle of substantial unity in the Lockean sense of "individual substance." But we can and should also count it as a principle of *substantial* unity if we take it as given that Persons are substances if any things are.

Let me try to illustrate this. Suppose we put aside thought-experiments again, and draw an unbroken line to represent my actual human life from my first coming into existence as a human being. We may then consider the segment from t_1, a moment ten years ago, to t_2, a moment five years ago:

[1]

t_1 t_2

―――――――――――――――――――――――|

my life from t_1 to t_2

We can now add a line, above my basic human lifeline, to represent, schematically, the *Person* that I am, that is, the Person that I am considered specifically at t_2 and considered specifically with respect to [**A**], my actions and experiences between t_1 and t_2.[11] This will be a broken line and will look something like this:

[2]

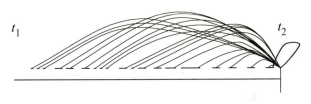

the view of t_1–t_2 from t_2: my (forensic) Consciousness at t_2 with respect to t_1–t_2

The dashes of the fragmented upper line represent pieces of the lower line: action-and-experience-involving pieces of which I am now Conscious. The curving lines represent the fact that I am at t_2 Conscious of some of the periods of time between t_1 and t_2.[12] Note that there is a line from t_2 to t_2 representing my Consciousness of my currently occurring experiences at t_2 ("thinking consists in being conscious that one thinks," 2.1.19).

Now consider the view of t_1–t_2 from t_3, the present moment, and see what time has wrought.

---

[11] And so not considered with respect to my substantial composition between t_1 and t_2, insofar as this involves more than the existence of the relevant actions and experiences (for the qualification, see p. 9).

[12] They represent "psychological connectedness," in Parfit's sense.

[3]

t_1 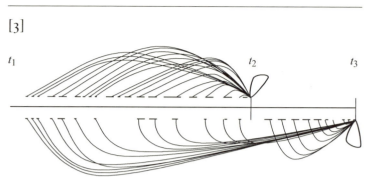 t_2 t_3

the view of t_1–t_2 from t_3: my (forensic) Consciousness at t_2 and t_3
with respect to t_1–t_2

The view from t_2 is represented as before by everything
above my continuous lifeline; the view from t_3 is represented
by everything below it. (The vertical line cutting the continuous horizontal lifeline marks the Person I was at t_2.) The
key change in my (forensic or [A]-related) Consciousness,
between t_2 and t_3, so far as the period from t_1 to t_2 is concerned, is marked by the fact that the lower gappy line is
sparser than the higher gappy line. This represents the fact
that I am at t_3 Conscious of fewer of the experiences that occurred between t_1 and t_2 than I was at t_2. So the Person that
I am at t_3 has changed not only because I've performed new
actions and undergone new experiences between t_2 and t_3,
but also because I'm no longer Conscious, at t_3, of some of
the actions and experiences that occurred between t_1 and t_2
of which I was still conscious at t_2.

The diagram represents a considerable thinning of the
lower dotted line relative to the higher one and may not be
accurate in this respect. For I may at t_3 still be Conscious of
almost all the things I was Conscious of at t_2. If we slightly
redefine "Conscious" so that it doesn't pick up everything
that I am still Concerned in, such as happy memories of

morally neutral experiences, but only picks up morally relevant items, it may be that not much has changed at t_3, Consciousness-wise, when it comes to the period between t_1 and t_2. In particular, it may be that not much has changed in my heart (to use Locke's biblical terms), all of whose secrets will be laid open on the Day of Judgment. I think that Locke doesn't expect the field of my Consciousness to change much from t_2 to t_3, so far as the morally important events in my life prior to t_2 are concerned.

That said, it's important that his view does allow change in the content of my field of Consciousness over time, relative to the actions and experiences of any period of past time. I may for example steal plums between t_1 and t_2, and no longer be Conscious of this action at t_3, and so no longer be properly punishable for it at t_3 (which may be the Day of Judgment). Consciousness may contain an involuntary natural mechanism that operates somewhat like a statute of limitations. One may forget many things precisely because they can appropriately be forgotten, because one is no longer Concerned in them (rather than ceasing to be Concerned in them simply because one has forgotten them and is therefore no longer Conscious of them). And one may perhaps *remember* things although one is no longer *Conscious* of them in the relevant sense, i.e. no longer Concerned in them in the moral-responsibility-engaging sense. One may not have to ask for 137,467 other offenses to be taken into consideration on the Day of Judgment, when receiving one's doom (i.e. all the offenses of the human being one is), for one may no longer be Concerned in many of them.

Chapter Eleven

Psychological Connectedness

I'LL RETURN TO THIS QUESTION in chapter 19. For the moment, note that this account of Locke's view can be reexpressed in Parfit's terms, according to which

(1) a person [**P**] at t_2 is (directly) *psychologically connected* to a person [**P**$_x$] at t_1 if—to take the case of memory—[**P**] can now remember having some of the experiences that [**P**$_x$] had at t_1,

and

(2) a person [**P**] at t_2 is *psychologically continuous* with [**P**$_x$] if there is some unbroken overlapping chain of such direct connections ([**P**] being psychologically connected to some [**P**$_i$], [**P**$_i$] to some [**P**$_j$], [**P**$_j$] to some [**P**$_k$], and so on, all the way back to [**P**$_x$]).

Clearly, [**P**] can be psychologically continuous with [**P**$_x$] even if [**P**] isn't psychologically connected to [**P**$_x$]. Equally clearly, [**P**] can be psychologically connected with [**P**$_x$] even if [**P**] isn't psychologically continuous with [**P**$_x$] (see Parfit 1984: 205–6). When it comes to memory, however, Locke isn't interested in the (transitive) relation of memory-link-based psychological continuity that has interested many of the "neo-Lockeans." He's only interested in the (nontransitive) relation of psychological connectedness.[1]

The psychological connectedness that matters to Locke is, furthermore, and crucially, narrower—more fine-grained— than psychological connectedness as ordinarily understood; and this is not simply because Consciousness isn't the same as memory. The point was made in chapter 8 and is worth repeating. Suppose that $[\mathbf{P}_x]$ performs two actions A1 and A2 at the same time at t_1. Locke's position, which is clearly correct on his terms, given the constantly reiterated forensic point of his account of Personal identity, is that $[\mathbf{P}]$ at t_2 can be Conscious of A1, and so psychologically connected to $[\mathbf{P}_x]$ at t_1 as the performer of A1 in such a way as to be the same Person as $[\mathbf{P}_x]$ at t_1, and so morally responsible for A1,

---

[1] In a letter to Arnauld in 1687, Leibniz writes of people's "recollection, consciousness or power to know what they are, upon which depends the whole of their morality, penalties and punishments" (1687: 160), agreeing thus far with Locke. "The intelligent soul that knows what it is," he continues, "and *is capable of pronouncing this **me** which says so much*, not only remains the same metaphysically ... , but it also remains morally the same and constitutes the same personality. For it is the memory and knowledge of this me that makes it liable to punishment and reward" (1686: §34). In his discussion of Locke's *Essay*, however, he decisively rejects Locke's Consciousness criterion: "if an illness had interrupted the continuity of my bond of consciousness, so that I did not know how I had arrived at my present state even though I could remember things further back, the testimony of others could fill in the gap in my recollection. I could even be punished on this testimony if I had done some deliberate wrong during an interval which this illness had made me forget a short time later. And if I forgot my whole past, and needed to have myself taught all over again, even my name and how to read and write, I could still learn from others about my life during my preceding state; and, similarly, I would have retained my rights without having to be divided into two persons and made to inherit from myself. All this is enough to maintain the moral identity which makes the same person" (ibid.). For a good discussion, see Thiel 2011, chap. 6.

while not being Conscious of A2—while not being psychologically connected to [$\mathbf{P}_x$] at t_1 as the doer of A2 in such a
way as to be the same Person as [$\mathbf{P}_x$] at t_1.[2] Plainly, then, [$\mathbf{P}$]'s
connection at t_1 to [$\mathbf{P}_x$] at t_1 is not a connection to [$\mathbf{P}_x$] at t_1
überhaupt, for if it were, this would yield a contradiction.
The crucial connection is to the doing of A1 at t_1 and not to
the doing of A2. On Locke's theory, it doesn't matter a jot
that there's only one human being involved. [P] can be the
same Person as [$\mathbf{P}_x$]-doing-A2 ("[$\mathbf{P}_{x/A2}$]") and not the same
Person as [$\mathbf{P}_x$]-doing- A1 ("[$\mathbf{P}_{x/A1}$]").

This is the point that has already been made about Nestor.
Perhaps one stole from a till with one hand and wrote a
check for charity with another, losing all memory and Consciousness of the latter act but not the former. If so, one will
not be responsible for the latter act, but only for the former,
on the Day of Judgment—unless the latter breaks back into
Consciousness (as we may surely hope it will) when the secrets of one's heart are laid open.

> —*This isn't possible.* [$P_{x/A1}$] *is not only the same* human being
> *as* [$P_{x/A2}$] *but also the same* Person, *simply because she is (we
> may suppose) fully Conscious of what she is doing at* t_1. *And this
> means that we can again generate a contradiction. For even if
> we allow ourselves for purposes of argument to treat* [$P_{x/A1}$] *and*
> [$P_{x/A2}$] *as potentially different Persons, in spite of the fact that
> there is only one human being, and equally only one human
> subject of experience, so that* [P] *at* t_2 *can be the same Person as
> one of them and not the other; still* [$P_{x/A1}$] *and* [$P_{x/A2}$] *must be
> the same person by Locke's own Consciousness criterion,
> given that* [P] *is fully Conscious of what she is doing at* t_1; *so*
> [P] *cannot be identical with* [$P_{x/A1}$] *and not also with* [$P_{x/A2}$].

---

[2] "Do an action" strikes me as incorrect, but I follow Locke's usage.

This seems a good objection; and there is perhaps no better way to understand Locke's overall theory of personal identity than to realize that it simply fails. That it is not any sort of objection is, in fact, at the heart of his idea. The point was made, in effect, by Locke's *per-impossibile* Nestor case, although this was misinterpreted: "person," once again, "is a forensic term, appropriating actions and their merit."[3]

This is not to say that there are no remaining difficulties, and indeed there are. Something still remains to be explained, something to do with continuity. One can put the point by saying that what the case shows is that there is a respect in which one's diachronic identity as a Person [P] can come apart from one's diachronic identity as a subject of experience [S]. This, though, is not a weakness in Locke's account. It is, rather, an essential part of its point as a theory of responsibility. One must, perhaps, grant that the same subject of experience [S] performed both A1 and A2, and given that one is the [S] that performed A1, one is also the [S] that performed A2. Nevertheless, one is not now the same Person as the Person that performed A2, although one is the same Person as the Person who performed A1. This is so simply because one is no longer Concerned in A2.

I think the case makes Locke's notion of a Person particularly clear. One can put the point by saying that [S] is a continuing thing, a temporal continuant (which may have been carried by many different substances during the course of its existence), in a respect in which [P] isn't. Or perhaps

---

[3] Here again we encounter a sense in which many of the so-called neo-Lockeans of our time (of whom Shoemaker and Parfit are perhaps the main representatives) aren't really Lockeans at all. For their conception of how mental links and mental continuities constitute a person as a diachronically continuous entity is not compatible with the possibility just described.

one does better to say that (i) [S] is a continuing thing, a standard temporal continuant, and that there is *therefore* a fundamental *sense* in which (ii) [P] is also a standard temporal continuant, given that [S] is a fundamental component of [P]; while adding that (iii) there is nonetheless a respect in which an [S]-*considered-specifically-qua-[P]* is *not* a temporal continuant. For the pick and choose of one's Consciousness may be extraordinarily fine-grained, when it comes to the past, in precisely such a way as to give rise to the present case of A1 and A2: if Consciousness "makes personal identity," then it identifies [P] at t_2 with $[\mathbf{P}_{x/A1}]$ at t_1 and not with $[\mathbf{P}_{x/A2}]$ at t_1.

We seem to have been led into some strange forms of expression. But the facts in question are no odder than the fact you can't remember everything you did, and the fact that you may no longer be rightly held responsible for everything you did. And it looks as if Locke's theory of personal identity may be completely right, considered specifically as a theory of moral responsibility—given the assumption that the notion of moral responsibility is a coherent one at all.[4]

---

[4] It depends crucially on the force of the doctrine of the heart, as in "the secrets of all hearts shall be laid open" (§22). If what I have forgotten in the case described by Leibniz in note 1 above (p. 89) remains in or on my heart, then it seems to me that Locke's doctrine is correct.

Chapter Twelve

Transition (Butler Dismissed)

LOCKE HAS DEFINED Personal identity in terms of the reach of Consciousness in beings who qualify as Persons (being in particular fully self-conscious, able to think of past and future, and "capable of a law"). A person in this sense, a Person, is not just a type of standard temporal continuant whose diachronic identity conditions amount to nothing more than the standard temporal-continuity conditions of other known kinds of objects (living or not, material or not). A Person is indeed an object of a certain sort, and must exemplify a certain sort of temporal continuity, if it is to continue to exist, given the opening paragraphs of Locke's chapter "Of identity and diversity" (§§1–3). And Locke assumes that any candidate Person has such continuity, considered as a subject of experience. But ... a Person is also an object-considered-specifically-in-respect-of-a-certain-property. It's a subject-of-experience-considered-in-the-Ciceronian-Hobbesian-Pufendorfian way (pp. 19–20 above), or, in Locke's version of this idea, a subject of experience considered—at any particular time at which it is considered—specifically in respect of the reach of its field of Consciousness at that time.

I hope that it is by now reasonably plain what Locke's theory of personal identity is meant to be and do—or at least not less plain than it is in Locke's own version. One has before one in the present, let us suppose, a subject of experience; a subject of experience that counts as a Person by Locke's functional-capacity definition of Person (pp. 63–67); a subject of experience that is, therefore, a moral being.[1] With this subject of experience now before one, one can ask which parts of its continuous past—which stretches back to infancy and beyond—are features or aspects or parts of the Person that it now is? On Locke's terms, this is the question "Which features or aspects or parts of the past of this subject of experience, this subject of experience that is the Person before us now, are contained in this subject of experience's overall field of Consciousness?" It is in answering this question—in moving, one might say, from the *Person*=subject of experience before us to the matter of establishing the forensic *Personal identity* of the Person=subject of experience before us—that one sees how it is that certain past actions and experiences come to be or remain features or aspects or parts of the Person=subject of experience who stands before us now in the present (i.e. come to be or remain parts or aspects of this Person's "Personal identity"). This procedure for establishing Personal identity is plainly different from the procedure of establishing personal identity in our ordinary person₁ or human-being or human-subject-of-experience sense of "person," because personal identity in this ordinary sense may be fully constituted independently of how Consciousness constitutes Personal identity in Locke's forensic, capital-letter sense.

The principal remaining task is to consider §13, in which Locke argues that a person can survive a change in its thinking substance even if its thinking substance is immaterial.

---

[1] This Person could conceivably have just lost all memory and Consciousness of its past—forever—and still be a Person.

This paragraph has been widely thought to involve a major error on Locke's part, and it's certainly not as clear as one might wish. Before continuing, though, I want to put aside Butler's well-known objection.

It's enough to quote it to see that it is irrelevant. Butler begins by saying that although

> consciousness of what is past does thus ascertain our personal identity to ourselves, yet to say, that it makes personal identity, or is necessary to our being the same persons, is to say, that a person has not existed a single moment, nor done one action, but what he can remember; indeed none but what he reflects upon. (1736: 440–41)

Here he incorrectly identifies consciousness with memory.[2] He continues, famously,

> And one should really think it self-evident, that consciousness of personal identity presupposes, and therefore cannot constitute, personal identity; any more than knowledge, in any other case, can constitute truth, which it presupposes.
> This wonderful mistake …

The wonderful mistake, though, is Butler's, not Locke's. Butler's remark has nothing to do with what Locke is talking about.[3] Butler is indeed "marvellously mistaken," in Law's words (1769: 21), in thinking that Locke should have made

---

[2] He appears to compound the error by wrongly taking Consciousness, already wrongly taken to be memory, to be only occurrent memory: "indeed none but what he reflects upon." This is low behavior for a philosopher and makes one think poorly of bishops, especially when one remembers Bishop Berkeley's contribution. The good Bishop Law counterbalances them to a considerable extent; but he has been forgotten.

[3] Apart from everything else, while Locke speaks of consciousness of actions, of past existence, of pleasure and pain, good and harm, of thinking, of one's body, he never speaks of consciousness of personal identity.

such a mistake; as is Reid when he writes that Locke's "doctrine upon this subject has been censured by Bishop Butler, in a short essay subjoined to his *Analogy*, with whose sentiments I perfectly agree" (1785: 275 [§3.6]), and many others since. Personal identity through time, understood as human subject-of-experience identity through time, is indeed presupposed. It's taken as given by Locke, as I've remarked several times (although he's very interested in arguing—in §13 and §15—that it's compatible with radical change of substantial realization). In saying that Consciousness constitutes Personal identity, he's merely offering a criterion for picking out those parts of such a subject's past that that subject is still responsible for. Locke's terms may be somewhat misleading; I record another source of misunderstanding in the last three paragraphs of chapter 18. But really Berkeley, Butler, and Reid have no excuse.

Chapter Thirteen

"*But next ... *": *Personal Identity without Substantial Continuity*

SUPPOSE, as I suspect Locke suspected, that materialism is true, and that one's whole psychological being—one's character, personality, memory, and so on—is wholly located in one's brain (see p. 9, n. 5). Suppose further that all the individual material particles composing one's brain have over the years been replaced many times.[1] Is this something to worry about, personally speaking? Plainly not. This is how things actually are with us (so Locke suspects, and so most of us today believe), and it doesn't put our continuing existence in question in any way at all. The [S] that one is, the subject of experience that one is, survives the process of complete substantial turnover with its diachronic continuity

[1] In the average human body, a trillion atoms are replaced every millionth of a second (Greene 2004: 441); according to one estimate, half of the molecules that make up one's liver at any time are gone five days later. The replacement rate for the brain is not known, but one estimate is that there is a complete turnover over a two- to three-week period (the brain is unusual in that neuronal cells are preserved; only their components are replaced).

untouched. So too, the person that one is (in the ordinary lowercase sense of the word "person") survives the process of complete substantial turnover with its diachronic continuity untouched.

This gives a fundamental insight into the essence of personal identity—to anyone who allows that the materialist story is even so much as coherent. For it appears to show conclusively that personal identity or sameness of *subject of experience* across time, personal identity across time understood in the lowercase, nonforensic, non-Lockean sense as sameness of subject of experience across time, doesn't require *sameness of substance or substantial composition* across time, any more than the diachronic continuity of an individual animal life requires sameness of substance or substantial composition. There is, it appears, a deep sense in which we are, considered as persons (where persons are considered as things that persist through significant periods of time), remarkably insubstantial entities, remarkably insubstantial relative to many conventional conceptions of substance, although we do of course always require some substantial realization or other, and must exemplify some sort of causal continuity between two different times if we are to be the same person/subject of experience at both those times. There's a sense in which we are, considered as persons, "Consciousnesses" in the count-noun sense of §23, most essentially *informational entities*, although, again, we do of course always require some substantial realization or other, and also some sort of causal continuity, something that ensures our identity across time, even if it involves exotic migrations across substances, through Teletransporters, and so on.[2]

---

[2] For the Teletransporter thought-experiment, see Parfit 1984. Briefly, one's body is scanned by a machine, and information sufficient to build a body qualitatively identical with one's present body out of new matter is transmitted across space to Mars. Causal continuity—indeed physical

To see this, it's enough to take materialism seriously, as Locke did, and think it through. I think it's one of Locke's principal ideas in his discussion of Personal identity. Again Ayers's phrase seem apt: a person is indeed a principle of unity, a fundamental principle of unity, a principle of diachronic unity, but it is at the same time, in a fundamental sense, a nonsubstantial principle of unity.[3] What Locke wants most, in the dialectical context of his time, and given his materialist and mortalist or thnetopsychist sympathies, is to show that one doesn't have to rely on a single continuing immaterial, immortal soul to span the gap—to preserve Personal identity—between death and resurrection.[4]

He puts the general point about the possible independence of Personal identity and substantial-composition identity clearly in §12, in which he makes the point that materialists can—must—allow full transmission of Personal identity (a persisting capacity for Consciousness, certainly, but also subjecthood, personality, memory) across complete change of substance. He goes straight on to the immaterialist case

continuity—is assured. It's true that, for a time, one exists only as a packet of radio waves. But so far as the continuing existence of one's personality (say) is concerned, this is hardly less robust, as a form of physical existence, than the bioelectrochemically complex activity in one's brain that constitutes the preservation of one's personality under normal circumstances (which include constant replacement of the constituent atoms of one's brain).

[3] It may count as a substantial principle of unity from an Aristotelian point of view.

[4] On the matter of immortality, Locke is clear on the point that "immortality is not at all owing nor built on immateriality as in its own nature incorruptible." See his discussion of 1 Corinthians 15:40–55 in his "Adversaria Theologica 94" (Nuovo 2002: 29–30). When we die, we die entirely. If in the end we are to have immortality, it will be something we acquire only at the resurrection. We are at present wholly corruptible entities. That, according to Locke, is why St. Paul states that "this corruptible must be *changed* & *put on* incorruption & this mortal must *put on* immortality" (ibid.). See also Johnston 2010: 91–93.

in §13, in which he claims that for all we can know a priori
there could be a similar transmission of Personal identity
across change of substance even if a persisting capacity for
Consciousness (subjecthood, personality, memory) is wholly
located or realized in (carried in, resident in) immaterial
substance. After all, we're all continuing Persons, and if
materialism is true, as materialists suppose, then there are
processes of *transubstantial transmission and transfer* that
allow that Persons may continue in existence even if their
substantial composition is wholly changed.[5] So why, he
asks, should this not also be possible in the immaterial case?
How can we rule this out a priori? For all we know, there
can be Personal identity across time without substantial-
composition identity across time in the immaterial case
just as in the material case. If so, we don't have to rely on a
single continuing immaterial substance in order to preserve
a Person's identity between death on earth and the Great
Day. Certainly the continuing *subject of experience* [S] is [M]
+ [I]-borne, or at the very least [M]-borne. And *the whole
Lockean Person* [P], i.e. the continuing subject of experience
[S] *together with the forensic load* [A] that [S] carries by
reason of its Consciousness of [A], is [M] + [I]-borne, or
at the very least [M]-borne. Nevertheless [M] and [I] can
change and pass away while [P] (= [S] + [A]) persists. (Note
that the present point is not only that a single continuing
immaterial substance isn't—for all we know—necessary for
preservation of Personal identity between death and the Day
of Judgment; it's equally that a single continuing immaterial
substance isn't—for all we know—sufficient either.)

The general idea is clear enough, especially when placed
in its mortalist context, but the interpretation of §13 is

[5] This is not of course transubstantiation in any magical or Christian
sense.

difficult, so I'll take it sentence by sentence. I hope it will become clearer why it's useful to distinguish [S] and [A], in discussing Locke's notion of a Person [P], but those who aren't interested in the detailed discussion of §13 may now skip to chapter 19 (p. 139).

[§13 s1] Locke's general question in §13, as remarked, is whether "personal identity can … be preserved" across "change of … substance," a question to which he has already replied in the affirmative, in general terms, in §10: the question "whether we are the same thinking thing; i.e. the same substance or no … concerns not *personal identity* at all." He starts §13 by assuming for purposes of argument that all thinking substance is immaterial. He does this because he's just dealt with "those who place thought in a purely material animal constitution" in §12. He's already noted that materialists "conceive personal identity preserved in something else than identity of substance" (§12), and it follows from this—given the assumption, which Locke makes, that all substance is either material or immaterial— that the only case that remains to be addressed is the case of those who place thought in an *im*material substance.

However it goes in detail, Locke's account must provide for something whose reality is in his time publicly pre-supposed on all sides, i.e. our personal responsibility over time up to and including the Day of Judgment, when we're resurrected with bodies that can't plausibly be thought to be particle-for-particle identical with our bodies at any time of our lives.[6] Now nearly everyone in Locke's time thinks that the question "What makes Person [P] on the Great Day the

---

[6] There is a well-stocked account of the many attempts to deal with this problem in Martin and Barresi 2006.

same person as myself now?" is quickly and simply answered by saying that the existence of [**P**] on the Great Day involves the same immaterial-soul component—[**I**]—as my existence on earth does now. In Locke's time, furthermore (and still today), an immaterial substance like [**I**] is taken to be "simple," i.e. to have no parts, and it is accordingly assumed that [**I**]'s continuance in existence can't involve any change of substantial composition (since any change would have to involve a numerically different substance). Plainly [**I**] is a terrific, *nec plus ultra* identity-preserver.

Almost all of Locke's contemporaries accept the view that I as a living person today consist of [**M**] + [**I**].[7] And once Locke has further explained his forensic use of the word "person," most of them will be prepared to accept that I as a Person also consist of [**A**]. Most of them will also allow that I won't have the same [**M**] on the Day of Judgment, because I'll be made of different material particles. But they'll then point out that I will have the same [**I**], and affirm that this will already be enough to guarantee that I have the same [**A**]. This is the context in which Locke is writing, and it explains why he pursues his fundamental (mortalism-friendly) aim— to remove an objection to materialism without questioning the story of our personal responsibility on the Great Day— by arguing that Personal identity across time doesn't or needn't require the persistence of anything (like [**I**]) whose continuance involves no change of substantial composition.

He has to show this, given his fundamental aim, because the materialists who "place thinking in a system of fleeting animal spirits" are already committed to denying that the

---

[7] Although my [**I**] guarantees my *identity* between death and resurrection, I also need some [**M**], at the resurrection, to be a *person* again. See p. 12, n. 10.

persistence of a single continuing substance is necessary for personal responsibility. They're already committed to the view that persons can survive change in their thinking substance (given that they hold that persons' thinking substance is wholly material). This means that if it can be shown that the continuance of something whose existence involves no change of substantial composition is after all necessary for my presence on the Day of Judgment, the immateriality of thinking substance will in effect be guaranteed (given, as always, that acceptance of the story of the Day of Judgment is mandatory).

From this perspective, then, Locke is seeking to block an argument from (i) the taken-for-granted or nonnegotiable fact of personal responsibility on the Day of Judgment to (ii) the immateriality of thinking substance. To do this he has to show that *individual-thinking-substance identity* across time isn't necessary for *Personal identity* across time, and so isn't necessary for *Personal responsibility* across time. He sees, correctly, that the only way to do this decisively, in the context of his times, is to establish the possibility that a Person can survive change in thinking substance even when it's assumed that all thinking substance is immaterial.

[§13 s2] Having restricted attention to immaterial substance in [s1], Locke raises the question "whether the consciousness of past actions can be transferr'd from one thinking substance to another" (I'll call this "transfer of Consciousness of [A]," although strictly speaking [A] also includes one's present actions and experiences). He answers, as he must if his argument is to succeed, that this is possible so far as we know. It can't be ruled out a priori. It may be impossible in fact, he says; transfer of Consciousness of [A] may in fact be impossible so far as immaterial substances

Locke *Essay Concerning Human Understanding* 2.27.13

[s1] But next, as to the first part of the question, whether if the same thinking substance (supposing immaterial substances only to think) be changed, it can be the same person.

[s2] I answer, that cannot be resolved, but by those, who know what kind of substances they are, that do think; and whether the consciousness of past actions can be transferred from one thinking substance to another.

[s3] I grant, were the same consciousness the same individual action, it could not: but it being but a present representation of a past action, why it may not be possible, that that may be represented to the mind to have been, which really never was, will remain to be shown.

[s4] And therefore how far the consciousness of past actions is annexed to any individual agent, so that another [agent] cannot possibly have it, will be hard for us to determine, till we know what kind of action it is, that cannot be done without a reflex act of perception accompanying it, and how performed by thinking substances, who cannot think without being conscious of it.

[s5] But that which we call the *same consciousness*, not being the same individual act, why one intellectual substance may

not have represented to it, as done by itself, what it never did, and was perhaps done by some other agent, why I say such a representation may not possibly be without reality of matter of fact, as well as several representations in dreams are, which yet, whilst dreaming, we take for true, will be difficult to conclude from the nature of things.

[s6] And that it never is so, will by us, till we have clearer views of the nature of thinking substances, be best resolved into the goodness of God, who as far as the happiness or misery of any of his sensible creatures is concerned in it, will not by a fatal error of theirs transfer from one to another, that consciousness, which draws reward or punishment with it.

[s7] How far this may be an argument against those who would place thinking in a system of fleeting animal spirits, I leave to be considered.

[s8] But yet to return to the question before us, it must be allowed, that if the same consciousness (which, as has been shown, is quite a different thing from the same numerical figure or motion in body) can be transferred from one thinking substance to another, it will be possible, that two thinking substances may make but one person.

[s9] For the same consciousness being preserved, whether in the same or different substances, the personal identity is preserved.

are concerned. But we can't know this with certainty. We in our ignorance of the nature of things certainly can't produce any demonstrative reason why it can't happen. Locke has by this time already established that a Person can survive change in its material or [M]-constitution, so all he needs to do, to complete his argument that Personal identity across time is independent of substantial identity across time, is to establish (or at least show that we can't rule out) the possibility that a Person can survive change in its immaterial or [I]-constitution.

One of the principal intuitive difficulties in the idea of transfer of Personal identity between immaterial substances, as opposed to material substances like brains, is that in the material case, Personal-identity-preserving change of substance is a matter of gradual replacement of parts. In the immaterial case, by contrast, the Person or subject must presumably undergo total replacement of substance in a single moment—given that immaterial substances are supposed to be metaphysically simple entities with no parts.[8] This, however, doesn't give us any conclusive a priori reason to think that is impossible. Nor in fact is the supposition of immedi-

---

[8] I put aside, here, Kant's neat use of the notion of *elanguescence* in his "Refutation of Mendelssohn's Proof of the Permanence of the Soul" (1781/1787: B413–15). Note that nothing rules out the idea that immaterial substances could be composite, in their own nonspatial way. *Indivisibility* is a property that believers in immaterial substances have wanted these substances to have, and have often stipulated them to have, simply because they think it guarantees *incorruptibility*, and hence (so they suppose) *immortality* (Kant gives a very clear account of this motivation in his First Paralogism in A (1781/1787: A349). It isn't, however, a priori that immaterial substances have this property, as Descartes knew, even if it is a priori that they're not *spatially* divisible.

ate transfer forced on us. We can also imagine that the process takes hours, while the Person is asleep, or even years, while the Person is in a state of unconsciousness, or the rest of the passage of the world is suspended.

[§13 s3] If the Consciousness of past action A1 that is transferred from one substance to another (in such a way as to be "the same consciousness" after the transfer as before) is supposed to be A1 itself, then clearly the transfer would be impossible. For A1 has already happened; that is, it's already existed as a property or modification of a certain particular individual immaterial substance, and it—numerically that very action A1—can't possibly also be a property or modification of a different immaterial substance, let alone occur at a different time.[9] Forestalling this objection, Locke stresses that of course he doesn't mean this by "the same consciousness." He's concerned with the case in which there is a present Conscious "representation" of past A1, an episode of experiencing A1 as one's own, or reliving A1, of just the kind we have in the normal course of things in having autobiographical memories. To put it in a version of his words:

---

[9] "Were the same consciousness the same individual action" is compressed, and arguably has another reading (which doesn't, however, change the overall role of [s3] in the larger argument): given that representations are themselves actions, it's possible that Locke is thinking of "the same consciousness" as an action other than A1: as A1-representing representation/action A3, say. But then (A1-representing representation/action) A3 is a property or modification of the new substance and can't possibly be numerically identical with any A1-representing representation/action A2 on the part of the previous substance. (The idea that "the same consciousness" might also refer to a capacity for representation of A1 may be lurking somewhere.)

here "same consciousness" means a present representation of a past action/experience, and, given that this is so, it hasn't been shown that it is actually impossible for the mind to represent something that never happened as having happened.

The second half of this claim is very loose, however, because it's obviously possible if taken literally. Whatever exactly "the mind" refers to, it's obvious that a mind can represent something that never happened as having happened. Locke makes the point himself in [s5]: restricting his attention to our representations of ourselves, he points out that many of the representations of ourselves that we have when dreaming are false, although we take them to be true while we're dreaming.

We know, then, that Locke has put things loosely in the second half of this claim in [s3]. He isn't pointlessly asserting that we can't prove the impossibility of something that happens (as he himself acknowledges) all the time. So we can take it that he means something more specific by the second half of the claim, and, given the first two sentences of the paragraph, it seems clear what this is. His claim is that we can't rule out the possibility that a thinking immaterial substance—[I_1], say—might as a result of some causal process of transmission that Locke calls a "transfer" represent itself as having done or experienced something, A1, that it, [I_1], didn't do or experience, something that was in fact done or experienced by some other thinking substance, say [I_2]. And we already know that Locke wants to show that this isn't impossible. He wants to show that it's not impossible in order to show that we can't rule out the possibility that the existence of a single Person might involve first one immaterial substance and then another. He's assuming for the sake of argument that "he has in himself an immaterial spirit, which is that which thinks in him" (§14), but questioning whether it need always be the same one. The question is "what makes the same *person*, and not whether it be the same identical substance, which always thinks in the same *person*" (§10).

Chapter Fourteen

"And therefore . . . ": *[I]-transfers,*
[Ag]-transfers, [P]-transfers

[§13 s4, s5] So far, perhaps, so good. We now arrive at the
main problem. At first Locke seems to use the terms "agent,"
"thinking substance," and "intellectual substance" in [s4]–
[s6] in a way that allows that a Person may survive change
of agent or thinking substance or intellectual substance.
I'll call this the *bare-immaterial-substance* use of the terms
"agent," "thinking substance," and "intellectual substance"
(I hope not too confusingly), or, more simply, the *non-Person*
use. We know that Locke wants to establish that a Person
can conceivably survive change of immaterial substance, and
since a Person obviously can't survive a change of Person,
we know that Locke needs the non-Person use so long as
he's trying to show that a Person can survive change of immaterial substance.

At other times, however, Locke seems to use the terms
"agent," "thinking substance," and "intellectual substance"
in such way that a change of agent or thinking substance or
intellectual substance would be a change of Person, so that a
Person couldn't survive the change. I will call this the *Person
use*. Clearly the two uses are in conflict, and the second risks

opening up the contradictory possibility that a Person could survive a change of Person.

Here is the beginning of the passage in which the uses occur:

> [s4] And therefore how far the consciousness of past actions is annexed to any individual *agent*, so that another cannot possibly have it, will be hard for us to determine, till we know what kind of action it is, that cannot be done without a reflex act of perception accompanying it, and how performed by *thinking substances*, who cannot think without being conscious of it.
>
> [s5] But that which we call the same consciousness, not being the same individual act [this is what was ruled out in [s3]], why one *intellectual substance* may not have represented to it, as done by it self, what it never did, and was perhaps done by some other *agent*—why I say such a representation may not possibly be without reality of matter of fact, as well as several representations in dreams are, which yet, whilst dreaming, we take for true—will be difficult to conclude from the nature of things.

Here is the same passage reordered and thinned, but still in Locke's own words:

> [it] will be hard for us to determine how far the consciousness of past actions is annexed to any individual agent, so that another cannot possibly have it. … [It will be] difficult to conclude from the nature of things … why one intellectual substance may not have represented to it, as done by it self, what it never did, and was perhaps done by some other agent.

Here it is again, reworded:

We in our ignorance do not know whether Consciousness of an agent's past actions is connected or "annexed" to that agent in such a way that no other agent can possibly have it. We can't rule out the possibility that one thinking substance may have represented to it, as done by itself, an action that it never did, and that was perhaps done by some other agent.

The difficulty is this. Locke wants to establish that Personal-identity-preserving transfer of Consciousness of [A] is possible between two different *immaterial* substances. When he says that we can't know that "one *intellectual substance* may not have represented to it, as done by it self, what it never did, and was perhaps done by *some other agent*," it seems clear that "intellectual substance" and "agent" are being used to denote the same kind of entities—i.e. immaterial subjects across which Consciousness of actions can be transferred while Personal identity is preserved. It seems clear that Locke wants to establish that transfer of Consciousness of an action from one agent or thinking or intellectual substance to another *is* possible, as part of establishing his main point: that a Person or subject can possibly survive change of immaterial substance. This, so far, supports the immaterial-substance or non-Person reading of "agent," "thinking substance," and "intellectual substance."

[§13 s6] It seems no less clear, however, that he thinks that a transfer of Consciousness of an action from one of these entities could possibly be a transfer between *Persons*, and not just between immaterial substances.[1] For in the very next sentence, [s6], he says that such a transfer could lead to ter-

---

[1] In making this claim, Locke introduces the idea of what Shoemaker later called "quasi-memory."

rible injustice. The injustice would consist in one "sensible creature" being punished or rewarded for what another did because such a transfer had taken place. The problem is that only a transfer between Persons could be unjust.

The first thing I want to do, in order to try to deal with this problem, is to bracket an objection that initially seems devastating. This is the objection that the notion of a transfer of Consciousness of an action between Persons is incoherent, on Locke's view, given his claim that "consciousness [alone] makes Personal identity" (§10, §16). I believe this objection is mistaken and consider it in the next chapter.[2]

Having put this objection aside, I propose that we call a transfer of Consciousness of an action or experience from one Lockean "agent" to another an *[Ag]-transfer*; a transfer of Consciousness of an action or experience from one immaterial substance to another an *[I]-transfer*; and a transfer of Consciousness of an action or experience from one Person to another a *[P]-transfer*. For good measure, and for later use, let us call a transfer of Consciousness of an action or experience from one packet of material substance to another an *[M]-transfer*. Finally, let us use *[C]-transfer* to cover any transfer of Consciousness of an action or experience whatever. Later on it'll be helpful to introduce the term *[S]-transfer* for a transfer of Consciousness of an action or experience from one subject of experience to another. But not yet.

On these terms, Locke makes the following claims. First,

[1] **[I]**-transfers are possible so far as we know.

---

[2] It's connected to Butler's error, and the error of thinking that a Mackie-style memory-link-based account of personal identity in terms of psychological continuity is neo-Lockean.

We just don't know enough about the nature of minds (which we're temporarily assuming to be wholly immaterial) to know that this isn't possible ([s2]–[s3], [s5], [s8]). Second,

[2] [**Ag**]-transfers are possible so far as we know.

Again, we don't know enough about the nature of minds to know that this isn't possible: "how far the consciousness of past actions is annexed to any individual agent, so that another [agent] cannot possibly have it, will be hard for us to determine, till we know … " ([s4]). Third,

[3] [**I**]-transfers could be [**Ag**]-transfers.

It will, Locke says, "be difficult to conclude from the nature of things" that "one intellectual substance may not have represented to it, as done by itself, what it never did, and was perhaps done by some other agent" ([s5]). Note that [2] follows from [1] and [3], but is in any case asserted in [s4].

So far, everything seems compatible with the non-Person reading (or bare-immaterial-substance-reading) of "agent" / "intellectual substance," according to which we can simply identify [**I**] and [**Ag**], and say both that

[4] all [**I**]-transfers are [**Ag**]-transfers

and that

[5] all [**Ag**]-transfers are [**I**]-transfers

and so speak simply of [**I**]-transfers, while at the same time denying that

[6] [**I**]-transfers are [**P**]-transfers,

i.e. while holding that all [**C**]-transfers, while being transfers across *substance* (either [**M**]-transfers or [**I**]-transfers), are never [**P**]-transfers.

Now, however, we come to the claim, in [s6], that

[7] **[I]**-transfers could lead to injustice

and it follows from [7] that

[8] **[I]**-transfers could be **[P]**-transfers

for they couldn't otherwise involve injustice.

We haven't yet encountered an insuperable difficulty, because the overall picture may be this: **[I]**-transfers can happen, and they can happen without being **[P]**-transfers:

[9] **[I]**-transfers that are not **[P]**-transfers are possible so far as we know.

This after all is precisely the case whose possibility (the unknowability of whose impossibility) Locke wants to establish—the case in which Personal identity is preserved across change of immaterial substance. And we may include in this picture the idea that **[I]**-transfers may be somewhat *dangerous*—the idea that it may be possible for something to go wrong during an **[I]**-transfer, with the result that the process by which Consciousness of an action or experience is being transferred from one immaterial substance to another while remaining the property of a single Person goes awry, so that the action or experience goes instead from one Person to another different Person, with potentially "fatal" consequences.

In this case a coherent interpretation of the passage is still open (we're continuing to put aside the objection that Locke must hold the notion of **[P]**-transfer to be incoherent). For Locke can now say—he does say—that God in his goodness won't let such accidents happen. So we can still maintain the non-Person or bare-immaterial-substance reading of "agent." On this view, although **[I]**-transfers can take place without mishap, i.e. without involving [**P**]-transfers, they can also possibly be [**P**]-transfers; but it's all right, because God will make sure that none of them are.

However, when Locke goes on in [s6] to say that God in his goodness will *never* allow "one intellectual substance [to] have represented to it, as done by itself, what it never did, and was perhaps done by some other agent," it seems that we can no longer avoid the Person-reading of "agent" (/ "intellectual substance" / "thinking substance"), according to which [**I**] is equivalent to [**P**], so that

[10] all [**I**]-transfers are [**P**]-transfers.

For Locke now seems to be saying that although [**I**]-transfers are possible as far as we know, they will in fact always be [**P**]-transfers; so that the possibility he is arguing for ([**I**]-transfer without [**P**]-transfer) isn't in fact a possibility after all. And yet then, at the end of the paragraph, in [s8], he plainly reasserts the conclusion he wants, the conclusion that so far as we know,

[9] [**I**]-transfers that are not [**P**]-transfers are possible.

What should we make of this? One way to read him is as making a slip while his meaning remains quite clear. On this view his basic position is [9]. Consciousness of [**A**], and so identity of [**P**], can not only survive change of [**M**], i.e. material substance (as everyone agrees). Consciousness of [**A**], and so identity of [**P**], can also survive change of [**I**], i.e. immaterial substance (a radically new suggestion on Locke's part). All that matters to preservation of [**P**], in such a case of change of substance, is preservation of sameness of Consciousness of [**A**], and as far as we know sameness of Consciousness of [**A**] can be preserved across change of [**I**].

A second way to read him finds no slip. On this view, his position is the following. As things actually are, all [**I**]-transfers would in fact be [P]-transfers, so God has a reason to prevent them (at least when they're not morally neutral). Nevertheless [9] [I]-transfers that are not [P]-transfers are possible as far as we know. There is no logical or conceptual reason why we should think that Personal identity requires sameness of immaterial substance. This, again, is his central claim in [s8] and his goal in the paragraph considered as a whole. It's the claim that he first makes in [s3] and reasserts in [s8] after confronting the injustice objection.[3]

One possible case of transfer might involve $[I_1]$ and $[I_2]$ "carrying" $[P_1]$ and $[P_2]$ respectively—$[I_1]$ being "that which thinks in" $[P_1]$ and $[I_2]$ being "that which thinks in" $[P_2]$—until time t_1, at which point $[P_1]$ and $[P_2]$ instantaneously switch [I]-components, so that $[I_2]$ is henceforth that which thinks in $[P_1]$ and $[I_1]$ is that which thinks in $[P_2]$. It's helpful to substitute "$[S_1]$" and "$[S_2]$" for "$[P_1]$" and "$[P_2]$," when considering this case. This allows one to bracket all [P]-related forensic issues to do with Consciousness of particular actions, and get a clear picture of the *subject-of-experience-hood(s)* of $[P_1]$ and $[P_2]$ being carried along in $[I_1]$ and $[I_2]$ until t_1. We have, then, $[I_1]$ and $[I_2]$ carrying $[S_1]$ and $[S_2]$ respectively until t_1, then switching, so that $[I_2]$ is that which thinks in $[S_1]$ and $[I_1]$ is that which thinks in $[S_2]$.

Another possibility is that $[S_1]/[P_1]$ jumps at t_1 from $[I_1]$ to $[I_2]$, where $[I_2]$ has hitherto been a blank or vacant unit of soul-substance. Again, each of us might travel along a series of [I]-units, in the way that is perhaps envisaged by Descartes when he says that

it is quite clear to anyone who attentively considers the

---

[3] See also §§24–25. The achievement of the paragraph, if it succeeds, is to show that as far as we know, a Person's possession of a single continuing immaterial soul is neither necessary nor sufficient for the coherence of the story of the Day of Judgment.

nature of time that the same power and action are needed
to preserve anything at each individual moment of its duration as would be required to create that thing anew if it
were not yet in existence. Hence the distinction between
preservation and creation is only a conceptual one (*Meditations* 1641: 1.33)

and

from the fact that we now exist it does not follow that
we shall exist a moment from now, unless there is some
cause—the same cause which originally produced us—
which continually reproduces us, as it were, that is to say,
which keeps us in existence (*Principles* 1644: 2.190).

Things could get indefinitely more complicated. Who are we
to rule on the matter, in "this vast and stupendious universe"
(2.2.3)? All that justice requires, though, is that actions and
experiences don't stray from their Persons. Anything that's
compatible with that, substance-wise, is fine; anything at all.

Chapter Fifteen

"A fatal error of theirs"

WHETHER OR NOT either of the two proposed readings is right, Locke's intention in §13 seems plain. But now we face the famous objection that was deferred in the last chapter. For Locke holds that Consciousness is a sufficient condition of personal identity—that "consciousness [alone] makes personal identity" (§§10, 16). And that appears to mean that unjust [P]-transfers are impossible—in which case one can't need to appeal to God to stop them. It seems that Locke's theory of personal identity rules out the possibility that there could be "fatal errors" of this sort.[1] If so, he's inconsistent in thinking that such a fatal error is even possible (conceivable). He's made a very large mistake.

Spelled out a little, the argument runs as follows. A [C]-transfer is a transfer of Consciousness of an action from one entity to another, an entity which we may assume to be a Person. But if Consciousness alone is really a sufficient condition of Personal identity, as Locke asserts, then

[11] [C]-transfers can't possibly be unjust.

---

[1] The "error" is fatal because it concerns one's fate in the largest sense—one's fate on the Day of Judgment.

For whatever entity (Person) a [C]-transfer is a transfer to, the action it brings Consciousness of is, on transfer, immediately and ipso facto an action on the part of the entity (Person) to which the action is transferred.

Consider a [C]-transfer that it initially seems right to describe as a transfer of an action from one person [P_1] to another person [P_2]. On the present reading of Locke, what happens is that the action that we think of as [P_1]'s action is (becomes) at the moment of transfer *immediately and wholly an action on the part of [P_2]*, in such a way that there's no injustice whatever in treating it as an action on the part of [P_2], and as not in any sense an action on the part of [P_1]. On this view, whatever intuitive grounds we may have for saying that [P_2] at t_2 has been lumbered with an action that is not really its own action are immediately obliterated by the fact that [P_2] is now Conscious of that action. Locke seems to emphasize the point in the very next paragraph, arguing that if one somehow became Conscious of one of the actions of the Greek hero Nestor, then that action would ipso facto become one's own. One would be literally the same (moral and legal) Person as Nestor, at least as far as that action was concerned, simply by reason of that Consciousness.

The more one thinks about Locke's chapter, however, the more unimpressive this objection (this reading of Locke) appears. This brings me to my last main exegetical point.

Let us call Locke's theory of personal identity taken independently of the injustice claim the *radical theory*. The radical theory consists of what I'll call the *radical claim*, i.e. "consciousness [alone] makes personal identity," taken in isolation, i.e. without consideration of the injustice claim. The radical theory entails that

[11] [C]-transfers can't be unjust

because if any [C]-transfer brings you an action, then that action is ipso facto and immediately really and truly your action, for which you may therefore be justly punished or equally rewarded.[2]

It's widely held that Locke's theory of personal identity is the radical theory. If this is right, then Locke is guilty of contradiction in claiming that a Person could suffer injustice in a [C]-transfer.[3] It seems, furthermore, that he can't possibly retain the idea that there could be injustice without presupposing and relying on a notion of what a Person is that is not only (i) independent of and prior to the notion of Person set out in the radical theory, but also (ii) in direct conflict with it. He is therefore open to the charge of *circularity*, or of partly *begging the question*, and also the charge of *inconsistency*.[4]

Locke is open to these charges if his theory of personal identity is just the radical theory. It follows, I think, that it isn't. I'm going to argue that there is indeed a respect in which he is presupposing a notion of what a person is that is independent of the notion of person set out in the radical theory, but that there's no circularity or inconsistency, because he never endorses the (in fact grotesque) radical theory in the first place.

The central point is already in place: throughout his discussion of Personal identity, Locke simply *assumes* the diachronically continuous existence of a subject of experi-

---

[2] This is already enough to realize that Locke can't mean to espouse the radical theory.

[3] Locke specifies that God would only have reason to prevent transfers of Consciousness in cases in which the actions had consequences for punishment and reward; his focus is very much on "person" as a forensic term.

[4] This circularity objection has nothing to do with Butler's feeble objection.

ence [**S**], a human subject of experience, say, a Person whom we may call *John*. He takes John's diachronic identity or continuity as a subject of experience as given, while stressing that it isn't a function of the diachronic identity or continuity of his substantial realizers.

We have, then, John, a human subject of experience who satisfies the definition of Personhood given in §9 and §26 (see pp. 63–67), and is therefore a Person. Since John is a Person, we may raise the question of his *Personal identity*, i.e. the *forensic* question "Which actions is John responsible for, praiseworthy or blameworthy for?" Where should we look? Which actions are relevant?

Here is the crux: *we already have* a sharply bounded set of actions with respect to which we may raise the question of John's forensic/Personal identity. Which set is this? It's the complete, lifelong set of actions of John the subject of experience, a set of which the actions of which John is Conscious (and which therefore form part of his Personal identity) form a small subset. John the human subject of experience may have switched souls, or switched bodies, like the cobbler and the prince, so that he's no longer the same *man* or *human being* as before, in the basic sense of being the same person$_1$.[5] But he's still the same *subject of experience*, in Locke's scheme. This is taken for granted, and when we ask which set of actions we must pick from, when we try to identify the set of actions he's Conscious of (and so responsible for, and so constituted as a Person by), it is, again, simply the complete set of actions and experiences of John the human subject of experience. John the Person, considered now, is the Person whose *Personal identity* (a

5 For the point that a different soul-substance means a different human being see p. 7 n. 2.

forensic matter) is wholly and solely a matter of which of those of the actions and experiences of John-the-human-subject-of-experience he is Conscious of now. There isn't any mysterious duplication or ghosting here, giving rise to Persons that are somehow additional to subjects of experience. John the Person standing before us now *is* John the human subject of experience standing before us now. John the Person is simply John the human subject of experience considered specifically with respect to his overall moral or forensic status. End of story. We have a clear and consistent and arguably deeply plausible account of what a Person's "Personal identity" consists in, where their "Personal identity" is a forensic matter.

I'll rerun the argument. We need to consider the "consciousness makes personal identity" claim in context, and a key part of the context is, precisely, the injustice claim, the claim that a [C]-transfer could involve injustice

[12] [C]-transfers could be unjust.

This is directly contrary to the radical claim, which entails

[11] [C]-transfers can't be unjust.

We can restate the clash without explicit reference to injustice, because a [C]-transfer can't be unjust unless it is a [P]-transfer. This being so, [12] entails

[13] [C]-transfers could be [P]-transfers,

and [13], too, is directly contrary to the radical claim. For the radical claim not only entails [11] but also and more simply

[14] [C]-transfers can't be [P]-transfers.

For suppose we have two Persons $[P_1]$ and $[P_2]$ and an action A of $[P_1]$, and suppose that after a time $[P_1]$ ceases to be

Conscious of A and that (by some strange causal process) [P_2] becomes Conscious of A. It will of course be extremely natural for us to call this a [C]-transfer from one Person to another, but it won't really be any such thing, on the terms of the radical theory, because there'll no longer be any sense in which A is [P_1]'s action after [P_1] loses Consciousness of it, nor any sense in which A won't be wholly [P_2]'s action, after [P_2] becomes Conscious of it.

We may take it, then, that the radical claim entails [14], and that [14] is accordingly one neat way to sum up the radical theory. Anyone who believes that Locke espouses the radical theory must think that his claims about possible [C]-transfers between Persons, and about dangers of injustice, are a slip. But if these two claims are a slip, they're a very obvious and massive slip. I think this refutes the view (widespread outside the domain of history of philosophy, and also in various regions within it) that Locke held the radical theory.

There are, nevertheless, various matters that invite comment. I'll go over the issue again. I'll restate the supposed difficulty and try to give its strongest form. I think there's still enough allegiance to the mistaken view of Locke to make this worthwhile. I accept that what follows will seem grossly repetitious in that bright and surely imminent future when Locke is properly understood.

Chapter Sixteen

A Fatal Error of Locke's?

SUPPOSE THAT immaterial substance $[\mathbf{I}_1]$ exists at time t_1, and is "that which thinks in" $[\mathbf{P}_1]$, and that $[\mathbf{P}_1]$ A-s at t_1 (i.e. performs a certain action A or has a certain thought or other experience E). In §13 Locke is canvassing the possibility that $[\mathbf{P}_1]$, existing at t_1 and t_2 and beyond, can at t_1 be $[\mathbf{I}]$-constituted (i.e. constituted, immaterial-substance-wise) wholly by immaterial substance $[\mathbf{I}_1]$ that A-s at t_1, and can now at t_2 be wholly $[\mathbf{I}]$-constituted by a numerically distinct immaterial substance $[\mathbf{I}_2]$. The idea is that the Person who at t_2 has $[\mathbf{I}_2]$-based Consciousness of that earlier A-ing at t_1 is the very same Person as the Person who engaged in $[\mathbf{I}_1]$-based A-ing at t_1 and had $[\mathbf{I}_1]$-based Consciousness of that A-ing at t_1.

This is *[I]-transfer without [P]-transfer*, in the terms introduced earlier—i.e. $[\mathbf{I}]$-transfer preserving Personal identity. Locke's claim in §13 is that if we consider the idea that Personal identity might survive $[\mathbf{I}]$-transfer from an a priori point of view, we find no more conceptual difficulty in it than in the idea of $[\mathbf{M}]$-transfer preserving Personal identity, i.e. in the familiar materialist idea that you now, a Person considered at t_2, are the same Person as a Person who A-d at t_1 although you're made of entirely different material particles than the Person who A-d at t_1.

So far all is clear. Locke is arguing exactly as we'd expect him to, given his aim. He's arguing that for all we know, [**I**]-transfer is possible in such a way that the existence of a single Person [**P**$_1$] from t_1 to t_2 can successively (and non-overlappingly) involve the existence of two immaterial substances.

But now he presents himself with a difficulty. To claim that [**I**]-transfer is possible, he proposes, is to open up the possibility that it could go wrong, in such a way as to lead to injustice. Introducing yet another new term, "sensible creature," to refer to a subject of experience who is a Person (because capable of being held morally responsible), Locke considers the possibility that sensible-creature subject of experience [**S**$_1$] could at t_2 be held responsible for A-ing at t_1, because Conscious of that A-ing, although it didn't actually A at t_1. Thus [**S**$_1$] (a sweet and reasonable creature, say) might be lumbered with the heinous action of sensible creature [**S**$_2$], and wrongly punished on the Day of Judgment—the consequences lasting, perhaps, for eternity. And [**S**$_2$] (a monstrous wicked creature, perhaps) might acquire from fallible sensible creature [**S**$_3$] a marvellous action that, perhaps, redeems [**S**$_2$] for all eternity—an action that, in becoming [**S**$_2$]'s, is, necessarily, taken away from [**S**$_3$], who is, lacking it, a lost soul. Locke explicitly considers this sort of possibility, grants that it can't be ruled out once it has been allowed that [**I**]-transfer is possible, and says that, until we know enough to rule it out a posteriori (doubtless never), we can base our certainty that it will never happen on the goodness of God, who, being good, would never allow such a fatal error.

Locke must be supposing that these sensible creatures are Persons, as just remarked, because he's taking them to be proper objects of punishment, and the objection (already stated) is immediate.

—It is your own view, Mr Locke, that Consciousness alone is sufficient for personal identity: that for any thing x, if person [P] is Conscious of x, then x is [P]'s, and that this is so whatever else is true of [P] and x.[1] The trouble is that "is Conscious of," in your use, is a kind of "success" or "factive" verb. In other words

(i) *[P]* is Conscious of *x*

implies not only

(ii) *[P] experiences x as its* own

but also

(iii) *x* is [**P**]'s *own.*

You make this as plain as could be when you discuss the case of Nestor in §14, and it's worth dramatizing the idea in another way. Imagine an immaterial-substance-based subject of experience [S$_x$] considered at t$_2$. Now imagine a thousand incoming transfers of Consciousness to [S$_x$], so that [S$_x$] becomes Conscious at t$_1$ of a thousand actions performed at past times by a thousand different immaterial-substance-based subjects of experience. On your view, [S$_x$] will continue to be a single person throughout this process, and all the actions and experiences of action will now be the actions and action-experiences of one single person—[S$_x$]. In actual fact such things don't happen, as you say, but your theory allows that they're possible. This, it seems, is the— absurd—price you're prepared to pay to make room for the possibility that a person can survive change in immaterial substance just as it can survive change in material substance.

The first thing to say in reply, on Locke's behalf, is that when

---

[1] Recall that *x* may be anything at all that one can experience as one's own in the distinctive from-the-inside way: an action, an experience, a body, a limb, an immaterial soul.

he claims that Consciousness "makes personal identity" in §10, he's discussing our actual case, the case of human beings. His question is this: "Which of the many, many past actions and experiences of the living, experiencing *human subject of experience* that we have been since birth are still part of the (forensic) *Person* we now are, in such a way that we're still answerable for them?" It's to this question that Locke's answer is that "consciousness makes personal identity." The question of responsibility is settled by taking the great set of all the actions and experiences of the subject of experience that one is and indeed the human being that one is (for there has in fact been no cobbler-prince monkey business), and asking which of them one is now Conscious of, i.e. which of them one still experiences as one's own in the special way that constitutes Consciousness. The Nestor case is a dramatic restatement of this point, and a large part of its force derives precisely from the fact that such a case is in fact impossible. It's a *per-impossibile* case designed to make the force of the notion of Consciousness clear: if, *per impossibile*, one really did somehow become Conscious of one of Nestor's actions, one would indeed be the same person as Nestor, as far as that particular action was concerned; *that's* how strong the notion of Consciousness is. Locke's deeper aim, as always, is to show that materialists (and mortalists) can give a solid account of our presence and responsibility on the Day of Judgment, by showing that Consciousness can reach across time, in such a way as to found Personal responsibility or identity, in the absence of strict substantial identity.

To say that Locke is discussing our actual case, in spite of his thought-experiments, is to take the first key step toward the sense in which he is indeed, as remarked on page 121, "presupposing and relying on a notion of what a Person is that is not only (i) independent of and prior to the notion of Person set out in the radical theory, but also (ii) in direct conflict with it." It's true that the radical theory allows for the possibility of freaks like [S$_x$], but this isn't a problem for Locke. On the contrary: it provides a good way of showing that he doesn't have a problem. The fact that the radical theory allows for freaks like [S$_x$] is enough to show (as clearly as the "fatal error" passage does) that the unqualified attribution of the radical theory to Locke is mistaken. To feel the torque of Locke's philosophical imagination in 2.27 of the *Essay* is to see that if he had entertained the radical theory, he'd have been onto the consequence that it allowed freakish creatures like [S$_x$] in a flash.

For suppose the thousand actions or experiences transferred to [S$_x$] have no punishment-and-reward consequences, so that God has no reason to prevent them, but that they're quite fantastically disparate, coming from a thousand different cultures, two sexes, and several different sexual orientations. There can be no characteral coherence in a subject of experience so constituted. It's natural to think that there can't really be a person there at all, a single entity that we can think of as a person, either in Locke's special Person sense or our most ordinary sense.

Now reintroduce moral considerations, and suppose that the actions and experiences do have punishment-and-reward consequences, and that some of them are saintly while others are unspeakable. In this case, too, the actions and experiences will have radically incompatible from-the-inside characters. The best of them will essentially involve— be experientially infused with—an outlook on life that makes the worst of them impossible and vice versa. It won't be possible to attribute this set of actions and experiences to a single person/Person. There'll be nothing intelligible as a person, no single entity of a sort fit for judgment.

It seems, then, that the radical theory is incoherent. It's incoherent relative to the idea that a certain sort of psychological integration is necessary if one is to have a person at all—a responsible person. Considerations of basic characteral coherence place limits on what can intelligibly count as a single person; the radical theory allows, incoherently, that any possible collection of actions and experiences whatever, however disparate, may be the actions and experiences of a single person.

Obviously Locke didn't make this point against the radical theory. For him, the question of Personal identity was a question about the responsibility of an already given subject of experience (whose identity was not, however, to be taken to be grounded in identity of substance). He never entertained the possibility of the radical theory. If he had, he would quickly have noticed its incoherence.

Chapter Seventeen

Circularity?

I'VE ARGUED that one must place the radical claim that "consciousness [alone] makes personal identity" in context—a context which, crucially, contains the injustice claim. No reading of Locke can be right unless it interprets the force of the radical claim in a way that renders it consistent with the injustice claim. There is in that sense no problem of inconsistency. There's only an inadequate reading of Locke that makes it seem that there's an inconsistency.

Suppose this is accepted. The charge of circularity or question-begging remains, inasmuch as Locke's notion of what Personal identity is must contain something over and above what is contained in the radical claim. If you accept that there's overwhelming reason to doubt that the radical claim can be taken independently of the injustice claim, you face the question of what the radical-claim-independent component of Locke's notion of Personal identity amounts to.

I've already answered this question. In raising the question of personal identity, Locke assumes the existence of a diachronically continuous subject of experience [S] that qualifies as a Person by virtue of possessing the capacities definitive of Personhood set out in §9 and §26. His two points are, again, (1) the diachronic identity of such a thing doesn't depend on the identity or continuity of any substance, although causal continuity is presumably required; (2) what such a thing is responsible for, at any given time, is the set of actions and experiences it is Conscious of, at that time.

The unfortunate $[S_x]$ helps us to think further about the general issue (even though we have no reason to think any such case occurred to Locke), for our natural reaction to $[S_x]$ expresses an aspect of our concept of a person that Locke takes for granted in his overall theory, and that goes beyond the bare assumption of the existence of a continuing subject of experience. It can be reexpressed as follows. A person (and equally a Person) can't be just an action-and-experience-pot into which one can put absolutely any action and experience.[1] In addition to being a cognitively sophisticated "sensible creature" (§13), capable of a law, and of happiness and misery, a person (Person) is, necessarily, something that has a certain personality or moral-characteral coherence. This is something Locke takes for granted, in assuming a continuing human subject of experience as the entity for whom the question of Personal identity (i.e. the question of responsibility) arises.

The next point is that he may—should—be allowed to take this for granted. Otherwise we no longer really have any idea what we're talking about. Or rather: we're certainly not talking about persons (Persons) or personal identity (Personal identity). No account of Locke's views can be correct if it attributes to him a theory of what persons are, and of what their persistence through time involves, that threatens to conflict with this basic assumption about the nature of persons—the assumption that they have, necessarily, a certain moral-characteral coherence. To say

---

[1] Actions, equally, are vastly experientially rich entities whose incompatibilities are such that they can't all be put into one pot.

that to make this basic assumption is to beg the question is like saying that one begs the question if one takes it that any account of what it is to know that p must have the consequence that p is true if known.

Once again we may conclude that Locke never endorsed the radical theory of Personal identity. It's given ex hypothesi, in the story about [S$_x$] and the thousand experiences, that there's a single *subject of experience* presented to us, when the time comes for moral judgment; but this isn't enough to give us good reason to think that there's a single *person* or *Person*, a single *moral entity*, for a person (Person) is, again, necessarily something that has some sort of overall moral character, or at least characteral coherence. This Locke naturally and rightly presupposes. He takes for granted a conception of persons that rules out stewpot persons. The charge of circularity or question-begging fails, because it arises only relative to the mistaken idea that Locke endorses the radical theory.

The characteral coherence condition, as an adequacy condition on any satisfactory account of persons, is so basic that it isn't explicitly or separately stated; it's simply carried along in the assumption that we have to do with a continuing human subject of experience when we raise the question of its Personal identity, a subject of experience whose diachronic identity is a given. Locke presupposes this unit of assessment—a human subject of experience—even as he explicitly declines to draw on the diachronic identity conditions supplied by the sortal term "human body" or "individual substance."[2]

The claim that "consciousness makes personal identity,"

---

[2] He declines by allowing that Persons can conceivably swap whole bodies ([M]-components) in an instant, and also, for all we know, souls ([I]-components).

then, is simply the claim that the actions that you'll be responsible for on the Day of Judgment, as a human subject of experience, will be all and only those of the actions of the human subject of experience that you are of which you are then Conscious. Plainly a transfer to you of Consciousness of an action that wasn't performed by you, the subject of experience that you are, could be unjust.

When I first started thinking about §13, I thought Locke might have been responding to an objection that had been put to him by some member of his discussion group without having sufficiently worked it through, and that he might have made a mistake. But there's no mistake, only carelessness of expression. It's not insignificant, I think, that the objection to the fatal error passage in §13 was first raised only in 1951, by Anthony Flew (as far as I and the Locke scholars I've consulted know), even though Locke's theory was subjected to the fiercest scrutiny and discussion, first by his wonderfully disputatious and intensely adversarial contemporaries, and then by his immediate and not so immediate successors. The reason for this, perhaps, is that no one at that time misunderstood him on this point, even if they misunderstood him on many others. It didn't occur to anyone—reasonably enough—that Locke might endorse anything that might allow for stewpot persons.[3]

---

[3] Evidence of an earlier occurrence of the objection wouldn't show that it wasn't a radical misreading, because Locke was radically misread, and polemically and constructively misunderstood, from the very beginning.

Chapter Eighteen

The Distinction between [P] and [S]

ONE MIGHT finally put the point—somewhat tendentiously—
by saying that Locke isn't sufficiently clear about the
difference between his definition of a *Person*, considered as
a kind of thing, and his definition of Personal *identity*. It's
not sufficiently clear that he raises the forensic question of
Personal identity—i.e. the question of what a Person is morally
and legally responsible for—after, or at least independently
of, the question of what a *Person* is.

On this account of things, Locke first defines what it takes
to be a Person. He gives a definition according to which we
(of course) qualify as Persons, for to be a Person is simply to
be a *subject of experience* of a certain sophisticated sort [S], a
subject of experience with the capacities set out in (1)–(9) on
pages 63–67 above.

We may provisionally say, then, that [P] = [S], although
this equation will shortly cause problems, where [S] is
assumed to be a continuing thing, a continuing thing that
is able to survive radical change of substantial realization.
Locke doesn't propose Consciousness as the metaphysical
determinant of what constitutes [S]'s continuing identity
or existence over time. He doesn't, in other words, propose

Consciousness as the determinant of what constitutes [**P**]'s identity or existence over time *as a subject of experience*. Consciousness is rather what determines [**S**]'s (and so [**P**]'s) *forensic* identity over time (in addition to determining exactly which substance or substances constitute [**P**] at any given time—see chapter 8). [**S**]'s continuity over time is—again—given. If the assumption that the [**S**] that is [**P**] is a continuing thing involves a circularity, then Locke is guilty of circularity. But he isn't, because—to repeat—he isn't proposing Consciousness as the determinant of [**S**]'s identity over time, but only of [**S**]'s moral and legal responsibility over time (together with [**S**]'s substantial constitution at a time), where [**S**] is already given as a continuant. He's assuming [**S**]'s continuity over time, while stressing the point that [**S**] may possibly be radically differently substantially realized at different times.

With this definition of a Person in place, Locke raises the forensic question of *Personal identity*—the question of what a Person is morally and legally responsible for. His answer to the question of what a Person is, is, as remarked, [**S**]: a Person is a subject of experience [**S**] of a certain sophisticated sort, one that can, for example, "consider it self as it self, the same thinking thing at different times and places" (§9) and is "capable of a law" (§26). His answer to the forensic question of the Personal identity of a Person [**S**] is [**A**]: the (temporally gappy) set of actions and experiences, extending up to the present moment, of which the Person [**S**] is Conscious, and for which it is therefore morally and legally responsible, and which literally forms a part of [**P**].

Certainly the [**S**] and the [**A**] aspects of [**P**] are in some tension. For suppose I'm Person [**P**] = [**S**]. [**S**] is by assumption a long-term continuant. It seems, though, that the claim that Consciousness of [A] constitutes my forensic Personal identity doesn't just entail that for any and all the actions and experiences in my [A], I'm identical with the subject-agent who performed them or underwent them. It also presumably entails that I'm *not* identical with the subject-agent of any actions and experiences of which I'm not Conscious. But the [S] that I am, a long-term continuant, is the subject-agent of many past actions and experiences of which I'm no longer Conscious, actions and experiences that are therefore not in my [A]. Let [A*] denote the complete set of all the actions and experiences of [S]. We may then say that there is a vast number of actions and experiences in [A*] that are not in [A]. It follows that the full account of the forensic *Personal identity* of the [P] that I am, which is established by reference to my [A], has the consequence that I'm often not the same *Person* as the [S] that I am, since I'm not the subject-agent of many of [S]'s actions—all those that are in [A*] but not in [A]. But that contradicts the starting assumption that [P] = [S].

The trouble is that my forensic Personal identity is massively gappy, although I am, as a Person, a continuant. So if one tries to work out what I am as a *Person* solely by reference to what Locke has offered as a criterion of *Personal identity* ("consciousness makes personal identity"), one comes up with gaps, contradictions, inconsistency. If one wrongly takes the Consciousness criterion of Personal identity to be a way of establishing what a Person is over time, then the assumption that Persons are continuants not only seems to beg the question, but also turns out to be incompatible with the gappy entity that emerges.

Plainly we should have sympathy for those who have misinterpreted Locke, although most of them have had none for him. The fact remains that there is no inconsistency, no contradiction, no question-begging—only misunderstanding of Locke's aims. There is a respect in which the terms "Person" and "Personal identity" pull apart, in Locke's scheme of things, but in a perfectly coherent way.

Chapter Nineteen

Concernment and Repentance

HAVING PUT her unanswerable question to those who think that Lockean consciousness is the same as memory (see p. 75 above), Marya Schechtman goes on to say that on Locke's view, "past events can become part of present consciousness by affecting us in the present along the dimension of pleasure or pain" (1996: 112). This is right enough, correctly understood.[1] It seems, however, that this isn't the only way for past events to become part of present Consciousness. For it seems that one may be Conscious of a past experience simply insofar as one experiences it as one's own—this alone being the deep core of Consciousness—while having no particular feelings of pleasure or pain with regard to it; rather as one can be (occurrently) Conscious of a part of one's body as one's own while having no particular present feelings of pleasure or pain with regard to it.

There are, in fact, various possibilities, when it comes to awareness of one's past. One may now remember stealing

---

[1] One can doubt the implication that Consciousness itself involves, rather than being inevitably accompanied by, Concernment (see p. 51 above). Locke, furthermore, is only concerned with past events accessible through from-the-inside memory (memory of other past events can cause us pleasure or pain).

plums and being flogged as a boy with some amusement, and with whatever pleasure is inseparable from amusement, while no longer experiencing the action as one's own in such a way that one feels it would be appropriate for one to be punished for it, or indeed (and connectedly, in Locke's view) in such a way that it would *be* appropriate for one to be punished for it. One can also, perhaps, be Conscious of a past action, good or bad, and have a correct view of its moral quality, and be concerned in it in the accountability-engaging way, so that it's appropriate for one to be punished or rewarded for it, while feeling no particular present pleasure or pain in the contemplation of it. If an action or experience is to attract punishment or reward, one must be Conscious of it, but although this is a necessary condition of attracting punishment or reward, on Locke's view, it may not be sufficient; for many things, such as warm memories, may be morally neutral, although they involve Consciousness and Concernment. One may also hope that one will not be punished for all one's wrongdoings even when one is still Conscious of them in a Concernment-involving way. For God has a reputation for mercy.

Another case involves a complication Locke didn't consider, and which arguably raises a doubt about the adequacy of his account. Suppose one is given to guilt. It seems plain that one can continue to feel guilty about an action performed as a child although one is not in fact still related to it in an accountability-engaging way. But guilt (apart from being a painful emotion) is surely a form of Concernment, and entails Consciousness; and Consciousness entails same Personhood; and same Personhood entails present accountability and punishability. It seems, then, that current guilt about a past action entails accountability and punishability for that action even when the guilt is inappropriate, neurotic, or absurd, and punishment is equally inappropriate.

A quick answer to this, in the spirit of Locke's theory, is that one will be all right on the Day of Judgment. This is because one's conscience, on that stupendous occasion, will get things in proportion and excuse one (see §22). One will see clearly that one is no longer implicated in or accountable for one's childish misdeed, and one will no longer feel guilty.[2] The secrets of one's heart being laid open, this is what will appear.

This seems right. Chronic guilt of this sort is, however natural, a form of moral (and almost invariably self-indulgent) ignorance that won't be able to survive on the Great Day.[3]

But one (or Locke) can also deal with this case in another way. One can allow that the childish misdemeanor will still feature on the long list of things for which one is theoretically accountable, simply insofar as one is Conscious of it, while insisting that one won't actually be punished for it (God, for one, wouldn't dream of doing so). Reid's general will surely not be punished for stealing the plums, even if he not only remembers it but still feels bad about it, and is to that extent still Concerned in it in such a way that it's still part of the Person he is.[4] In childhood, after all, we haven't yet attained the so-called age of responsibility, and this is

[2] Leibniz differs from Locke in not requiring that we ourselves, in addition to God, should get everything right on the Day of Judgment (1704: 243 [2.27.22]). Locke doesn't, though, require that we be able to remember everything that we've forgotten, on the Day, contrary to what Leibniz suggests (ibid.).

[3] Questions about the Great Day can always be converted into earthly questions about one's overall moral status or standing.

[4] He was soundly flogged at the time. Enough is enough.

a fact to which divine law will surely not pay less attention than human. There are vicious eschatologies that fry babies for being unbaptized and mandate punishment for all the misdemeanors of childhood. Religion, after all, is a human creation. But what will doubtless happen on the Great Day is that the old general's heart and conscience, enlightened by the grandeur of the occasion, will excuse him, with considerable good humor, and so, surely, and in any case, and once again, will God.[5]

It may help to introduce the notion of one's final account—the bill, the rap sheet, the list of chargeable items that one has as a human subject of experience on the Day of Judgment.[6] The only actions or experiences that are up for punishment or reward are the ones listed on one's final account; and what is on one's account is of course a function of what one is then Conscious of (Consciousness being inevitably accompanied by moral-emotional Concernment).[7] Vast quantities of one's life's actions and experiences are unrecorded. (If one's whole life flashes before one's eyes, few events will snag on one.) Those that remain are all and only those one still feels involved in, in such a way as still to feel that they're something that *one* did or experienced, where *"one"* means the person one feels or experiences oneself to be in the natural present-day (person$_2$-related) sense of "person" that doesn't simply equate it with "human being"; and where

---

[5] I'm sorry to say that St. Augustine was keen on original sin and thought that babies could commit sins. His anti-Pelagianism has a highly neurotic quality and clearly serves some psychological need in him.

[6] In §14 Locke imagines a thinking being losing all consciousness of its past "and so as it were beginning a new account from a new period."

[7] One might say, in other terms, that it will be a matter of what one "identifies with" in the past, where this identification is not a matter of choice or intentional action, and obviously doesn't require having a positive attitude to the thing identified with.

this feeling or experience is not a matter of one's choice, but a matter of what shows in one's heart when its secrets are laid open. This tiny subset of the vast set of actions of the human being that one is constitutes the Person (the accountable moral entity) one now is, so far as one's past actions are concerned: "that with which the Consciousness of this present thinking thing can join it self, makes the same person, and is one *self* with it, and with nothing else."[8] Tying punishment and reward to actual Consciousness and Concernment isn't going to allow anyone to get away with anything they shouldn't get away with, for what one is Conscious of—what one still feels Concerned or involved in—is, again, not something one can do anything about, on Locke's view. It's not under the control of the will, it's not something one can fake away—not in one's heart.[9]

We have, then, the idea of an account, an accounting, in which one's actions and experiences are registered. But Locke's overall picture is also deeply and plausibly informed—it seems to me—by the idea that one's overall forensic condition, one's fundamental moral standing, at any time, either now or on the Day of Judgment, lies in one's overall moral character or moral being at that time, and not just in the bag of actions and experiences that one retains—by still being Conscious of them—from one's life as a human being. One way to read Locke is as holding bluntly

[8] §17; "so far as one's past actions are concerned" brackets the rest of what constitutes one as a Person—one's material and/or immaterial constitution.

[9] "What if criminals rob a bank, put the money in a Swiss bank account, have their memories wiped by a professional criminal hypnotist, and wake up knowing only about the money in the bank?" This old objection to Locke's claim that moral responsibility for *x* entails Consciousness of *x* can be filed away with the observation that this maneuver will fail to delete the action from the secret registers of their hearts.

that one's bag of actions and experiences itself constitutes—wholly constitutes—one's overall moral character or being or forensic Personhood. I think that there is another way of presenting things that is no less plausible and no less Lockean in its overall spirit.

According to this proposal, (a), the set of actions and experiences of which one is still Conscious in the accountability-entailing way is at least partly a function of (b), one's present overall moral character or moral being considered (insofar as it can be) independently of the set of actions and experiences. Thus—roughly—it's because one now has this overall moral outlook that it's no longer true to say that one is properly held accountable for this particular pathetic and regrettable past action A1, although one is still accountable for this other wrong past action A2. Given one's present overall moral outlook, A1 is really no longer part of "who one is." One can either express this by saying one is no longer Conscious of A1, no longer identified with A1 in the accountability-engaging way (although one may well remember A1), or one can say that although one is still Conscious of A1, because one still experiences it as one's own in the basic way, so that it is still on one's account, nevertheless one will not actually be punished for it, because the opening of one's heart will reveal that one is no longer identified with it (identification being a matter of Concernment) in the accountability-engaging way.

I think this is an important part of Locke's overall picture, or at least of a broadly speaking Lockean picture. There is, however, no need to restrict oneself to just one of the two ways of presenting things just described. They're formally opposed, for one claims that the set of actions and experiences of which one is Conscious constitutes one's whole moral being, while the other claims that facts about which actions and experiences one is still correctly said to be Conscious of depend at least partly on one's moral being or character considered as something whose existence is at least partially independent of whatever set of actions and experiences one is Conscious of. Fruitful moral thinking may move easily between the two.

We need, in any case, to understand Locke's picture in a way that allows him to accommodate something that he would surely wish to accommodate: the idea that repentance—*metanoia*—can cancel out or detach one from a past wrongdoing in such a way that one won't be punished for it on the Day of Judgment, or indeed on some earlier, sublunary occasion, even though one remembers perfectly well what one did.[10] In such a case, one will still *remember* the wrongdoing, but one won't be punished for it because one won't be *Conscious* of it. Or at least: one won't experience it as one's own in the Concernment-involving way. Not because one has already paid in full in the coin of earthly punishment (although this is one possibility), but because one has repented in such a way that the link of moral Concernment is broken.[11] In this case, one could say that the action is no longer on one's final account at all; or, as before, that although it is still on one's final account, simply because one still remembers it and apprehends it as one's own doing, one won't actually be punished for it.

[10] What about Consciousness without memory? One may have a general memory of an occasion in one's past, and feel some uneasiness about it, on account of some action A that one then performed, although one cannot remember what one did, or even that one did anything in particular. Here again, it seems natural to say that one's uneasiness is (occurrent) Consciousness of A, although there's also a clear sense in which one doesn't remember A—not before one's heart opens.

[11] There seems to be no similar device of cancellation for meritorious actions. See below.

This won't quite do, however, because it seems clear that one may still be *Concerned* in the action, in feeling extremely sad about the harm one did to others, say, even when one is no longer *morally* Concerned in it—even when true repentance has broken the link of punishment-incurring moral Concernment.[12]

At this point Locke may wish to crack down on these speculations, which go beyond what he explicitly considered, and insist that genuine, from-the-inside, autobiographical remembering can't come apart from moral-Concernment-implying Consciousness. It seems to me, though, that what we're now faced with are various terminological choices, not substantive philosophical issues. One possibility is to take it that the fundamental definition of

[1] being Conscious of (action) x

is simply

[2] experiencing x as one's own,

where "as one's own" is to be understood in an affectively neutral sense that need not involve any sort of

[3] identificatory Concernment with x.

One can then grant that

[4] from-the-inside remembering of x

---

[12] St. Augustine was sixteen when he raided a pear tree with his friends—considerably older, no doubt, than Reid's fictional boy. Fortunately, he moderated his belief in original sin with a robust notion of repentance and had no doubt that God had forgiven this particular sin along with many others. God "melted away my sins like ice"—even though "I only picked [the pears in order] that I might steal" and enjoyed doing wrong "for no other reason than that it was wrong" (397–98: 49–51 [§§2.6–7]).

is by definition remembering which involves experiencing *x* as one's own. One can grant, in other words, that [4] entails [2], which entails [1].

If Locke were to make this terminological choice, he would I think have to concede that [1], Consciousness, can detach from [3], Concernment, and that it's Concernment that makes the essential link to punishability. And he might further have to allow that Concernment isn't sufficient for punishability, only necessary, given the case of repentant sadness. Alternatively, the gap can be closed by appeal to God's mercy. On this view one is indeed still punish*able* for absolutely everything one is Conscious of, and one is still Conscious of absolutely everything one experiences as one's own, even if one now experiences it as one's own only in a wholly affectively neutral, wholly morally disengaged way. Nevertheless, God won't actually punish one for any of the things from which one has disengaged.

This is one terminological choice among others, made to suit a case that Locke didn't consider in print (his official position is that Consciousness and Concernment never come apart), and it raises a question about the minimal or thinnest form of Consciousness.[13] Imagine that one once performed some action, good or bad, and that one now feels about it rather as Henry James felt about his novel on page 5 above. One feels, in the Jamesian way, that the person who performed the action is in effect a different person from the person one is now. Could this nonetheless be a case of (Lockean) Consciousness? It doesn't seem so, because Locke says that Consciousness of a past action requires being

[13] This can also be taken as a question about the minimal form of "from-the-insideness" or "immediate givenness"—once this last notion is allowed to have application beyond the sphere of one's present experience.

able to "repeat the idea of [the] past action with the same consciousness [one] had of it at first" (§10), and it seems plain that this ability has been lost in the Jamesian case, so that there is no sufficient sense in which the action is still constitutive of one's moral identity, still lodged somewhere in one's heart.

The repeatability requirement in §10 places an extremely strong demand on Consciousness, requiring it to have the power and supposedly undistorted accuracy of Proustian "involuntary memory." And one possibility, of course, is that our capacities for recall will be exceptionally vivid on the Day of Judgment, so that we fulfill the repeatability requirement even for actions from which, in life, we are genuinely Jamesianly detached.[14] We can put this idea aside, though, for a much weaker notion of Consciousness of past actions and experiences is sufficient for Locke's purposes, and the important point is rather this: if Consciousness is genuinely lost, in the way that it seems to be in the Jamesian case, then Locke's theory gives the right result. The person one is now can't be rightly punished for the action of which Consciousness has been lost.

This core idea lifts easily out of its eschatological context, and seems better expressed in an entirely nonreligious and nonepistemological way. It's simply the idea that there is at any time a fact of the matter about a person's overall moral

[14] As Garrett notes (2003: 117, 120, n. 25 and 26), Locke takes human memory to be a far more reliable and powerful instrument than it usually appears to us to be. "As when our senses are actually employed about any object, we do know that it does exist; so by our memory we may be assured, that heretofore things, that affected our senses, have existed. And thus we have knowledge of the past existence of several things, whereof our senses having informed us, our memories still retain the *ideas*; and of this we are past all doubt, so long as we remember well" (4.11.11).

nature, shape, constitution, or being, whether or not it is ever revealed or made the basis of action. This is an idea that has considerable resonance and plausibility for many people. One's moral identity is not simply a matter of an accumulated bag of actions. It's something that can change (e.g. improve) over time, and not just by a change in the proportion of good and bad actions in the bag. And this improvement can be not only correlative with, but also partly constitutive of, one's losing touch with some of one's past actions in such a way that one is no longer appropriately punished for them.[15]

[15] Throughout this discussion, I'm putting aside the fact that the notion of desert appears in the final analysis to be incoherent. See e.g. Strawson 1986, Parfit 2011: ch. 11.

Chapter Twenty

Conclusion

THERE'S A FURTHER reason why the idea of a person's overall moral nature or identity may be useful in a Lockean framework. When materialists or mortalists address the troublesome question of what guarantees personal identity between death and resurrection, they face a difficulty. Locke has, indeed, his famous answer in terms of Consciousness, but the idea that the Consciousness of John on the Great Day (John$_{GD}$) is numerically the same Consciousness as the Consciousness of John on earth (John$_E$) still seems to require, for its coherence, the idea that there be some form of individuality-preserving continuity linking John$_E$ and John$_{GD}$. Locke finds no problem in the idea that God may give each of us a brand-new body on the Great Day.[1] This won't matter, so long as our personality and memory information and mental capacities and Consciousness are somehow preserved. But how will these things be preserved, if no immaterial soul persists between one's death and one's resurrection?

---

[1] "The sentence shall be justified by the consciousness all persons shall have, that they themselves, *in what bodies soever they appear*, or *what substances soever that consciousness adheres to*, are the same that committed those actions, and deserve that punishment for them" (§26).

When Locke explicitly considers the matter in 2.27, he has the soul provide the link, in a conventional manner:

> And thus may we be able without any difficulty to conceive, the same person at the resurrection, though in a body not exactly in make or parts the same which he had here, the same consciousness *going along with* the soul that inhabits it (§15).

But he himself queries the idea that the identity of a Person across time depends on there being a single continuing soul (even after he has allowed for argument, in §13, that the existence of a Person essentially involves the existence of immaterial substance). There must be *causal continuity* of some sort, in order for a Person considered at one time to be the same Person as a Person considered at a later time, and so for a Person on the Day of Judgment to be the same as a Person previously on earth, and it must be causal continuity of a sort that preserves the moral and cognitive capacities (including Consciousness) that are constitutive of being a person. But beyond that anything goes.

If the soul dies along with the body, as the thnetopsychists suppose, then we can perhaps imagine God as database, storing all our Personal details and guaranteeing full continuity in causal transmission. This kind of preservation of Personal identity is certainly no worse than its preservation through sleep or change of material particles. In fact, given God's fabled capacities, it is surely better. Some may think it unjust to punish the new-bodied Person John$_{GD}$, in this case, because it simply won't be true that *he* performed the actions of the original-bodied Person John$_{E}$. On Locke's view, however, this reaction reveals an unreconstructedly *lumpen* picture of what a Person is. For here is a

moral entity, a Personal identity. Why exactly can't it survive storage as data (data storage will always involve some
substantial realization or other)? On this view, it's not as if
some new person, or some other already existing person,
is being unjustly punished or rewarded when this moral
entity is reanimated in a new body and punished or rewarded.
It is *this very* moral entity that is now being brought back
to life.

The greater difficulty, perhaps, arises when we renounce
the storage option, or claim that God has no need of it—that
God can re-create $John_E$ out of completely new materials,
in creating $John_{GD}$. God can't coherently be supposed to do
this, however, unless $John_{GD}$ is in some way *based* on $John_E$
and in this case, it seems, the storage and transmission conditions are already sufficiently fulfilled.[2]

What about a case in which genuine from-the-inside
autobiographical memory of performing some action A
has decayed into merely factual (but still autobiographical)
memory? One no longer remembers A-ing from the inside,
but one still remembers that one A-d (see p. 41). Can this be
a case of Consciousness?

At first it seems not, for the reason just given: Conscious-

---

[2] The feeling that it would be unjust to punish or reward $John_{GD}$ for
what $John_E$ did is likely to rearise. Some may then reply that $John_E$'s moral
identity has been re-created, and is justly susceptible of punishment and
reward, even if $John_E$ himself has not been re-created. On this view, it is
overall moral identities, good or bad, rather than particular actions and
experiences, that are justly punished and rewarded, and that are, indeed,
most properly speaking called "Persons." Priestley (another convinced
thnetopsychist) introduces an idea of this kind in his *Disquisitions Relating
to Matter and Spirit*, distinguishing between "the identity of the man" and
"the identity of the person" (1777: 156–57). It may deserve further inves-
tigation, whatever its ultimate cogency.

ness of a past action requires being able to repeat the idea of the past action with the same Consciousness one had of it at first, which plainly seems to require "from-the-insideness." It's not clear that this is the right thing to say, however, because it seems clear that one can still feel directly morally Concerned in, and responsible for, an action one knows one did, although one doesn't remember the doing of it at all. And if this is so, then it looks as if one still has an immediate moral-Concernment-involving connection to the action, in which case it must be true to say that one is Conscious of it, on Locke's terms. It seems clear that one still "owns" it in this case, both in the old (and Lockean) sense of acknowledging it and in the literal sense: "one owns [it], as [one's] own" (§17).

In this case of fading memory, one might say that there is still *Concernment*, of the accountability-engaging sort, without requiring that there be *Consciousness*, of the sort that requires from-the-inside givenness (let alone highly accurate from-the-inside givenness). Alternatively, one could maintain the unbreakable link between Consciousness and Concernment by saying that this Concernment isn't the real thing. It's not Concernment in the requisite Lockean sense, *L-Concernment*, as it were; it's only Jamesian Concernment, *J-Concernment*, i.e. Concernment of a sort that can be said to exist even when one is in a condition of Jamesian remoteness from one's past action or experience (p. 5), or when from-the-inside memory has decayed to factual memory. It's not, however, clear that Locke would have wished to say that one shouldn't be punished, on the Day of Judgment, if one's L-Concernment had faded to J-Concernment, or if one's from-the-inside memory had faded to merely factual memory. It seems better for him to say that there is only one relevant kind of Concernment, while allowing that Concernment doesn't after all require rich experiential from-the-inside access (strong repeatability, full action replay).[3]

On this view, we retain the equation of [1], to be Conscious of x, with [2], to experience x as one's own, and allow that [2] is sufficient for [3], identificatory Concernment in x, while also allowing that [2] needn't involve experiencing x from the inside in the rich experiential way (this side of the Day of Judgment, at least). It seems plain that one can still feel Concerned in and responsible for an action or experience, still take it to be one's own in the crucial sense, even when one has no rich experiential from-the-inside access to it.[4]

It is, perhaps, a connected point that there seems (as noted) to be a large asymmetry in our initial intuitions about punishment and reward. Many agree that true mental distance from past wrongdoing can render punishment wholly inappropriate, but find it much less clear that similar distance from good

---

[3] There are many complexities. John's feelings of self-disapprobation may be nothing more than an internalization of the sensed—or feared—disapprobation of others, and have no independent existence. John may continue to feel responsible for something insofar as he thinks of himself as located in the public, interpersonal sphere, although something crucial has drained out of the feeling (and possibly quite rightly) in his private sphere, his *forum internum*.

[4] One can retain the "from the inside" locution if one wishes. All one has to do is to drop the rich experiential requirement and allow that feeling responsible for an action/experience that one apprehends as one's own is already sufficient for experiencing it from the inside. For an enlightening comparison of Locke and Kierkegaard in this respect, see Stokes 2008.

deeds renders praise and reward wholly inappropriate. This asymmetry can't be maintained within the strictly Lockean framework, and some will think the framework gives the right result. Others may seek to defend the asymmetry. Others again may insist that what is most fundamental, when it comes to Concernment in past good actions, is simply their coherence with one's present character and outlook. So long as one is the same kind of Person as the Person who did the good thing one did, the same kind of Person as the Person out of whom that action flowed, then one is still Concerned in it in the relevant sense and is appropriately praised and rewarded for it.

Unfortunately, this line of thought runs equally well in the case of bad actions. The softer-hearted won't be able to justify their lopsidedness of attitude by reference to characteral coherence, for all that it plays a considerable and interesting part in our moral thinking. They won't be able to justify their intuition that one's past good deeds should continue to count for something when one has gone downhill, even when one's bad deeds should cease to count for anything when one has gone the other way. Nor will they be able to justify an inclination to overlook the bad action done out of character while continuing to give weight to the good action done just as far out of character.[5] But the idea of forgiveness—an idea that has, of course, no necessary connection with religious belief, which diminishes it—may give them what they need. Another possibility is that final judgment is geared simply to one's moral essence, one's overall state of

[5] Such cases strike Maxim Gorky vividly in his remarkable autobiography. See e.g. 1913–1923/2001: 602.

moral being considered (at least in principle) independently of one's great tally of actions.

Many other cases and responses can be imagined; they go far beyond those that Locke considers.[6] There is much more to say. Leibniz makes many subtle comments in response to Locke.[7] Here, though, I will go no further.

---

[6] It seems, for example, that a Person could in principle survive complete loss of [A] as well as complete changeover of [M] and [I]. There could still be the same [S] after radical, Day-of-Judgment-proof amnesia, an [S] who still qualified as a *Person* by the definition of Person, despite lacking any forensic "account" and having, in that sense, no *Personal identity* at all. See e.g. Dainton 2008.

[7] Leibniz c. 1704: 2.27. See Thiel 2011, chap. 6.

Postface

LOCKE'S THEORY of personal identity links four fundamental notions: *identity, consciousness, concern,* and *responsibility*. In this postface I survey the links in a general fashion.

Although Locke's theory of personal identity is part of his chapter on the general subject of identity and diversity, it is first and foremost a theory of moral and legal responsibility.

A theory of moral and legal responsibility requires a theory of personal identity, on Locke's (and indeed most people's) view, because only persons can be morally and legally responsible for anything:

(1) [theory of responsibility → theory of personal identity].

But Locke's theory of personal identity is no less fundamentally a theory of concern or concernment—a theory about what is (necessarily) of concern to each of us, given our interests as creatures "capable of happiness or misery" (§17).

For this reason alone, it must be a theory of moral and legal responsibility. For nothing is of more concern to each of us individually, on Locke's view, than the nature or extent of our legal and moral responsibility.

A sufficient reason for this, in the framework in which Locke is writing, is that one's existence continues on from this earthly life into another life of potentially unbounded duration whose quality, happy or miserable, is determined by what one is morally responsible for in this earthly life.

(2) [theory of concern → theory of responsibility].[1]

It follows from (1) and (2) that a theory of concern must be a theory of personal identity:

(3) [theory of concern → theory of personal identity].

A theory of concern is bound to be a theory of personal identity in being a theory of responsibility.

This, though, is an indirect connection between concern and personal identity. There's a separate and direct reason why (3) is true. It's a matter of simple definition, in Locke's scheme, that what is of concern to one has to do with oneself. It has to do centrally with "one's own person" and, derivatively, with what is related to one (as one's family or one's property, say). Strictly speaking, all that is of concern to each of us, on Locke's terms, is "our pleasure or pain; i.e. happiness or misery; *beyond which we have no concernment*" (4.11.8). To know what concerns one, therefore, one must know what one is; one must know one's boundaries, as it were. One must know what constitutes one or one's self, and to know that, on Locke's view, is to know what constitutes one as a person. (He uses the terms "self" and "person" interchangeably.)

It follows that a theory of concern must be a theory of personal identity, in Locke's framework, even if one's moral responsibility has nothing to do with one's happiness and

---

[1] One can accept (2) without believing in any afterlife.

misery. (1) and (2) entail (3), but (3) can be established without reference to them. So a theory of what concerns one must be a theory of personal identity twice over, in Locke's scheme. For nothing is of more concern to us (given Locke's Christian eschatological framework) than where we stand in matters of moral responsibility: "nothing of pleasure and pain in this life, can bear any proportion to the endless happiness, or exquisite misery of an immortal soul hereafter" (*Essay* 2.21.60).

On one view, the fundamental chain of ideas begins with the notion of *concern*. It runs from there to the notion of *moral responsibility* and on to the notion of *personal identity* (although the link between concern and personal identity provided by moral responsibility can as noted be skipped). The notion of personal identity links in turn to the notion of *consciousness*, which links back to the notion of *concern* in the way described in chapters 5–6 above. That said, *identity* is the fundamental topic of the chapter in which Locke's theory of personal identity appears, and the four terms are equally crucial.

I've said something about responsibility and concern. What about consciousness and identity? Locke's fundamental and well-known claim about personal identity is that "consciousness makes personal identity" (§10). By "consciousness of x," he means a certain sort of special mental relation that one can have to something x, which involves experiencing x in a certain immediate kind of way in which one can experience something only if it is one's own (chapter 6). More particularly, he means a mental relation one can have to precisely two sorts of things: first, portions of substance, which may be either material or immaterial, and secondly, actions including thought and other mental goings-on.

If you're conscious of something, then, in Locke's special sense of the word, the thing you're conscious of is either (i) you as a whole, the person you are, or (ii) part of what constitutes you as a whole, the person you are, in a sense of "constitute" that allows that your actions and mental goings-on, as well as portions of substance, can be literally part of what constitutes you as a person.

If you're conscious of an action, for example, in Locke's special sense of the word "conscious," then you are (necessarily) the person whose action it is or was, and the action falls under (ii). The action is on Locke's terms part of what constitutes you, the person or moral entity that you are. If you're conscious of a mental going-on, you are (necessarily) the person whose mental going-on it is or was, and the mental going-on again falls under (ii) on Locke's terms, being part of what constitutes you, the person or moral entity that you are. So too, if you're conscious of a portion of matter, the portion of matter is (necessarily) either part of or all of the body of the person you are and falls under (ii), being part of what constitutes you, the person or moral entity that you are. The same is true, mutatis mutandis, if you're conscious of a portion of immaterial "soul-substance."

It's this fact about the special restricted meaning Locke gives to the word "conscious" that explains why his notion of consciousness, i.e. Consciousness (p. 30), connects directly to the notion of concern, in his account. If you're Conscious of something, then it is by definition—necessarily—you, or part of you, as just remarked. And if it's you, or part of you, then it's necessarily of concern to you, in Locke's view. Thus, the fundamental notions form a circle: concern, moral responsibility, personal identity, Consciousness, concern. One can also run the circle differently: Consciousness, identity, concern, responsibility, Consciousness. This characterization of the heart of Locke's theory of personal identity may seem at first oblique and hard to understand, when placed next to other more popular characterizations, but it is I think apt.

Presented in this way, Locke's notion of concern—his way of understanding what is of concern to us—may seem narrowly self-interested. But one shouldn't mistake a definition for a moral position. The notion of concern with which he operates plays the theoretical role it's designed to play without excluding wider notions of concern with which Locke would no doubt have sympathized. Above all, it has to be understood in the light of the unique position one is in when it comes to determining one's fate in the "afterlife."

Appendix One

"Of Identity and Diversity"

An Essay concerning Human Understanding:
Book 2, Chapter 27

by John Locke

This version of 2.27 of Locke's *Essay* in modern English expands slightly on the text on a few occasions when it seems helpful to do so, and uses some of the simple if unbeautiful semi-technical terminology of present-day analytic philosophy. I would welcome suggestions and corrections.

There are very few paragraph breaks within Locke's numbered paragraphs. I've introduced many more in order to make it easier to pair parts of his text with their modern renderings. I've marked Locke's own internal paragraph breaks by prefixing an asterisk to their first words. I've also numbered the individual sentences of the famously difficult §13, and added a number of footnotes. The paragraph headings are Locke's own in the case of paragraphs 1–6, 8–10, 21, 26, and 28. Otherwise they are additions to or expansions of his headings.

I've capitalized "Person," "Consciousness," and "Concernment" and their cognates in the modern rendering in line with their capitalization in the main text of the book.

Locke's discussion of personal identity begins in §9.

§1 *WHEREIN IDENTITY CONSISTS*

Another occasion, the mind often takes of comparing, is the very being of things, when considering any thing as existing at any determined time and place, we compare it with it self existing at another time, and thereon form the ideas of *identity* and *diversity*.

When we see anything to be in any place in any instant of time, we are sure, (be it what it will) that it is that very thing, and not another, which at that same time exists in another place, how like and undistinguishable soever it may be in all other respects: and in this consists *identity*, when the ideas it is attributed to vary not at all from what they were that moment, wherein we consider their former existence, and to which we compare the present.

For we never finding, nor conceiving it possible, that two things of the same kind should exist in the same place at the same time, we rightly conclude, that, whatever exists anywhere at any time, excludes all of the same kind, and is there it self alone. When therefore we demand, whether anything be the same or no, it refers always to something that existed such a time in such a place, which 'twas certain, at that instant, was the same with it self and no other. From whence it follows, that one thing cannot have two beginnings of existence, nor two things one beginning, it being impossible for two things of the same kind, to be or exist in the same instant, in the very same place; or one and the same thing in different places. That therefore that had one beginning is the same thing; and that which had a different beginning in time and place from that, is not the same but diverse. That which has made the difficulty about this relation, has been the little care and attention used in having precise notions of the things to which it is attributed.

§1 *The nature of identity*

Another way in which we often compare things is in respect of their very existence—as for example when we consider an individual thing as existing at a given time and place and compare it with itself existing at another time, and on that basis form the ideas of identity and diversity.[1]

When we see that something is in a given place at a given moment of time, we are certain that it is that very thing and is not some other thing that exists in another place at the same time. This is so whatever sort of thing it is, and however similar and indeed indistinguishable it and the other thing are in all other respects. And this is what identity is: it is correctly attributed to those things[2] that we find not to have changed at all when we consider their existence at some moment in the past and compare this with their present existence.[3]

Given that we never find two things of the same kind in the same place at the same time, and do not think that this is possible, we rightly conclude that anything that exists at any place or any time excludes all other things of the same kind from that place at that time, and is the only thing of that kind present at that place and time. So when we ask whether some thing X considered at time t_1 and some thing Y considered at time t_2 are the same single thing,[4] we are always asking this about something that existed at a certain time and place and was then certainly identical with itself and nothing else. It follows that one thing cannot have two beginnings of existence any more than two things can have one beginning, because it is impossible for two things of the same kind to be or exist at the same instant in the very same place, or for one and the same thing to exist at the same instant in two different places. For any X and Y, therefore, if they share a spatio-temporal beginning of existence then they are the same thing, and if they have different spatio-temporal beginnings they are not the same thing, but different things. All the difficulties that have arisen about the relations of identity and difference stem from lack of sufficient care and attention in giving a precise specification of the things that are being compared in respect of identity and difference.

[1] I.e. difference, non-identity, distinctness.

[2] It's simplest to replace "ideas" by "things" here; Locke sometimes uses "idea," which we take to be a term that applies only to mental phenomena, in contexts where we would expect a term like "thing" or "property."

[3] "Identity" standardly means diachronic identity in Locke's time. Note that as it stands, this is a definition of what was then called "strict" identity, which allows no change at all.

[4] It's diachronic identity that is at issue: see the previous note and the first sentence of the paragraph.

§2 *IDENTITY OF SUBSTANCES*

We have the ideas but of three sorts of substances; 1. God. 2. Finite intelligences. 3. Bodies. First, God is without beginning, eternal, unalterable, and everywhere; and therefore concerning his identity, there can be no doubt. Secondly, finite spirits having had each its determinate time and place of beginning to exist, the relation to that time and place will always determine to each of them its identity as long as it exists. *Thirdly, the same will hold of every particle of matter, to which no addition or subtraction of matter being made, it is the same.

For though these three sorts of substances, as we term them, do not exclude one another out of the same place; yet we cannot conceive but that they must necessarily each of them exclude any of the same kind out of the same place: or else the notions and names of identity and diversity would be in vain, and there could be no such distinctions of substances, or anything else one from another. For example, could two bodies be in the same place at the same time; then those two parcels of matter must be one and the same, take them great or little; nay, all bodies must be one and the same. For, by the same reason that two particles of matter may be in one place, all bodies may be in one place:

[*Identity of modes*] which, when it can be supposed, takes away the distinction of identity and diversity, of one and more, and renders it ridiculous. But it being a contradiction, that two or more should be one, identity and diversity are relations and ways of comparing well founded, and of use to the understanding.

All other things being but modes or relations ultimately terminated in substances, the identity and diversity of each particular existence of them too will be by the same way determined: only as to things whose existence is in succession, such as are the actions of finite beings, v.g. *motion* and *thought*, both which consist in a continued train of succession, concerning their diversity there can be no question: because each perishing the moment it begins, they cannot exist in different times, or in different places, as permanent beings can at different times exist in distant places; and therefore no motion or thought, considered as at different times, can be the same, each part thereof having a different beginning of existence.

§2 *THE IDENTITY CONDITIONS OF SUBSTANCES*

We have ideas of only three sorts of substances: [1] God. [2] Finite intelligences. [3] Bodies. God, first, is without beginning, eternal, unalterable, and everywhere, so there can be no doubt about his identity. Secondly, each finite spirit has a determinate time and place at which it begins to exist, and its relation to that time and place will always determine its identity, as long as it exists. Thirdly, the same will hold of every particle of matter, so long as there is no matter added to it or subtracted from it.

Although these three sorts of substances, as we call them, are not debarred from occupying the same place, we take it that two substances *of the same kind* cannot possibly occupy the same place; for otherwise the notions of identity and diversity (the terms "identity" and "diversity") would be useless, and there would be no way of distinguishing one substance from another, or indeed of distinguishing anything from anything else. If, for example, two bodies could be in the same place at the same time, then those two parcels or portions of matter, large or small, would have to be one and the same. In fact all bodies would have to be one and the same; for if two particles of matter can be in one place, then all bodies can be in one place.

[*The identity of modes*] If we suppose this, we destroy altogether—render ridiculous—the distinction between identity and diversity, between singularity and plurality. It is, however, a contradiction to say that two or more things could be one thing, and it follows that the relational or comparative notions of identity and diversity are in fact sound and of use to the understanding.

Since all that exist apart from substances are modes or relations,[5] which are themselves ultimately ontologically grounded in substances, it follows that the identity and difference of all particular modes or relations will be determined in the same way as the identity and difference of substances. Now things that exist successively in time, like the actions[6] of finite beings (such as motion and thought), are unquestionably numerically diverse, for their existence simply consists in a continued train of succession. Each of them perishes the moment it begins, and so cannot possibly exist at a different time or place, in the way that enduring things can. It follows that if we consider a motion (or thought) X that exists at a time t_1, and a motion (or thought) Y that exists at a different time t_2, we know that X and Y cannot possibly be the same. For each part of a train of motion or thought has a different beginning of existence.

---

[5] I.e. properties.

[6] "Action" has a wide use; it covers mental occurrences as well as intentional bodily actions. I'll sometimes use the clumsy term "action/experience" to keep this point in view. Locke standardly uses "thought" in the wide Cartesian sense to denote all conscious mental occurrences (see e.g. §9 below), and one question is whether "action" covers all conscious occurrences, including those, like sensations, that we ordinarily think of as passive, or whether it sometimes refers more narrowly only to mental goings on for which one might be held to be responsible. See p. 15 above.

§3 *PRINCIPIUM INDIVIDUATIONIS*

From what has been said, 'tis easy to discover, what is so much inquired after, the *principium individuationis*; and that it is plain is existence it self, which determines a being of any sort to a particular time and place incommunicable to two beings of the same kind. This though it seems easier to conceive in simple substances or modes; yet when reflected on, is not more difficult in compound ones, if care be taken to what it is applied:

v.g. let us suppose an atom, i.e. a continued body under one immutable superficies, existing in a determined time and place; 'tis evident, that, considered in any instant of its existence, it is, in that instant the same with it self. For being, at that instant, what it is, and nothing else, it is the same, and so must continue, as long as its existence is continued; for so long it will be the same, and no other. In like manner, if two or more atoms be joined together into the same mass, every one of those atoms will be the same, by the foregoing rule: and whilst they exist united together, the mass, consisting of the same atoms, must be the same mass, or the same body, let the parts be ever so differently jumbled: but if one of these atoms be taken away, or one new one added, it is no longer the same mass, or the same body.

In the state of living creatures, their identity depends not on a mass of the same particles; but on something else. For in them the variation of great parcels of matter alters not the identity: an oak, growing from a plant to a great tree, and then lopped, is still the same oak; and a colt grown up to a horse, sometimes fat, sometimes lean, is all the while the same horse: though, in both these cases, there may be a manifest change of the parts: so that truly they are not either of them the same masses of matter, though they be truly one of them the same oak, and the other the same horse. The reason whereof is, that, in these two cases of a mass of matter, and a living body, *identity* is not applied to the same thing.

§3 *THE PRINCIPLE OF INDIVIDUATION*

We now have the means to settle the long disputed question about the principle of individuation of things.[7] It is now plain that their principle of individuation is simply: existence itself. This is already sufficient to pin any kind of being down to a particular time and place that cannot be shared with or co-occupied by any other being of the same kind. At first this point seems easier to grasp in the case of simple substances or modes. Reflection, however, shows that it is no more difficult in the case of compound ones, so long as one takes care.

Thus consider an atom, i.e. a continuously existing body with one unchanging surface existing at a specific place and time. When it is considered at any instant of its existence it is evident that it is at that instant the same thing as itself. For, being at that instant what it is, and nothing else, it is the same thing as itself, and must continue to be the same thing as itself for as long as it continues to exist.[8] By parity of reasoning, if two or more atoms are joined together into the same lump of matter,[9] every one of them will be the same as itself. It follows that for so long as these atoms exist united together, the lump or body that they jointly constitute will be numerically the same lump or body, simply because it consists of the same atoms—however much they are jumbled up. If, however, even one of these atoms is taken away, or a new one added, it will no longer be the same lump of matter or the same body.

When it comes to living creatures, however, their identity across time does not depend on their being a lump of matter that consists of the same particles. It depends rather on something else. For living creatures can retain their identity across time even if there is a huge change in or turnover of their component parts. An oak that grows from a plant to a great tree and is then pruned or pollarded is still the same oak. A colt that grows up and becomes a horse and is sometimes fat, sometimes thin, is for all that the same horse. In both these cases there can be an obvious change in their component parts across time, so that neither of them is strictly the same mass of matter (considered through time), while they undoubtedly remain the same oak and the same horse, respectively. The reason for this is that in these two cases—a lump of matter and a living body—the notion of identity is not applied to the same thing.[10]

---

[7] Locke doesn't recognize abstract objects.

[8] He doesn't simply say "identical with itself" because identity is a diachronic notion. See n. 3

[9] "Mass" doesn't mean "mass" as in physics, it means roughly "parcel of matter," "a grouping together." I'll use "lump."

[10] Parfit has said that he would rather his wife be made of different particles than that his wedding ring should be.

§4 *IDENTITY OF VEGETABLES*

We must therefore consider wherein an oak differs from a mass of matter, and that seems to me to be in this; that the one is only the cohesion of particles of matter any how united, the other such a disposition of them as constitutes the parts of an oak; and such an organization of those parts, as is fit to receive, and distribute nourishment, so as to continue, and frame the wood, bark, and leaves, etc. of an oak, in which consists the vegetable life.

That being then one plant, which has such an organization of parts in one coherent body, partaking of one common life, it continues to be the same plant, as long as it partakes of the same life, though that life be communicated to new particles of matter vitally united to the living plant, in a like continued organization, conformable to that sort of plants.

For this organization being at any one instant in any one collection of *matter*, is in that particular concrete distinguished from all other, and is that individual life, which existing constantly from that moment both forwards and backwards in the same continuity of insensibly succeeding parts united to the living body of the plant, it has that identity, which makes the same plant, and all the parts of it, parts of the same plant, during all the time that they exist united in that continued organization, which is fit to convey that common life to all the parts so united.

§4 *THE IDENTITY CONDITIONS OF PLANTS*

We must therefore consider the question of how an oak differs from a lump of matter. The answer seems to me to be this. The latter is only a clumping together of particles of matter united any old how. The former, by contrast, is a specific arrangement of particles of a kind that constitutes the parts of (e.g.) an oak. These parts are organized in such a way that they receive and distribute nourishment and so maintain and make up the wood, bark, leaves, etc., of the oak that themselves jointly constitute the life of the oak.

An individual plant, then, is one that has an organization of parts of the sort just described, existing in one united body and partaking of one common life. It continues to be numerically the same plant for as long as it partakes of the same life: as long as its organization continues to be the organization characteristic of that sort of plants, its diachronic identity is not in any way put in question by the fact that its continuing life is communicated to new particles of matter that become part of it.

And given that this particular organization—i.e. this particular, concrete instance of a certain type of organization—exists at a given instant in a given collection or "concretion"[11] of matter, it is thereby distinguished from all other such particular, concrete instances of organization: it is an individual life.[12] And given that it has (relative to that instant) continuous existence both in the past and the future—its continuous existence being constituted by the continuity of the process of individually insensible parts becoming successively united to the living body of the plant— the plant is numerically the same plant across time, and all its parts are parts of the same plant, so long they are parts of its continued organization.

[11] "Concrete" here is a noun meaning "concretion" (a "grown-togetherness" or "stuck-togetherness").

[12] In one sense, all oaks have the same organization: they all have the same single type of organization. In another sense, all oaks have or are different single organizations: each one is a different individual "token" of the same single organization type.

§5 *IDENTITY OF ANIMALS*

The case is not so much different in *brutes*, but that any one may hence see what makes an animal, and continues it the same. Something we have like this in machines, and may serve to illustrate it. For example, what is a watch? It is plain 'tis nothing but a fit organization, or construction of parts, to a certain end, which, when a sufficient force is added to it, it is capable to attain. If we would suppose this machine one continued body, all whose organized parts were repaired, increased, or diminished, by a constant addition or separation of insensible parts, with one common life, we should have something very much like the body of an animal, with this difference, that in an animal the fitness of the organization, and the motion wherein life consists, begin together, the motion coming from within; but in machines the force, coming sensibly from without, is often away, when the organ is in order, and well fitted to receive it.

§5 *THE IDENTITY CONDITIONS OF ANIMALS*

The case of non-human animals is sufficiently similar to that of plants for one to see, on the basis of what has already been said, both what constitutes an animal and what constitutes its continued existence as the same animal. Something similar also holds true of machines, which can serve here as an illustration. What, for example, is a watch? It's plain that it is nothing but an organization or construction of parts designed for a certain specific end, an end which it is capable of attaining when a sufficient force is applied to it. If we think of this machine as one continuously existing body all of whose organized parts are repaired, increased or diminished by a constant addition or separation of insensible parts, and have one common "life," then we have something very like the body of an animal. The difference is simply this: in an animal, the fitness of its organization for a certain end, and the motion in which its being alive consists, begin together: the motion comes from within. In machines, by contrast, the force is applied from outside,[13] and may be absent even when the organ is in full working order.

---

[13] We wind up the watch.

§6 *THE IDENTITY OF MAN*

This also shows wherein the identity of the same *man* consists; viz. in nothing but a participation of the same continued life, by constantly fleeting particles of matter, in succession vitally united to the same organized body. He that shall place the *identity* of man in anything else, but, like that of other animals, in one fitly organized body taken in any one instant, and from thence continued under one organization of life in several successively fleeting particles of matter, united to it, will find it hard to make an embryo, one of years, mad, and sober, the same man, by any supposition, that will not make it possible for Seth, Ismael, Socrates, Pilate, St. Austin, and Caesar Borgia, to be the same man.

For if the identity of soul alone makes the same man, and there be nothing in the nature of matter, why the same individual spirit may not be united to different bodies, it will be possible, that those men, living in distant ages, and of different tempers, may have been the same man: which way of speaking must be from a very strange use of the word *man*, applied to an idea, out of which body and shape is excluded: and that way of speaking would agree yet worse with the notions of those philosophers, who allow of transmigration, and are of opinion that the souls of men may, for their miscarriages, be detruded into the bodies of beasts, as fit habitations with organs suited to the satisfaction of their brutal inclinations. But yet I think no body, could he be sure that the soul of Heliogabalus were in one of his hogs, would yet say that hog were a *man* or Heliogabalus.

§6 *THE IDENTITY CONDITIONS OF HUMAN BEINGS*[14]

This also shows what the identity of a human being[15] consists in: it consists in nothing but the participation in the same continuing life of constantly fleeting particles of matter that are in succession vitally united to the same organized body.[16] Anyone who supposes that the identity of human beings consists in anything other than what the identity of other animals consists in—that is, the continuing life of an appropriately organized body whose continuing existence involves many material particles that fleetingly and successively make up a body of that particular type or organization—will find it very hard to give an account of how an embryo and a grown up (a grown up who is mad at one time, perhaps, sober at another) can be or count as the same human being while retaining the resources to exclude the possibility that Seth, Ismael, Socrates, Pilate, St. Austin, and Caesar Borgia, might all be the same human being.[17]

For if [a] identity or sameness of the soul is supposed to constitute sameness of the human being all by itself, and if [b] there is nothing in the nature of matter that excludes the possibility that the same individual soul can be united to different bodies,[18] then [c] there is no way of excluding the possibility that all these men, living at very different times and having different characters, are in fact the same man. This, however, would be a very strange use of the expression "human being." It would mean that the concept HUMAN BEING did not include anything about body and shape. It would also fit very badly with the theories of those philosophers who believe in the possibility of transmigration, and think that the souls of wrongdoing human beings may pass into the bodies of beasts (these bodies, equipped as they are with organs suitable for the satisfaction of these souls' brutal inclinations, being fit habitations for them). Even if one could be sure that the soul of Heliogabalus[19] was in one of one's hogs, one certainly would not say that the hog was a human being, or Heliogabalus.

[14] "Man" means human being. I'll use "human being" even when it seems clumsy.

[15] I.e. a human animal considered just as such.

[16] It's hard to improve on Locke's definition. It's a familiar point that all the molecules of our bodies are constantly being replaced (although there is some doubt about whether this is true of the ova), and half the molecules that now constitute your liver will be gone in five days' time. There's uncertainty about the turnover rate for the brain; some say it's a few weeks. It's worth thinking about what having a personality, a character, a "self," actually consists in, given that this is so. See p. 98 above.

[17] This is the first appearance of Locke's claim that identity of soul or "soul-substance" doesn't entail identity of human being ("man"). The list includes some very good and some very bad men.

[18] [b] would be generally granted in Locke's time, and [a] was a popular view.

[19] A dissolute Roman emperor.

§7 *IDEA OF IDENTITY SUITED TO THE IDEA IT IS APPLIED TO*

'Tis not therefore unity of substance that comprehends all sorts of *identity*, or will determine it in every case: but to conceive, and judge of it aright, we must consider what idea the word it is applied to stands for: it being one thing to be the same *substance*, another the same *man*, and a third the same *person*, if *person*, *man*, and *substance*, are three names standing for three different ideas; for such as is the idea belonging to that name, such must be the *identity*: which if it had been a little more carefully attended to, would possibly have prevented a great deal of that confusion, which often occurs about this matter, with no small seeming difficulties; especially concerning *personal identity*, which therefore we shall in the next place a little consider.

§7 *ONE CANNOT ANSWER QUESTIONS OF IDENTITY INDEPENDENTLY*
OF CONSIDERING HOW THE THING WHOSE IDENTITY
IS IN QUESTION IS BEING CONCEIVED OF

Unity of substance, then, isn't the only thing that is at issue when the diachronic identity of a thing is at issue. Facts about the unity or the sameness of a substance cannot decide the question of identity in every case. To get questions of diachronic identity right, when, using the word "Q," we say of some Q considered at time t that it's the same thing as some Q considered at some other time t_1, we have to consider what idea or concept the term "Q" stands for.[20] Given that "person," "human being" and "substance" are three words expressing three different concepts, it will be one thing for something X at time t_1 to be the same *substance* as something Y as time t_2, another thing for X at t_1 to be the same *human being* as Y at t_2, and yet another for X at t_1 to be the same *Person* as Y at t_2. *Questions about the identity of something X are a function of the concept that is expressed by "X."* If this fact had been a little more carefully attended to it might have prevented a great deal of the confusion and seeming difficulty that surrounds the matter of identity, especially in the case of Personal identity, which I will now briefly consider.

[20] "Considered at time t" and "considered at some other time t_1," convey the point that identity, i.e. diachronic identity, is in question.

§8 *Same man*

An animal is a living organized body; and consequently, the same animal, as we have observed, is the same continued life communicated to different particles of matter, as they happen successively to be united to that organized living body. And whatever is talked of other definitions, ingenious observation puts it past doubt, that the idea in our minds, of which the sound *man* in our mouths is the sign, is nothing else but of an animal of such a certain form:

since I think I may be confident, that whoever should see a creature of his own shape or make, though it had no more reason all its life, than a cat or a parrot, would call him still a man; or whoever should hear a cat or a parrot discourse, reason, and philosophize, would call or think it nothing but a cat or a parrot; and say, the one was a dull irrational man, and the other a very intelligent rational parrot.

A relation we have in an author of great note is sufficient to countenance the supposition of a rational parrot.

I had a mind to know from Prince Maurice's own mouth, the account of a common, but much credited story, that I had heard so often from many others, of an old parrot he had in Brazil, during his government there, that spoke, and asked, and answered common questions, like a reasonable creature: so that those of his train there, generally concluded it to be witchery or possession; and one of his chaplains, who lived long afterwards in Holland, would never from that time endure a parrot, but said, they all had a devil in them. I had heard many particulars of this story, and assevered by people hard to be discredited, which made me ask Prince Maurice what there was of it. He said, with his usual plainness, and dryness in talk, there was something true, but a great deal false, of what had been reported. I desired to know of him, what there was of the first; he told me short and coldly, that he had heard of such an old parrot when he came to Brazil, and though he believed nothing of it, and 'twas a good way off, yet he had so much curiosity as to send for it, that 'twas a very great and a very old one; and when it came first into the room where the prince was, with a great many Dutchmen about him, it said presently, *What a company of white men are here!* They asked it what he thought that man was, pointing to the prince. It answered, *Some General or other*; when they brought

§8 *SAME HUMAN BEING*

An animal is a living organized body. For the same animal to exist at different times, therefore, is (as observed) for the same continuing life to exist at different times, by being communicated to different particles of matter that are successively united to the organized living body in question. Other definitions may be offered, but thorough and precise reflection shows that the idea in our minds that is expressed by the sound "human being" in our mouths is nothing other than the idea of an animal of a certain form.[21]

If we were to see a creature of our own shape or make, I think I may be confident that we would call it a "human being" even if it never displayed any more reason than a cat or a parrot. And if we were to hear a cat or a parrot discourse, reason, and philosophize, we would not call it anything other than a cat or a parrot. We would say that the human being was a dull irrational human being, and the parrot a very intelligent rational parrot.

In support of the supposition of a rational parrot, consider an incident related by a very well known author.

---

[21] Locke seems nonetheless to hold that the idea of the soul is included in our conception of what a human being is, if not in our imagistic idea of a human being; he later says that "the body, as well as the soul, goes to the making of a man" (§15).

---

it close to him, he asked it, *D'ou venes vous?* It answered, *De Marinnan.* The Prince, *A qui estes vous?* The Parrot, *A un Portugais.* Prince, *Que fais-tu la?* Parrot, *Je garde les poulles.* The Prince laughed and said, *Vous gardez les poulles?* The Parrot answered, *Ouy, moy et je scay bien faire;*and made the chuck four or five times that people use to make to chickens when they call them. I set down the words of this worthy dialogue in French, just as Prince Maurice said them to me. I asked him in what language the parrot spoke, and he said in Brazilian; I asked whether he understood Brazilian; he said No, but he had taken care to have two interpreters by him, the one a Dutchman, that spoke Brazilian, and the other a Brazilian that spoke Dutch; that he asked them separately and privately, and both of them agreed in telling him just the same thing that the parrot had said. I could not but tell this odd story, because it is so much out of the way, and from the first hand, and what may pass for a good one; for I dare say this Prince, at least, believed himself in all he told me, having ever passed for a very honest and pious man; I leave it to naturalists to reason, and to other men to believe as they please upon it; however, it is not, perhaps, amiss to relieve or enliven a busie scene sometimes with such digressions, whether to the purpose or no.

I have taken care that the reader should have the story at large in the author's own words, because he seems to me not to have thought it incredible; for it cannot be imagined that so able a man as he, who had sufficiency enough to warrant all the testimonies he gives of himself, should take so much pains, in a place where it had nothing to do, to pin so close, not only on a man whom he mentions as his friend, but on a Prince in whom he acknowledges very great honesty and piety, a story which if he himself thought incredible, he could not but also think ridiculous.

The Prince, 'tis plain, who vouches this story, and our author who relates it from him, both of them call this talker a parrot: and I ask any one else who thinks such a story fit to be told, whether if this parrot, and all of its kind, had always talked, as we have a prince's word for it, this one did, whether, I say, they would not have passed for a race of *rational animals*, but yet whether for all that, they would have been allowed to be men, and not parrots? For I presume 'tis not the idea of a thinking or rational being alone, that makes the idea of a *man* in most people's sense; but of a body so and so shaped joined to it: and if that be the idea of a man, the same successive body not shifted all at once, must as well as the same immaterial spirit go to the making of the same *man*.

I have taken care to give the story in full in the author's own words to show that he did not seem to think it incredible. He was a very able man, and had, in addition, the resources to back up his accounts of his experiences. It cannot be imagined that he would have taken such pains to tell such a story—a story that served no other purpose in his book—if he himself thought it incredible, and therefore also ridiculous; especially given that the story's protagonist is someone whom he mentions not only as a friend but also as a prince of very great honesty and piety.

Both the prince, who vouches for this story, and the author, who got it from him, plainly call this talker a parrot. Assuming that such a story can be taken seriously, let us suppose that parrots had always talked (as we have a prince's word for it that this one did). I believe that we would then grant that parrots were a race of rational animals. But we would not for a moment grant that they were human beings and not parrots. For it is surely not simply the idea of a thinking or rational being that makes up (constitutes) the idea of a human being in most people's understanding. The idea of a human being also (essentially) includes that of a body of such and such a shape. This being so, it is not enough to have the same immaterial spirit at time t_1 as at time t_2 in order to have the same human being. One must also have the same successive body "not shifted all at once."[22]

---

[22] With "not shifted all at once" Locke anticipates §15 below, in which a soul shifts instantaneously from one human body to another in such a way that we can't say that we have to do with the same human being, when we have to do with the same soul, although we do (he claims) have to do with the same Person. There can be and is successive and continuous partial replacement or "shifting" of parts, in the case of an animal body, but they can't all be shifted at once for there to be bodily continuity of the kind necessary for the sameness of a human being across time.

§9 *Personal identity*

This being premised to find wherein *personal identity* consists, we must consider what *person* stands for; which, I think, is a thinking intelligent being, that has reason and reflection, and can consider it self as it self, the same thinking thing, in different times and places; which it does only by that consciousness, which is inseparable from thinking, and as it seems to me essential to it: it being impossible for any one to perceive, without perceiving, that he does perceive.

§9 *PERSONAL IDENTITY*

It follows from the principle laid down in §7[23] that we must consider what the word "person" stands for, in order to work out what Personal identity consists in. A Person, I propose, is [1] sentient or conscious, i.e. a subject of experience;[24] it is [2] capable of cognition;[25] [3] capable of reasoning; [4] aware of its own mental operations;[26] [5] and able to consider itself *as itself*[27] and as being the same subject of experience across time and in different places. [5] is made possible by [6] the *Consciousness*[28] or immediate or "from-the-inside givenness"[29] that is inseparable from all experience. It seems to me that it is essential to experience,[30] because it is impossible for anyone to experience anything without experiencing that he experiences.[31]

[23] Already put into practice in §8.

[24] "Sentient or conscious" replaces "thinking" used in the wide Cartesian sense ("intelligent" is not redundant).

[25] This replaces "intelligent"; the thing in question is not merely sentient.

[26] "Reflection" doesn't just mean "thoughtful" and isn't redundant. See pp. 63–64 above.

[27] Note that this is a definition of full or explicit self-consciousness, which is not entailed by the capacity for reflection noted in [4].

[28] "Con-scious" = knowing-with: a kind of accompanying awareness. This is the first occurrence of the word in the chapter. I capitalize it in the modern rendering because it has a special sense in Locke. See p. 33ff above.

[29] A clumsy but useful phrase. This phenomenon is well discussed in the Phenomenological tradition, in which, following Husserl, it is often called "first-personal givenness" (see e.g. p. 34 above).

[30] A natural way to read the "only" in "which it does only by that consciousness" is to take it to state that Consciousness is a necessary condition of the capacity described in [5]. It could also be taken to mean that Consciousness is a sufficient condition, but the claim would then be less plausible.

[31] Surely we can experience things without consciously experiencing that we experience them? Locke (following Aristotle and Descartes) agrees in as much as he certainly doesn't think that all awareness involves explicit conscious second-order awareness of his awareness. See next note.

§9 *PERSONAL IDENTITY (CONTINUED)*

When we see, hear, smell, taste, feel, meditate, or will anything, we know that we do so. Thus it is always as to our present sensations and perceptions: and by this every one is to himself that which he calls *self*: it not being considered in this case, whether the same *self* be continued in the same, or divers substances.

For since consciousness always accompanies thinking, and 'tis that, that makes every one to be, what he calls *self*, and thereby distinguishes himself from all other thinking things, in this alone consists *personal identity*, i.e. the sameness of a rational being: and as far as this consciousness can be extended backwards to any past action or thought, so far reaches the identity of that *person*; it is the same *self* now it was then; and it is by the same *self* with this present one that now reflects on it, that that action was done.

§9 *PERSONAL IDENTITY (CONTINUED)*

For when we see, hear, smell, taste, feel, meditate, or will anything, we know that we are doing so.[32] This is always how it is in the case of our *present* sensations and perceptions, and this is also what makes each Person experience his sensations and perceptions (actions) as his own when considering himself at times other than the present.[33] Note that in having this experience of something's being *me* in the past or future we have no thought about whether the persistence of our "self" involves one or several substances.

All experience, then, involves Consciousness in the present sense; and a subject of experience S's Consciousness of an experience is necessary and sufficient for that experience being, and being experienced by S as being, S's own experience, and not the experience of any other subject.[34] This, then, and this alone, is what Personal identity, i.e. the sameness of a rational being across time, consists in. S is the same Person as the subject of any past action or thought that S is conscious of in the sense of "Consciousness" just defined; and S performed any action that that subject of experience performed.[35]

---

[32] This we do ordinarily take to be true, and this is all that Locke means in his previous clause. He's talking about the "immediate givenness" or "from-the-inside givenness" of experience. Note again that "thinking" (also "perceiving") is used in the wide Cartesian sense to include sensing, feeling, meditating, willing.

[33] The extension of the thesis to times other than the present is implied by "continued."

[34] By definition, no one can be Conscious of anyone else's experience.

[35] Recall that the word "action" refers as much to mental occurrences as to bodily actions; this is so even though Locke sometimes explicitly distinguishes, as here, between actions and thoughts.

§10 *CONSCIOUSNESS MAKES PERSONAL IDENTITY*

But it is farther inquired whether it be the same identical substance. This few would think they had reason to doubt of, if these perceptions, with their consciousness, always remained present in the mind, whereby the same thinking thing would be always consciously present, and, as would be thought, evidently the same to it self. But that which seems to make the difficulty is this, that this consciousness being interrupted always by forgetfulness, there being no moment of our lives wherein we have the whole train of all our past actions before our eyes in one view: but even the best memories losing the sight of one part whilst they are viewing another; and we sometimes, and that the greatest part of our lives, not reflecting on our past selves, being intent on our present thoughts, and in sound sleep, having no thoughts at all, or at least none with that consciousness, which remarks our waking thoughts. I say, in all these cases, our consciousness being interrupted, and we losing the sight of our past *selves*, doubts are raised whether we are the same thinking thing; i.e. the same substance or no. Which however reasonable, or unreasonable, concerns not *personal identity* at all. The question being what makes the same *person*, and not whether it be the same identical substance, which always thinks in the same *person*, which in this case matters not at all. Different substances, by the same consciousness (where they do partake in it) being united into one person; as well as different bodies, by the same life are united into one animal, whose identity is preserved, in that change of substances, by the unity of one continued life.

§10 *Consciousness determines Personal identity*

It will now be asked whether identity of Person[36] necessarily involves identity of substance. Few would think that there was any reason to doubt this if all one's experiences, including the Consciousness that (partly) constitutes them, always remained present to one's mind—if, in other words, one was always Conscious of the totality of one's conscious existence. In this case one's self-identity across time would presumably be evident to one.[37] The difficulty, however, is created by the fact that this Consciousness is always being interrupted by forgetfulness. In fact there is never a time at which we have the whole sequence of all our past actions/ experiences simultaneously in mind. Even those of us with the best memories lose sight of one part of their past experience when considering another part—and we aren't usually reflecting on our past actions/experiences at all, but are intent on our present thoughts. We have, furthermore, no Conscious experience in sound sleep—or at least none with the Consciousness that is distinctive of waking life. In all these cases, then, our Consciousness is interrupted. We are not then Conscious of the past actions/experiences that make up our past existence, and doubts are accordingly raised about whether or not we are the same thinking thing, i.e. the same *substance*, as the subject of those past actions/experiences. But these doubts, reasonable or not, have nothing to do with the question of Personal identity. The question of Personal identity is about what makes entity X at t_1 the same *Person* as entity Y at t_2; it is not the question whether it is always the same *substance* that does the thinking in the same Person. When it comes to Personal identity, sameness of substance doesn't matter at all:[38] different substances may be united in or into one Person by being part of what realizes (and is therefore the object of) the same Consciousness just as different parts of matter can be united into one animal by being part of what realizes the same life, the identity of the animal being preserved, in spite of the change in its material parts, by the unity of its continuing life.

---

[36] This replaces Locke's "it," which might conceivably be thought to stand for "sameness of consciousness," although this seems ruled out by the next sentence.

[37] To understand Locke's approach is to see that this initially strange-seeming proposal is the natural first step for Locke to take.

[38] What Locke has principally in mind here, I think, is the fact that the substance of the brain is always changing, so that the substance that does the thinking in us is always changing if we're wholly material beings.

§ 10 *CONSCIOUSNESS MAKES PERSONAL IDENTITY*

For it being the same consciousness that makes a man be himself to himself, *personal identity* depends on that only, whether it be annexed solely to one individual substance, or can be continued in a succession of several substances. For as far as any intelligent being can repeat the idea of any past action with the same consciousness it had of it at first, and with the same consciousness it has of any present action; so far it is the same *personal self*.

For it is by the consciousness it has of its present thoughts and actions, that it is *self* to it *self* now, and so will be the same *self* as far as the same consciousness can extend to actions past or to come; and would be by distance of time, or change of substance, no more two *persons* than a man be two men, by wearing other clothes today than he did yesterday, with a long or a short sleep between: the same consciousness uniting those distant actions into the same *person*, whatever substances contributed to their production.

§10 *Consciousness determines Personal identity (continued)*

For since it is sameness of Consciousness that makes certain past experiences one's own in the way that certain present experiences are one's own,[39] Personal identity (across time) depends only on this sameness of Consciousness. It doesn't matter whether this sameness of Consciousness involves only one individual substance, or whether it is continued in a succession of several substances. As long as an intelligent being can rehearse or re-experience any past action/experience with the same "from-the-inside" Consciousness it had of it when it first occurred, and with the same from-the-inside Consciousness that it has of any present action/experience, then it is the same Person as the intelligent being that performed that action (had that experience).[40]

For it is the Consciousness it has of its present thoughts and actions that makes it be itself to/for itself in the present; in just the same way it will be the same self (Person) as any self (Person) whose actions/experiences it is Conscious of, be they past or future. So long as there is sameness of Consciousness, distance in time or change of thinking substance will no more result in there being two Persons than a human being's change of clothes overnight will result in there being two human beings (whether their sleep is short or long). Sameness of Consciousness will make those distant actions/experiences the actions/experiences of the Person who is present now, whatever substances contributed to their production.

---

[39] This is a long spelling out of "makes a man be himself to himself," but the explicit references to time are implicit in Locke's word "same," for sameness, here, is essentially a matter of sameness across time. Note that Locke's primary definition of Consciousness is by reference to present experience (see p. 72 above; the common identification of Lockean consciousness with memory is wrong in several ways).

[40] The Consciousness does not have to be just as vivid, qualitatively speaking. It just has to be true that one experiences the action as one's own. See p. 148 above.

§11 *PERSONAL IDENTITY IN CHANGE OF SUBSTANCES*

That this is so, we have some kind of evidence in our very bodies, all whose particles, whilst vitally united to this same thinking conscious self, so that we feel when they are touched, and are affected by, and conscious of good or harm that happens to them, are a part of our *selves*: i.e. of our thinking conscious *self*. Thus the limbs of his body are to every one a part of *himself*: he sympathizes and is concerned for them. Cut off a hand, and thereby separate it from that consciousness, we had of its heat, cold, and other affections; and it is then no longer a part of that which is *himself*, any more than the remotest part of matter. Thus, we see the *substance*, whereof *personal self* consisted at one time, may be varied at another, without the change of personal *identity*: there being no question about the same person, though the limbs, which but now were a part of it, be cut off.

§11 *PERSONAL IDENTITY ACROSS CHANGE OF SUBSTANCE [1]*

The body provides some evidence for this, for all those of its constituent particles that are "vitally united" to the thinking Conscious subject that is oneself, in such a way that one feels something when they are touched, and is consciously affected by them, and aware of good or harm that happens to them, are a part of oneself, i.e. the thinking Conscious subject that one is. Thus the limbs of one's body are a part of oneself: for one sympathizes and is *Concerned* for them.[41] If one's hand is cut off, and thereby separated from the Consciousness one has of its heat, cold, and other affections, then it is no longer a part of that which is oneself, any more than the remotest part of matter is. We see, then, that the substance of which a Personal self is constituted at one time may be different at another time[42] without there being any change in Personal identity. For there is no doubt that we still have the same *Person*, when someone's limbs are cut off.

---

[41] This is the first use in this chapter of the key notion of Concernment, although its special connection with the question of Personal identity has already been made clear earlier in the *Essay* (2.1.11). Note that this Concernment is *proof* that they are part of oneself, given how "Concernment" is understood.

[42] Locke is a bit loose, here, given his explicit references to different times, but his meaning is clear.

§12 *PERSONAL IDENTITY IN CHANGE OF SUBSTANCES*

But the question is, whether if the same substance, which thinks, be changed, it can be the same person, or remaining the same, it can be different persons?

*And to this I answer first, this can be no question at all to those, who place thought in a purely material, animal, constitution, void of an immaterial substance. For, whether their supposition be true or no, 'tis plain they conceive personal identity preserved in something else than identity of substance; as animal identity is preserved in identity of life, and not of substance. And therefore those, who place thinking in an immaterial substance only, before they can come to deal with these men, must show why personal identity cannot be preserved in the change of immaterial substances, or variety of particular immaterial substances, as well as animal identity is preserved in the change of material substances, or variety of particular bodies: unless they will say, 'tis one immaterial spirit, that makes the same life in brutes; as it is one immaterial spirit that makes the same person in men, which the Cartesians at least will not admit, for fear of making brutes thinking things too.

§12 *Personal identity across change of substance [2]*

The question is now this: [a] If the substance which thinks is changed, can it still be the same Person?[43] [b] If the substance remains the same, can it be a different Person?[44]

The first part of my answer[45] is that *materialists* (those who place conscious experience wholly in a purely material animal constitution) can hardly ask question [a], because (whether or not materialism is true) they have to take Personal identity to be secured by something other than identity of substance; as animal identity is secured by identity of life, rather than identity of substance. So before the *immaterialists* (those who place conscious experience wholly in an immaterial substance) can confront the materialists they will have to show why *Personal* identity cannot be preserved across change or variation in *immaterial* substance as easily as *animal* identity can be preserved in the change or variation in *material* substances. Otherwise they will have to grant that the diachronic identity of the life of a non-human animal depends on the diachronic identity of an immaterial spirit just as diachronic Personal identity depends on diachronic identity of immaterial spirit in human beings. And the Cartesians certainly will not admit this, because they will then have to grant that non-human animals, too, are thinking things.

[43] I.e. does *same substance* entail *same Person?*
[44] I.e. does *same Person* entail *same substance?*
[45] This is a nice piece of argument.

§13 *Whether in the change of thinking substances there can be one person*

[s1] But next, as to the first part of the question, whether if the same thinking substance (supposing immaterial substances only to think) be changed, it can be the same person.

[s2] I answer, that cannot be resolved, but by those, who know what kind of substances they are, that do think; and whether the consciousness of past actions can be transferred from one thinking substance to another.

[s3] I grant, were the same consciousness the same individual action, it could not: but it being but a present representation of a past action, why it may not be possible, that that may be represented to the mind to have been, which really never was, will remain to be shown.

[s4] And therefore how far the consciousness of past actions is annexed to any individual agent, so that another cannot possibly have it, will be hard for us to determine, till we know what kind of action it is, that cannot be done without a reflex act of perception accompanying it, and how performed by thinking substances, who cannot think without being conscious of it.

[s5] But that which we call the *same consciousness*, not being the same individual act, why one intellectual substance may not have represented to it, as done by it self, what it never did, and was perhaps done by some other agent, why I say such a representation may not possibly be without

§13 *CAN THERE BE ONE PERSON ACROSS CHANGE IN
IMMATERIAL SUBSTANCE?*

The first part of the question raised in §12 is [a] whether a Person can survive a change of thinking substance. In answering it I will assume for the moment that only immaterial substances can think.[46]

To settle the question definitively one would need to know [i] the nature of thinking substances, and [ii] whether Consciousness of past actions/experiences can (given the nature of thinking substances) possibly transfer from one thinking substance to another.[47]

Now if "same Consciousness" meant "numerically the same individual episode of Consciousness," then plainly there couldn't be any such transfer. Here, though, it refers only to a present[48] representation of a past action/experience, and given that this is so, it hasn't been shown that it is actually impossible for the mind[49] to represent something that never happened as having happened.[50]

It will be hard for us, therefore, to determine the extent to which the Consciousness of an individual agent's past actions is tied to that agent in such a way that no other agent can possibly have it.[51] We cannot hope to know this until we know the nature of those actions that can't be done without a reflex act of perception accompanying them, and know how these actions are performed by thinking substances who cannot think without being Conscious of their thinking.[52]

So—given that "same Consciousness" does not here mean "numerically the same individual act"—it will be difficult for us, with our limited knowledge of the nature of things, to conclude that one thinking substance cannot possibly have represented to it, as done by itself, an action that it never did, and that was perhaps done by some other agent. It will be difficult to rule out the possibility that its representation

---

[46] The materialist approach is put aside because it follows immediately from the materialists' starting supposition that the answer to the question is yes.

[47] Locke aims to show that we can't in the present state of our knowledge rule out the possibility of this kind of transference in the case of immaterial thinking substances.

[48] And so numerically distinct.

[49] I take "the mind" to refer to the "thinking substance."

[50] Locke is loose here, because it's obvious that the mind can represent something that never happened as having happened. Given [s3], however, it's clear that his aim is to show that we can't rule out the possibility that an immaterial thinking substance I1 might represent itself as having done something that it, I1, didn't in fact do, and that some other substance I2 did. Locke wants to show that we can't rule this out in order to show that we can't rule out the possibility that the existence of a single *Person* P might involve first one immaterial substance, I1, and then another, I2. It's important that Locke takes the faculty of memory to be extremely reliable. He also takes it that memories are self-certifying, in the sense that they present as memories, this being part of their overall experiential character (see *Essay* 2.10; Garrett 2003).

[51] This is the first use of "agent" in 2.27. The only other use outside this paragraph occurs in §26. This is an interpretative crux; see pp. 110–113 above.

[52] All thinking (perception, experience) involves reflexivity inasmuch as "thinking consists in being conscious that one thinks" (2.1.19).

§13 *WHETHER IN THE CHANGE OF THINKING SUBSTANCES*
THERE CAN BE ONE PERSON (CONTINUED)

reality of matter of fact, as well as several representations in dreams are, which yet, whilst dreaming, we take for true, will be difficult to conclude from the nature of things.

[s6] And that it never is so, will by us, till we have clearer views of the nature of thinking substances, be best resolved into the goodness of God, who as far as the happiness or misery of any of his sensible creatures is concerned in it, will not by a fatal error of theirs transfer from one to another, that consciousness, which draws reward or punishment with it.

[s7] How far this may be an argument against those who would place thinking in a system of fleeting animal spirits, I leave to be considered.

[s8] But yet, to return to the question before us, it must be allowed, that if the same consciousness (which, as has been shown, is quite a different thing from the same numerical figure or motion in body) can be transferred from one thinking substance to another, it will be possible, that two thinking substances may make but one person.

[s9] For the same consciousness being preserved, whether in the same or different substances, the personal identity is preserved.

§13 *Can there be one Person across change in*
immaterial substance? (*continued*)

of itself as having done something may be false although it takes it to be true—just
as many of the representations of ourselves that we have when dreaming are false
although we take them to be true while we are dreaming.

[The case that matters is the case in which there really is an action, and in which
the agent X who actually did the action is not the agent, Y, that now represents itself as
having done it.][53] But until we have a clearer view of the nature of thinking substances,[54]
we should base our confidence that this will never happen on the goodness of God. For
God, being good, will not transfer Consciousness of any action/experience from one of
his sensible creatures to another if the transfer has any consequences for their happiness or misery: he will not transfer from X to Y Consciousness which draws reward or
punishment (and so happiness and misery) with it, through Y's having made a fatal error.[55]

Does this constitute an argument against those (the materialists) who place thinking in a system of fleeting animal spirits? I leave this for further consideration.

The fact remains—to return to the question before us—that it must be allowed
that if the same Consciousness (which is quite different from the same numerical figure or motion in body, as I have already shown) can be transferred from one thinking
substance to another, then it *will* be possible for two thinking substances to make up
[successively] one single Person.

For so long as the same Consciousness is preserved[56]—whether in the same substance or different substances—Personal identity is preserved.[57]

---

[53] This is so-called "quasi-memory" or "q-memory" (a term introduced by Shoemaker in 1970). The idea is that (i) the memory is in one sense a genuine memory, because someone really had the experience, (ii) the experience somehow directly causes the
memory in you, and yet (iii) it doesn't follow, from your having the memory in the from-
the-inside way, that you actually had the experience. Locke argues that such transfers
might be impossible in the nature of things, given the reflexive nature of all experience,
and the actual substantial nature of whatever it is that experiences (here assumed to be
immaterial). But, he says, we don't know enough about the nature of things to be able to
know with certainty that this is so. Still, he argues, it's enough for us, in our ignorance of
the nature of things, to assume that God wouldn't let this happen in any case in which
Consciousness carries punishment and reward with it.

[54] Which might show such a case to be impossible.

[55] A fatal error is an error which impacts on Y's happiness or misery by affecting his
overall fate on the Day of Judgment. The famous but misplaced objection to this passage
is that genuine transfer of Consciousness can't be unfair, on Locke's view, because one
is literally constituted as a Person by what one is Conscious of; so that if one becomes
Conscious of a new action it simply becomes part of the Person one is, whatever intuitive
reasons there are for saying that it was performed by a different Person. For discussion,
see pp. 119–24 above.

[56] Here "Consciousness" seems to function as a count noun. See the use of "Consciousnesses" in §23 below.

[57] Locke concludes that we can't rule out the possibility of transfer of Consciousness
from one immaterial substance to another, and so can't rule out persistence of Personal
identity across change of immaterial substance.

§14 *WHETHER, THE SAME IMMATERIAL SUBSTANCE REMAINING,*
THERE CAN BE TWO PERSONS

As to the second part of the question, Whether the same immaterial
substance remaining, there may be two distinct persons; which question
seems to me to be built on this, whether the same immaterial being, being
conscious of the action of its past duration, may be wholly stripped of all
the consciousness of its past existence, and lose it beyond the power of
ever retrieving it again: and so as it were beginning a new account from
a new period, have a consciousness that cannot reach beyond this new
state. All those who hold pre-existence, are evidently of this mind, since
they allow the soul to have no remaining consciousness of what it did in
that pre-existent state, either wholly separate from body, or informing any
other body; and if they should not, 'tis plain experience would be against
them. So that personal identity reaching no farther than consciousness
reaches, a pre-existent spirit not having continued so many ages in a state
of silence, must needs make different persons.

Suppose a Christian Platonist or a Pythagorean, should upon God's
having ended all his works of creation the seventh day, think his soul hath
existed ever since; and should imagine it has revolved in several human
bodies, as I once met with one, who was persuaded his had been the soul
of Socrates (how reasonably I will not dispute. This I know, that in the
post he filled, which was no inconsiderable one, he passed for a very rational man, and the press has shown, that he wanted not parts or learning)
would any one say, that he, being not conscious of any of Socrates' actions
or thoughts, could be the same person with Socrates? Let any one reflect
upon himself, and conclude, that he has in himself an immaterial spirit,
which is that which thinks in him, and, in the constant change of his body
keeps him the same; and is that which he calls himself: let him also suppose it to be the same soul that was in Nestor or Thersites, at the siege of
Troy, (for souls being, as far as we know anything of them, in their nature
indifferent to any parcel of matter, the supposition has no apparent absurdity in it) which it may have been, as well as it is now, the soul of any other
man: but he now having no consciousness of any of the actions either of
Nestor or Thersites, does he, or can he, conceive himself the same person

§14 *CAN THERE BE TWO PERSONS WITHOUT CHANGE*
OF IMMATERIAL SUBSTANCE?

The second part of the question raised in §12 is [b] whether there can be two distinct Persons given only one immaterial substance. I think that the question amounts to this. Can an immaterial substance that is Conscious of its past actions and existence be completely and irretrievably stripped of this Consciousness, and so as it were begin a new "account" from a new period, with a Consciousness that cannot possibly reach beyond this new period? All those who believe in pre-existence obviously think this, because they allow that the soul has no Consciousness of what it did in its pre-existent state—whether it then "informed" some other body or was wholly separate from body. (If they did not grant this, their claim would plainly be empirically indefensible.) Assuming, then, that a pre-existent spirit has not persisted through many ages in a state of silence,[58] it must make up different Persons; for one's Personal identity reaches no further than what one is Conscious of.[59]

Suppose a Christian Platonist or Pythagorean thinks that his soul has existed ever since the seventh day, because that is when God ended all his works of creation. And suppose that he believes that his soul has since returned in a number of different human bodies—like someone I once met, who was sure his soul had been the soul of Socrates (I won't discuss whether or not this was reasonable; he did, though, hold an important post, was considered a very rational man, and his publications testify to his scholarship and his abilities). Would any one say that he is in this case the same Person as Socrates, given that he is not Conscious of any of Socrates' actions or thoughts?[60] Suppose you examine yourself and conclude that you have in you an immaterial soul, and that this immaterial soul is [1] that which thinks in you, [2] that which makes it the case that you are one and the same throughout all the constant changes in your body, [3] that which you refer to when you say "myself." Suppose also that your soul is the one that was in Nestor or Thersites at the siege of Troy (the supposition has no obvious absurdity in it, because for all we know about souls they can attach to one portion of matter as well as they can to any other)—which is just as likely as Nestor's or Thersites' soul having been the soul of any other living human being. You now have no Consciousness of any of the actions of Nestor or Thersites. Do you—can you—suppose that you are the same

---

[58] I.e. with no Consciousness.

[59] I.e. since Personal identity reaches no further than Consciousness, there must be at least two different Persons in this case.

[60] Recall that one is, crucially, morally and legally responsible for the actions of any Person that one is.

§14 *WHETHER, THE SAME IMMATERIAL SUBSTANCE REMAINING,*
THERE CAN BE TWO PERSONS (CONTINUED)

with either of them? Can he be concerned in either of their actions? attribute them to himself, or think them his own more than the actions of any other man, that ever existed? So that this consciousness not reaching to any of the actions of either of those men, he is no more one *self* with either of them, than if the soul or immaterial spirit, that now informs him had been created, and began to exist, when it began to inform his present body, though it were never so true, that the same spirit that informed Nestor's or Thersites' body, were numerically the same that now informs his. For this would no more make him the same person with Nestor, than if some of the particles of matter, that were once a part of Nestor, were now a part of this man, the same immaterial substance without the same consciousness, no more making the same person by being united to any body, than the same particle of matter, without consciousness united to any body, makes the same person. But let him once find himself conscious of any of the actions of Nestor, he then finds himself the same person with Nestor.

§14 *CAN THERE BE TWO PERSONS WITHOUT CHANGE*
OF IMMATERIAL SUBSTANCE? (CONTINUED)

Person as either of them? Can you be *Concerned* in the actions of either of them? Can you attribute those actions to yourself, or think that they are any more your actions than the actions of anyone else who has ever existed? No. Given that you are not Conscious of any of the actions of either of those men[61] you are no more the same Person[62] as either of them than you would be if your soul had been created only when it began to "inform" your present body; and this is so even though we are now assuming that the soul that actually informs your body is numerically the same soul as the one that informed Nestor's or Thersites' body. This would no more make you the same Person as Nestor than would the fact some of the material particles that were once a part of Nestor were now a part of you. In the absence of sameness of Consciousness, sameness of immaterial substance no more makes a single Person out of the subjects of experience of two bodies to which it is united than sameness of material particle makes a single Person out of the subjects of experience of two bodies to which it is united.[63] If, however, you were ever to find yourself *Conscious* of any of the actions of Nestor (experiencing them as one's own from-the-inside), then you would indeed be the same Person with Nestor.[64]

[61] I.e. given that you don't experience any of their actions as your own in the immediate from-the-inside way.

[62] I use "Person" instead of "self." Here, as almost everywhere in Locke's chapter, the words are synonymous.

[63] I.e. of which it is (at different times) part.

[64] So far as that action, at least, is concerned; see p. 61 above.

§15 *THE BODY, AS WELL AS THE SOUL, GOES TO THE MAKING OF A MAN*

And thus may we be able without any difficulty to conceive, the same person at the resurrection, though in a body not exactly in make or parts the same which he had here, the same consciousness going along with the soul that inhabits it. But yet the soul alone in the change of bodies, would scarce to any one, but to him that makes the soul the *man*, be enough to make the same *man*.

For should the soul of a prince, carrying with it the consciousness of the prince's past life, enter and inform the body of a cobbler, as soon as deserted by his own soul, every one sees, he would be the same person with the prince, accountable only for the prince's actions: but who would say it was the same man? The body too goes to the making the man, and would, I guess, to everybody determine the man in this case, wherein the soul, with all its princely thoughts about it, would not make another man: but he would be the same cobbler to every one besides himself.

I know that in the ordinary way of speaking, the same person, and the same man, stand for one and the same thing. And indeed every one will always have a liberty to speak, as he pleases, and to apply what articulate sounds to what ideas he thinks fit, and change them as often as he pleases. But yet when we will enquire, what makes the same *spirit, man*, or *person*, we must fix the ideas of *spirit, man*, or *person*, in our minds; and having resolved with ourselves what we mean by them, it will not be hard to determine, in either of them, or the like, when it is the *same*, and when not.

§15 *THE BODY AS WELL AS THE SOUL IS PART OF
WHAT CONSTITUTES A HUMAN BEING*

It is therefore easy to make sense of the idea that we can have the same Person at the resurrection as in earthly life, even if the parts and structure of that Person's body are not exactly the same as they were on earth, given that the same Consciousness goes along with the soul-substance inhabits both bodies. That said, sameness of soul-substance isn't sufficient for sameness of human being (not unless one holds that a human being is—is nothing more than—a soul).

For suppose the soul of a prince, carrying with it the Consciousness of the prince's past life, enters and informs the body of a cobbler, the soul of the cobbler exiting the cobbler's body at the same moment. In this case it's plain that the cobbler is the same *Person* as the prince—i.e. that he is only accountable for the prince's actions. But none, surely, would say he was the same *human being* as the prince. The body as well as the soul is part of what constitutes a human being, and I think everyone will agree that in this case it settles the question: the cobbler is the same human being throughout this whole process. The fact that he has the prince's soul within him does not make him a different human being from the cobbler, and everyone (other than himself) will take him to be the same human being as before.

In everyday speech, of course, "same Person" and "same man" stand for one and the same thing, and we are all free to speak as we please. We can use speech sounds for whatever notion we like, and change them as often as we like. But when we want to work out the (diachronic) identity conditions of souls, human beings, or Persons, we need to focus mentally on the ideas of spirit, human animal, or Person and get a clear idea of what we mean by them. It will not then be hard for us to settle questions about their identity conditions, or the identity conditions of things like them.

§16 *CONSCIOUSNESS ALONE UNITES ACTIONS INTO THE SAME PERSON*

But though the same immaterial substance, or soul does not alone, wherever it be, and in whatsoever state, make the same man; yet 'tis plain consciousness, as far as ever it can be extended, should it be to ages past, unites existences, and actions, very remote in time, into the same person, as well as it does the existences and actions of the immediately preceding moment: so that whatever has the consciousness of present and past actions, is the same person to whom they both belong. Had I the same consciousness, that I saw the ark and Noah's flood, as that I saw an overflowing of the Thames last winter, or as that I write now, I could no more doubt that I, that write this now, that saw the Thames overflowed last winter, and that viewed the flood at the general deluge, was the same *self*, place that *self* in what substance you please, than that I who write this am the same *my self* now whilst I write (whether I consist of all the same substance, material or immaterial, or no) that I was yesterday. For as to this point of being the same *self*, it matters not whether this present *self* be made up of the same or other substances, I being as much concerned, and as justly accountable for any action that was done a thousand years since, appropriated to me now by this self-consciousness, as I am, for what I did the last moment.

§16 *Consciousness alone unites actions and experiences into the same Person*

Although sameness of *soul-substance* does not suffice for sameness of *human being* (wherever the soul-substance is, and whatever its state), sameness of *Consciousness* does suffice for sameness of *Person*. Past actions or experiences or existences, however remote in time, are as much part of the Person one is now as those of the immediate past, so long as one's Consciousness can extend to them.[65] Take any two actions, one past and one present. Whatever is Conscious of both of them is one single Person and is the agent of those actions.[66] Suppose I were Conscious of an experience of seeing Noah's Ark and the flood, in just the way that I am Conscious of having seen an overflowing of the Thames last winter, or of the fact that I am writing now. In that case I could no more doubt that I who write this now, he who saw the Thames overflow last winter, and he who saw the flood at the general deluge, are the same self or Person—whatever substantially constitutes or "realizes" this self or Person—than I can doubt that I who write this am the same self or Person now, while I write, as I was yesterday. (This is so quite irrespective of whether or not I consist of exactly the same substance, material or immaterial, as yesterday.) As far as being the same self or Person is concerned it simply doesn't matter whether the present self or Person be made up of the same or different substances. I am as much implicated and Concerned in and accountable for an action done a thousand years ago as I am for what I did a moment ago, so long as that action is "appropriated"[67] to me by my present self-Consciousness.

[65] So that one experiences them as one's own in the immediately given way. Plainly "*x* experiences *y* as its own" is not a "factive" verb (i.e. it doesn't entail "*y* is *x*'s own"); "*x*'s from-the-inside memory extends to *y* and *x* experiences *y* as its own" may be taken to be the relevant factive verb.

[66] It's logically impossible for two Persons to be Conscious of the same action, on Locke's view, because they would then be the same Person; see e.g. §17. So too we take experiences to be "logically private" in the sense that two people can't possibly have numerically the same one.

[67] First use of the verb "appropriate" in this chapter. To appropriate something is to make it one's own property, or acknowledge it as one's own (in French "mon propre main" means "my own hand").

Self is that conscious thinking thing, whatever substance made up of (whether spiritual or material, simple or compounded, it matters not) which is sensible, or conscious of pleasure and pain, capable of happiness or misery, and so is concerned for it *self*, as far as that consciousness extends. Thus every one finds, that whilst comprehended under that consciousness, the little finger is as much a part of it self, as what is most so. Upon separation of this little finger, should this consciousness go along with the little finger, and leave the rest of the body, 'tis evident the little finger would be the *person*, the *same person*; and *self* then would have nothing to do with the rest of the body.

As in this case it is the consciousness that goes along with the substance, when one part is separate from another, which makes the same *person*, and constitutes this inseparable *self*: so it is in reference to substances remote in time. That with which the *consciousness* of this present thinking thing can join it self, makes the same *person*, and is one *self* with it, and with nothing else; and so attributes to it self, and owns all the actions of that thing, as its own, as far as that consciousness reaches, and no farther; as every one who reflects will perceive.

§17 *THE IDENTITY OF A SELF OR PERSON DEPENDS ON CONSCIOUSNESS, NOT ON SUBSTANCE*

A self or Person is a Conscious thinking thing (again it doesn't matter what substance the thinking thing is made of, spiritual or material, simple or compound) that is sensible or conscious of pleasure and pain and capable of happiness or misery and is therefore Concerned for itself, as far as its Consciousness extends. One's little finger is as much a part of oneself as one's most essential part, so long as it is "comprehended under" one's Consciousness.[68] If one's little finger were cut off, and one's Consciousness went along with the finger and quit the rest of the body, then it would be the little finger that was the Person one was, the same Person that existed before the finger was cut off; and that Person or self (or: what constituted self for that Person) would have nothing to do with the rest of one's body.

When two parts of the body, say A and B, are separated from one another, then, it is the fact that the Consciousness goes along with A which makes it the case that A and not B is the same self or Person as the self or Person who existed previously (the self or Person being of course inseparable from itself). Exactly the same holds with respect to things remote in time: whatever the Consciousness of this present thinking thing can join itself with is *ipso facto* (part of) the same Person or self as this present thinking thing, and cannot be (a part of) any other Person or self. And, this being so, the Person attributes to itself—acknowledges as its own—all the actions of that thing, precisely to the extent that its consciousness reaches them and no further. This is obvious, on reflection.

---

[68] So long as it lies in one's field of Consciousness, so long as one would (for example) feel pain if it were injured.

§18 *Persons, not substances,*
THE OBJECTS OF REWARD AND PUNISHMENT

In this *personal* identity is founded all the right and justice of reward and
punishment; happiness and misery, being that, for which every one is
concerned for *himself*, not mattering what becomes of any substance, not
joined to, or affected with that consciousness. For, as it is evident in the
instance I gave but now, if the consciousness went along with the little finger, when it was cut off, that would be the same *self* which was concerned
for the whole body yesterday, as making part of it *self*, whose actions then
it cannot but admit as its own now. Though if the same body should still
live, and immediately from the separation of the little finger have its own
peculiar consciousness, whereof the little finger knew nothing, it would
not at all be concerned for it, as a part of it *self*, or could own any of its
actions, or have any of them imputed to him.

§18 *PERSONS, NOT SUBSTANCES, ARE THE OBJECTS*
OF REWARD AND PUNISHMENT

Personal identity understood in this way[69] is the foundation of all the right and justice of reward and punishment. When it comes to the happiness and misery that punishment and reward bring, one is Concerned only for oneself, and is unaffected by anything that happens to any substance that is not joined to or informed by one's Consciousness.[70] For as is evident in the example just given, if X's Consciousness went along with X's little finger when it was cut off, X would be the same self or Person as the one who was Concerned for X's whole body yesterday because the whole body was then part of itself, and could not deny that the actions of that body were its own. Suppose that this body continues to live and acquires its own Consciousness from the moment of its separation from the little finger—a Consciousness of which the little finger (the little-finger self or Person) knows nothing. In this case the little-finger Person will not be in any way Concerned for the body because that body will not be any part of itself. Nor will the little-finger Person acknowledge any of the actions of the new Person associated with the body as its own; nor will any of them be correctly imputed to it.

---

[69] I.e. as a strict function of the reach of Consciousness and Concernment. Locke's word "this" acknowledges that his use of "person" is in one way special. See also §26.

[70] This runs straight on from the previous paragraph, and is very compressed. In reality one's Concernment extends to other people, but in Locke's discussion of Personal identity it's restricted to oneself. The happiness and misery in question are the happiness and misery of punishment and reward in particular. What is in question is one's fate in the afterlife, which is necessarily one's principal Concernment.

§19 *WHICH SHOWS WHEREIN PERSONAL IDENTITY CONSISTS*

This may show us wherein *personal identity* consists, not in the identity of substance, but, as I have said, in the identity of *consciousness*, wherein if Socrates and the present mayor of Queinborough agree, they are the same person: if the same Socrates waking and sleeping do not partake of the same *consciousness*, Socrates waking and sleeping is not the same person. And to punish Socrates waking, for what sleeping Socrates thought, and waking Socrates was never conscious of, would be no more of right, than to punish one twin for what his brother-twin did, whereof he knew nothing, because their outsides were so like, that they could not be distinguished; for such twins have been seen.

§19 *This shows what Personal identity consists in*

This shows us what Personal identity consists in: not in identity of substance, but, as I have said, in identity of Consciousness. If Socrates and the present mayor of Queenborough have the same Consciousness, then they are the same Person. If Socrates awake and Socrates asleep do not have the same Consciousness, Socrates awake and Socrates asleep are not the same Person. To punish awake-Socrates for something that asleep-Socrates thought and that awake-Socrates was never Conscious of would be as wrong as punishing one twin for something done by the other that the first knew nothing about, simply on the ground that the two could not be distinguished by their outer appearance (there are such twins).

§20 *ABSOLUTE OBLIVION SEPARATES WHAT IS THUS
FORGOTTEN FROM THE PERSON, BUT NOT FROM THE MAN*

But yet possibly it will still be objected, suppose I wholly lose the memory of some parts of my life, beyond a possibility of retrieving them, so that perhaps I shall never be conscious of them again; yet am I not the same person, that did those actions, had those thoughts, that I once was conscious of, though I have now forgot them?

To which I answer, that we must here take notice what the word *I* is applied to, which in this case is the man only. And the same man being presumed to be the same person, *I* is easily here supposed to stand also for the same person. But if it be possible for the same man to have distinct incommunicable consciousness[71] at different times, it is past doubt the same man would at different times make different persons;

which, we see, is the sense of mankind in the solemnest declaration of their opinions, human laws not punishing the *mad man* for the *sober man's* actions, nor the *sober man* for what the *mad man* did, thereby making them two persons: which is somewhat explained by our way of speaking in English when we say such an one *is not himself*, or is *beside himself*; in which phrases it is insinuated, as if those who now, or, at least, first used them, thought, that *self* was changed; the *self* same person was no longer in that man.

---

[71] This should perhaps be "consciousness*es*," as in §23 below.

§20 *IF SOMETHING IS IRRETRIEVABLY FORGOTTEN IT IS SEPARATED*
FROM THE PERSON BUT NOT FROM THE MAN

Objection. Suppose I lose all memory of some parts of my life irretrievably, so that I may[72] never be Conscious of them again. Aren't I nonetheless the same Person as the Person who performed the actions and had the thoughts that I was once Conscious of—even though I have now forgotten them?

Reply. We need here to note what the word "I" is being applied to. In this case, it is being applied only to the human being, and since *same human being* is assumed to entail *same Person*, it is naturally supposed that "I" stands for the same Person as well as the same human being. If, however, a human being could possibly have distinct, mutually inaccessible fields of Consciousness at different times, that same single human being would certainly be different Persons at those different times.

This principle is backed by all the force and solemnity of the law, for human law does not punish a man who is mad for his actions when sane, nor a man who is sane for his actions when mad. It therefore treats the sane man and the mad man as two Persons. And this is reflected in our everyday idioms, as when we say of someone that he is "not himself" or is "beside himself." The implication of such phrases is that although we have the same human being we do not have the same self or Person.

---

[72] Locke's "perhaps" acknowledges those who think that you couldn't lose them in this way, so far as the Day of Judgment is concerned.

§21 *DIFFERENCE BETWEEN IDENTITY OF MAN AND OF PERSON*

But yet 'tis hard to conceive, that Socrates the same individual man, should be two persons. To help us a little in this, we must consider what is meant by Socrates, or the same individual man.

*First, it must be either the same individual, immaterial, thinking substance: in short, the same numerical soul, and nothing else.

*Secondly, or the same animal, without any regard to an immaterial soul.

*Thirdly, or the same immaterial spirit united to the same animal.

*Now take which of these suppositions you please, it is impossible to make personal identity to consist in anything but consciousness; or reach any farther than that does.

*For, by the first of them, it must be allowed possible that a man born of different women, and in distant times, may be the same man. A way of speaking, which whoever admits, must allow it possible, for the same man to be two distinct persons, as any two that have lived in different ages without the knowledge of one another's thoughts.

*By the second and third, Socrates in this life, and after it, cannot be the same man any way, but by the same consciousness; and so making *human identity* to consist in the same thing wherein we place *personal identity*, there will be no difficulty to allow the same man to be the same person. But then they who place *human identity* in consciousness only, and not in something else, must consider how they will make the infant Socrates the same man with Socrates after the resurrection.

But whatsoever to some men makes a *man*, and consequently the same individual man, wherein perhaps few are agreed, personal identity can by us be placed in nothing but consciousness, (which is that alone which makes what we call *self*) without involving us in great absurdities.

§21 *The difference between Personal identity*
and the identity of a human being

It remains hard to grasp the idea that Socrates could be numerically the same human being and yet be two different Persons, and it may be helpful to consider what is meant by "Socrates," or "numerically the same human being (considered as something existing at two different times)."

It must be either [1] numerically the same immaterial thinking substance—numerically the same single soul—and nothing else;

or [2] numerically the same animal, considered without regard to any immaterial soul;

or [3] numerically the same immaterial soul united to numerically the same animal.[73]

But whichever of these views you favor, it is impossible to make Personal identity consist in anything other than Consciousness, or reach any further than Consciousness.

Consider case [1]. In this case we would have to allow that a human being born of different women in two very different times could be the same human being. But to put things in this way is to allow that a single human being can be two different Persons, as distinct from each other as any two Persons who have ever lived, neither of whom has any from-the-inside access to the other's conscious life.[74]

Given [2] or [3], the only way in which Socrates in this life and Socrates after this life can be the same *human being* is by virtue of sameness of Consciousness.[75] On this view, that which constitutes the diachronic identity of a *human being* is the same thing as that which constitutes *Personal* identity; so there is of course no difficulty in allowing that if S at time t_1 is the same human being as S* at t_2 then S at t_1 is the same Person as S* at t_2. But those who locate the diachronic identity of a *human being* simply in Consciousness in this way won't be able to explain how it is that baby Socrates and Socrates after the resurrection can be the same human being.

There is, then, little agreement about the denotation of "human being," and there is accordingly little agreement about what makes it the case that a human being considered at t_1 is the same human being as a human being considered at t_2. But any view other than the view that Personal identity consists in nothing but sameness of Consciousness (Consciousness which is, after all, the very thing that gives rise to or constitutes what we call "self") leads to absurd consequences.

---

[73] The three options are: soul alone; body alone; or body and soul together. The third is the most common view at the time.

[74] This is one of the absurdities referred to at the end of the paragraph. He's made the case in (e.g.) §15.

[75] Body can contribute nothing to Socrates' diachronic sameness across this life and the next, because he won't have the same continuing animal life or body in the next life. This rules out [2]. It also means that body can contribute nothing as part of [3]. But then all that is left of [3] is [1]. But it's an essential part of [3] that [1] alone is not enough for sameness of human being.

§22 *But is not a man drunk and sober the same person?*

Why else is he punished for the fact he commits when drunk, though he be never afterwards conscious of it? Just as much the same person, as a man that walks, and does other things in his sleep, is the same person, and is answerable for any mischief he shall do in it.

Human laws punish both, with a justice suitable to their way of knowledge: because in these cases, they cannot distinguish certainly what is real, what counterfeit: and so the ignorance in drunkenness or sleep is not admitted as a plea. For though punishment be annexed to personality, and personality to consciousness, and the drunkard perhaps be not conscious of what he did; yet human judicatures justly punish him; because the fact is proved against him, but want of consciousness cannot be proved for him. But in the Great Day, wherein the secrets of all hearts shall be laid open, it may be reasonable to think, no one shall be made to answer for what he knows nothing of; but shall receive his doom, his conscience accusing or excusing him.

§22 ISN'T A MAN THE SAME PERSON WHEN DRUNK AND WHEN SOBER?

Why else is this man punished for wrong actions that he performs when drunk, even if he never has any Consciousness of them later on? In the same way, human beings who sleepwalk are the same Person when sleepwalking as they are when normally awake, and are responsible for any mischief they do when sleepwalking.

Human laws punish both, applying justice as best they can given the information available to them; for they cannot in these cases achieve certainty about what is real and what is fake. This is why the claim not to know what one did when one was drunk or asleep is not admitted as a plea. For even though punishment is essentially connected to Personal identity, and Personal identity to Consciousness, and even though the drunk really may really not have any Consciousness of what he did, still human judiciaries punish him justly, for there is proof that he performed the action in question, while it can't be proved that he now has no Consciousness of what he did. On the Day of Judgment, however, when the secrets of all hearts will be revealed, it is reasonable to expect that no one will have to answer for any action he knows nothing about (i.e. any action of which he has no Consciousness). Rather each will receive his judgment, his conscience accusing or excusing him.[76]

---

[76] His judgment will of course be just, and his conscience, fully laid open, will inevitably reveal the full truth about the extent of his field of Consciousness.

§23 *Consciousness alone unites remote
existences into one person*

Nothing but consciousness can unite remote existences into the same person, the identity of substance will not do it. For whatever substance there is, however framed, without consciousness there is no person: and a carcass may be a person, as well as any sort of substance be so without consciousness.

*Could we suppose two distinct incommunicable consciousnesses acting the same body, the one constantly by day, the other by night; and, on the other side the same consciousness, acting by intervals two distinct bodies: I ask in the first case, whether the *day* and the *night-man* would not be two as distinct persons, as Socrates and Plato; and whether in the second case, there would not be one person in two distinct bodies, as much as one man is the same in two distinct clothings?

Nor is it at all material to say, that this same, and this distinct *consciousness* in the cases above mentioned, is owing to the same and distinct immaterial substances, bringing it with them to those bodies, which whether true or no, alters not the case: since 'tis evident the *personal identity* would equally be determined by the consciousness, whether that consciousness were annexed to some individual immaterial substance or no.

For granting that the thinking substance in man must be necessarily supposed immaterial, 'tis evident, that immaterial thinking thing may sometimes part with its past consciousness, and be restored to it again, as appears in the forgetfulness men often have of their past actions, and the mind many times recovers the memory of a past consciousness, which it had lost for twenty years together. Make these intervals of memory and forgetfulness to take their turns regularly by day and night, and you have two persons with the same immaterial spirit, as much as in the former instance two persons with the same body. So that *self* is not determined by identity or diversity of substance, which it cannot be sure of, but only by identity of consciousness.

§23 *Only Consciousness can unite spatially-temporally remote phenomena into one Person*

Consciousness is the only thing that can make it the case that two spatio-temporally remote existences are part of the same Person. It is not enough that these existences involve the same substance, because whatever the substance, and whatever its constitution, there is no Person there (the substance is not part of any Person) if there is no Consciousness there. If a substance can be a Person although it does not involve any Consciousness then a corpse can be a Person.

Consider two cases: [1] first, two distinct Consciousnesses[77] which are incapable of communicating with each other and which animate and control the same body by turns, one by day, the other by night; [2] second, one single Consciousness animating two distinct bodies by turns, at regular intervals. In case [1], wouldn't the day human being and the night human being be two completely different Persons, as distinct as Socrates and Plato? And wouldn't there be only one Person in case [2], just as a human being remains the same single human being when he changes his clothes?

"The reason that there are two Consciousnesses in the first case, and one in the second, is that there are two immaterial substances in the first case, and only one in the second." No. This misses the point; it makes no difference whether or not this is so. Personal identity is—obviously—determined by sameness of Consciousness, whether or not the Consciousness in question is tied to one individual substance.

For suppose we grant that the thing which thinks in human beings is necessarily immaterial. Even so, this thinking thing may lose all Consciousness of its past and then later recover it. After all, we often forget our past actions, and the mind often recovers a memory of a past experience that it had lost for twenty years. Now make these periods of memory and forgetting occur by regular intervals, by day and by night. You then have two Persons with the same immaterial spirit, just as you have two Persons with the same body in [1] above. This shows that the question whether a self S considered at t1 is the same as or different from a self S* considered at t_2 is not determined by any facts about whether one or more substance in question. The question is simply this: do they have the same Consciousness?

---

[77] I take it that *a* Consciousness is a subject of experience. See p. 49 n. 14.

§24 *NOT THE SUBSTANCE WITH WHICH THE CONSCIOUSNESS MAY BE UNITED*

Indeed it may conceive the substance whereof it is now made up, to have existed formerly, united in the same conscious being: but consciousness removed, that substance is no more it self, or makes no more a part of it, than any other substance, as is evident in the instance, we have already given, of a limb cut off, of whose heat, or cold, or other affections, having no longer any consciousness, it is no more of a man's self than any other matter of the universe.

In like manner it will be in reference to any immaterial substance, which is void of that consciousness whereby I am my *self* to my *self*: if there be any part of its existence, which I cannot upon recollection join with that present consciousness, whereby I am now my *self*, it is in that part of its existence no more my *self*, than any other immaterial being. For whatsoever any substance has thought or done, which I cannot recollect, and by my consciousness make my own thought and action, it will no more belong to me, whether a part of me thought or did it, than if it had been thought or done by any other immaterial being anywhere existing.

§24 *PERSONAL IDENTITY IS NOT A MATTER OF THE SUBSTANCE WITH WHICH CONSCIOUSNESS MAY BE UNITED*

S may, in fact, suppose that all the substance of which it is now made up has come together before in such a way as to make up a single Conscious being S*.[78] But that substance, united in this way in the past to make up S*, is no more S, and no more a part of S, in the absence of S's Consciousness, than any other substance, as is evident in the case of the severed limb given in §11 above: once the limb is cut off, and one has no Consciousness of its heat or cold or other states, it is no more part of oneself than any other matter in the universe.

Exactly the same will hold true of any immaterial substance that carries no trace of that Consciousness by means of which I am aware of myself as myself.[79] If there is any part X of that substance's existence that I cannot by recollecting connect up with that Consciousness by means of which I am aware of myself as myself now, then X is no more part of myself than any other immaterial being is. Take anything whatever—call it Y—that some substance has thought or done. If I cannot recollect Y and be Conscious of it, then even if the substance that thought or did Y is now part of the substance that now constitutes me, Y will no more be mine than if it had been thought or done by any other immaterial being, wherever it exists.

[78] Both material and immaterial substance will be in question, given that we're now supposing that our existence involves both.

[79] And am therefore a self.

§25 *Consciousness unites substances, material or spiritual, with the same personality*

I agree the more probable opinion is, that this consciousness is annexed to, and the affection of, one individual immaterial substance.

*But let men according to their diverse hypotheses resolve of that as they please. This every intelligent being, sensible of happiness or misery, must grant, that there is something that is *himself*, that he is concerned for, and would have happy; that this *self* has existed in a continued duration more than one instant, and therefore 'tis possible may exist, as it has done, months and years to come, without any certain bounds to be set to its duration; and may be the same *self*, by the same consciousness, continued on for the future.

And thus, by this consciousness, he finds himself to be the *same self* which did such and such an action some years since, by which he comes to be happy or miserable now. In all which account of *self*, the same numerical substance is not considered, as making the same *self*: but the same continued consciousness, in which several substances may have been united, and again separated from it, which, whilst they continued in a vital union with that, wherein this consciousness then resided, made a part of that same self. Thus any part of our bodies vitally united to that, which is conscious in us, makes a part of our *selves*: but upon separation from the vital union, by which that consciousness is communicated, that, which a moment since was part of our *selves*, is now no more so, than a part of another man's *self* is a part of me; and 'tis not impossible, but in a little time may become a real part of another person.

And so we have the same numerical substance become a part of two different persons; and the same person preserved under the change of various substances. Could we suppose any spirit wholly stripped of all its memory or consciousness of past actions, as we find our minds always are of a great part of ours, and sometimes of them all, the union or separation of such a spiritual substance would make no variation of personal identity, any more than that of any particle of matter does. Any substance vitally united to the present thinking being, is a part of that very *same self* which now is: anything united to it by a consciousness of former actions makes also a part of the *same self*, which is the same both then and now.

§25 *Consciousness unites substances,*
material or spiritual, with the same Personality

I agree that it is more likely that this Consciousness (of mine) is bound up with, and is a property of, one individual immaterial substance; but people can rule on this as they wish, according to their various different theories. If one is capable of thought and reason, and of happiness or misery, one must grant: [1] that there is something that is oneself, one's self, the Person that one is, something that one is Concerned for, and would like to be happy (to flourish); [2] that this self (or Person) has existed for more than a single instant; [3] that it may therefore exist for months and years to come as it has done in the past (with no certain bound on its duration); [4] that it may be numerically the same self (or Person) in the future by virtue of involving the same Consciousness.

It is by virtue of this Consciousness, then, that one apprehends oneself to be numerically the same self or Person as the one that performed an action, years ago, that is now the cause of one's happiness or misery. Throughout this account of selves or Persons, it is not numerical sameness of *substance* across time that is taken to constitute numerical sameness of self or Person across time, but rather sameness and continuity of *Consciousness*. A number of different substances may be united in making up the substantial basis or "residence" of this Consciousness at one time, and may be separated from it at another time. So be it: at any time at which they exist in a state of vital union[80] with whatever this Consciousness resides in, they make up part of this same self or Person. Anything that is a part of one's body is a part of the self or Person that one is, so long as it is vitally united to that which is Conscious in one; but as soon as it is separated from a vital union with that which carries one's Consciousness through time, it is no more part of one than a part of a different self is a part of me, and it may in fact shortly become part of another Person.

So numerically the same substance may become a part of two different Persons, and the same Person may continue to exist across change of several substances. Imagine a spiritual substance stripped of all memory or Consciousness of its past actions and experiences, just as our own minds always lack memory of a large number of our own past actions and experiences, and sometimes of all of them. Adding or subtracting this spiritual substance to an existing Person could no more bring about any change in Personal identity than adding or subtracting a particle of matter. Any substance that is vitally united to the present thinking being now is part of the present Person or self. So too any past action that is united to this present Person or self by Consciousness is part of this same present Person or self, who is the same Person or self as the one who performed the action in the past.[81]

---

[80] See §4.

[81] When it comes to being part of a Person, there are two different basic principles of part-membership. One may be part of a Person P by being united to P (a) by vital union or (b) by Consciousness. For a *substance* to be part of a Person P at any given time is for it to be *vitally* united to whatever substance or substances P's Consciousness then "resides" in (material or immaterial). [2] For an *action or experience* to be part of P, by contrast, at any given time, is for it to be united to P by Consciousness, at that time. In §11 Locke suggests that being united by vital union entails being united by Consciousness.

§26 *Person a forensic term*

Person, as I take it, is the name for this *self*. Wherever a man finds what he calls *himself*, there I think another may say is the same *person*. It is a forensic term appropriating actions and their merit; and so belongs only to intelligent agents capable of a law, and happiness and misery. This personality extends it *self* beyond present existence to what is past, only by consciousness, whereby it becomes concerned and accountable; owns and imputes to it *self* past actions, just upon the same ground, and for the same reason, as it does the present.

All which is founded in a concern for happiness the unavoidable concomitant of consciousness, that which is conscious of pleasure and pain, desiring, that that *self*, that is conscious should be happy. And therefore whatever past actions it cannot reconcile or appropriate to that present *self* by consciousness, it can be no more concerned in, than if they had never been done: and to receive pleasure or pain, i.e. reward or punishment, on the account of any such action, is all one, as to be made happy or miserable in its first being, without any demerit at all. For, supposing a man punished now, for what he had done in another life, whereof he could be made to have no consciousness at all, what difference is there between that punishment and being created miserable?

And therefore conformable to this, the apostle tells us, that at the Great Day, when every one shall *receive according to his doings, the secrets of all hearts shall be laid open*. The sentence shall be justified by the consciousness all persons shall have, that they themselves in what bodies soever they appear, or what substances soever that consciousness adheres to, are the *same*, that committed those actions, and deserve that punishment for them.

§26 *"PERSON" IS A FORENSIC TERM*

"Person," as I take the word, denotes this self. I think that in every case in which a human being encounters something he calls himself, we may say that the something he encounters is the same Person (i.e. himself).[82] "Person" is a forensic term which has to do with ownership of actions and their merit. It follows that it applies only to agents who are capable of thought and reason, capable of grasping a law in such a way that they can understand themselves to be subject to it, and capable of happiness and suffering. Things that lie in the past can be part of what constitutes one as a Person considered now in the present only by means of Consciousness. To be Conscious of past actions is *ipso facto* to be Concerned in them and accountable for them. It is to acknowledge them as one's own and attribute them to oneself, and to do so for exactly the same reason, and on exactly the same grounds, as one attributes actions to oneself in the present.

What underlies all this is a Concern for happiness, which is an unavoidable concomitant of Consciousness. For a conscious entity that experiences pleasure or pain necessarily desires the happiness of that thing, the conscious self, that it is. When it comes to past actions of which it is not Conscious, therefore, it can be no more Concerned in (or about) them than if they had never been done. For, lacking the connection of Consciousness, these actions can be no part of itself considered now in the present. For it to receive pleasure or pain, i.e. reward or punishment, on account of any such action would be no different from its having been created happy or miserable at its origin, without any (merit or) demerit at all. For suppose a man were punished now for an action he had done in another life although he neither had nor could have any Consciousness of it. What difference would there be between such a punishment and simply being created miserable?[83]

Thus it is that the apostle tells us that on the great day, when everyone shall "receive according to his doings, the secrets of all hearts shall be laid open."[84] One's sentence will be justified given one's Consciousness that it was indeed oneself that performed the actions in question, and therefore deserves to be punished for them, whatever body one has and whatever substantial composition is the basis of one's Consciousness.

---

[82] This principle is trivial if Locke's "find" is taken as a success term.

[83] Here happiness and misery aren't a matter of particular feelings but of one's long-term fate as determined on the Day of Judgment.

[84] 1 Cor. 14:25 and 2 Cor. 5:10.

§27 *SUPPOSITIONS THAT LOOK STRANGE*
ARE PARDONABLE IN OUR IGNORANCE

I am apt enough to think I have in treating of this subject made some suppositions that will look strange to some readers, and possibly they are so in themselves. But yet I think, they are such as are pardonable in this ignorance we are in of the nature of that thinking thing, that is in us, and which we look on as our *selves*.

Did we know what it was, or how it was tied to a certain system of fleeting animal spirits; or whether it could, or could not perform its operations of thinking and memory out of a body organized as ours is; and whether it has pleased God, that no one such spirit shall ever be united to any but one such body, upon the right constitution of whose organs its memory should depend, we might see the absurdity of some of those suppositions I have made.

But taking, as we ordinarily now do (in the dark concerning these matters) the soul of a man, for an immaterial substance, independent from matter, and indifferent alike to it all, there can from the nature of things, be no absurdity at all, to suppose, that the same soul may, at different times be united to different bodies, and with them make up, for that time, one man: as well as we suppose a part of a sheep's body yesterday should be a part of a man's body to-morrow, and in that union make a vital part of Meliboeus himself as well as it did of his ram.

§27 *SUPPOSITIONS THAT LOOK STRANGE ARE PARDONABLE IN OUR IGNORANCE*

I realize, of course, that I have in discussing this question made some suppositions that will look strange to some readers. And perhaps they don't only look strange, but are strange. I think however that they are acceptable, given our ignorance of the nature of that thinking thing that is in us and that we take to be ourselves.

If we knew the nature of this thinking thing; if we knew how it is connected to a certain system of fleeting animal spirits; if we knew whether or not it could perform its operations of thinking and memory outside a body organized like ours; if we knew whether it has pleased God to make it the case that no single thinking thing is ever united to more than one such body, upon the right constitution of whose organs its memory depends; if we knew all this, then we might see that some of the suppositions I have made are in fact absurd or incoherent.

But so long as we remain in the dark about these matters, and make the standard assumption that the soul of a human being is an immaterial substance, independent from matter, not especially or essentially tied to any particular part of matter, then there is no absurdity or incoherence in the supposition that a single soul may at different times be united to different bodies, the soul and the body constituting a single human being during the period of time in which they are united. So too we can suppose that something that was a part of a sheep's body yesterday will be a part of a man's body to-morrow, and in that union make a vital part of Meliboeus (the man) himself, just as it did of his ram (the sheep).

§28 *The difficulty from ill use of names*

To conclude, whatever substance begins to exist, it must, during its existence, necessarily be the same: whatever compositions of substances begin to exist, during the union of those substances, the concrete must be the same: whatsoever mode begins to exist, during its existence, it is the same: and so if the composition be of distinct substances, and different modes, the same rule holds. Whereby it will appear, that the difficulty or obscurity, that has been about this matter, rather rises from the names ill-used, than from any obscurity in things themselves. For whatever makes the specific idea, to which the name is applied, if that idea be steadily kept to, the distinction of anything into the same, and divers will easily be conceived, and there can arise no doubt about it.

§28 *THE DIFFICULTY THAT ARISES FROM MISUSE OF WORDS*[85]

To conclude. [1] When any substance comes into existence, it is necessarily the same single substance for as long as it exists. [2] When anything that is a compound or concretion[86] or union of several substances comes into existence, it is necessarily the same compound or concretion for so long as its component substances are thus united. [3] When any mode or property begins to exist by being instantiated, it remains (numerically) the same for so long as it exists. [4] The same therefore holds for anything that is a compound of distinct substances and different modes. It is apparent, therefore, that the difficulty or obscurity that has so beset the issue of Personal identity arises from misuse of words rather than from any obscurity in things themselves. Whatever specific concept (or thing) a word is used to denote, it is easy to distinguish what is the same as what, and what is different, in a way that leaves no room for doubt, so long as the content of the concept (the nature of the thing) is held steady and constant.

---

[85] See also end of §1, §7, end of §15.

[86] A growing or sticking together.

§29 *CONTINUANCE OF THAT WHICH WE HAVE MADE
TO BE OUR COMPLEX IDEA OF MAN MAKES THE SAME MAN*

For supposing a rational spirit be the idea of a *man*, 'tis easy to know, what is the *same man*, viz. the *same spirit*, whether separate or in a body will be the same man.

Supposing a rational spirit vitally united to a body of a certain conformation of parts to make a *man*, whilst that rational spirit, with that vital conformation of parts, though continued in a fleeting successive body, remains, it will be the *same man*.

But if to any one the idea of a *man* be, but the vital union of parts in a certain shape; as long as that vital union and shape remains, in a concrete no otherwise the same, but by a continued succession of fleeting particles, it will be the same *man*.

For whatever be the composition whereof the complex idea is made, whenever existence makes it one particular thing under any denomination, the same existence continued, preserves it the same individual under the same denomination.

§29 *THE CONTINUING EXISTENCE OF A SINGLE HUMAN BEING
CONSISTS IN THE CONTINUING EXISTENCE OF AN ENTITY THAT
SATISFIES OUR DEFINITION OF WHAT A HUMAN BEING IS*

Thus suppose that the correct conception of a human being is that a human being is just (nothing but) a rational spirit. It is then easy to know whether one human being is numerically the same as another: if there is the same rational spirit then there is the same human being—whether or not the spirit is located in a body.

Suppose, alternatively, that a human being consists of a rational spirit that is vitally united to a body that has a certain specific structure. In that case the same single human being will continue to exist so long as that rational spirit and that body with that basic structure remain in vital union—even if the material particles that make up the body are constantly changing.

Suppose, finally, that the correct conception of a human being is that it is just a vital union of (material) parts in a certain shape. In that case the same human being continues to exist just so long as that vital union and shape[87] continues to exist in a "concrete" or compound that rmains the same although it consists of a continued succession of fleeting particles.

Take any complex concept C for which we have a word or name "N,"[88] and suppose that some portion of reality satisfies C in such a way that we can, given the existence of that portion of reality, say that a single particular N exists.[89] Then (numerically) the same single N continues to exist so long as that portion of reality continues to exist and to satisfy the criteria of identity associated with C.

---

[87] Locke treats "vital union and shape" as singular.

[88] E.g. the concept TIGER and the word "tiger."

[89] "N" is thus a *sortal* term, a count-noun that brings with it criteria of identity for things that satisfy the sortal concept C.

Appendix Two

A Defence of Mr. Locke's Opinion Concerning Personal Identity

by Edmund Law

A NOTE ON EDMUND LAW (1703–1787)

Edmund Law was born in 1703 in Lancashire, England. He graduated from St. John's College, Cambridge, in 1723, and was elected a fellow of Christ's College in 1727. His first publication was an *Essay on the Origin of Evil* (1731), a copiously annotated translation of Archbishop William King's theodicy *De origine mali*, which became the foremost treatment of the subject in English. Its latitudinarian approach strongly influenced the way in which the problem of theodicy was treated in eighteenth-century England, from Pope to Malthus. In the preface to the fifth edition (1781), Law remarked that Locke had always been one of his "chief guides" in philosophy.

In 1734 Law produced a major critique of a priori proofs of the existence of God, his *Enquiry into the Ideas of Space and Time* (1734). It took the form of a reply to John Jackson's book *The Existence and Unity of God Proved from his Nature and Attributes* (1734). Jackson (1686–1763) was a close follower of Samuel Clarke's Newtonian physico-theology, and Law, whose approach was fundamentally Lockean, was the major figure in a group of Cambridge divines who were extremely critical of Newtonian natural theology (among his friends at that time were David Hartley and the young William Paley).

Law's most influential work was *Considerations on the State of the World with Regard to the Theory of Religion* (1745). He argued that the human race, benefiting from divine education, progresses steadily in its understanding of both natural and revealed religion, even as it advances in other branches of knowledge. There's no conflict between the two enterprises; the one confirms the other; together they advance a deeper, unified understanding of the divinely created world. Law built on the ideas of earlier Anglican divines and gave a particularly succinct statement of the argument. He also argued that religion would be purified of all the corruptions it had acquired over previous centuries as this knowledge progressed. This work had a profound influence on Lessing, as can be seen in his own version of the argument, *Die Erziehung des Menschengeschlechts* (1771). A German translation of Law's work was printed in Leipzig in 1771.

Later editions contained a sermon originally preached in Durham Cathedral, "Reflections on the life and character of Christ," and an "Appendix concerning the use of the words soul and spirit in the holy scripture." This appendix developed Law's scripturally grounded defence of mortalism or thnetopsychism, or "soul-sleeping," the heterodox view, which he

---

* I have drawn here on Brian Young's entry on Law in the *Dictionary of National Biography*. See also Stephens 1996; Thiel 2011.

defended when examined for the degree of Doctor of Divinity in 1749, that the soul passed into a state of complete insensibility (whether sleep or death) at bodily death, to be restored to life and consciousness, by a special act of divine power, only at the resurrection. Paley, who wrote a biography of Law, considered mortalism to be Law's chief claim to recognition. The doctrine was also ably defended by Francis Blackburne, a long-standing friend of Law's from Cambridge, and provoked a good deal of pamphlet literature in the 1750s and 1760s.

In 1756 Law became master of Peterhouse, and instituted a notable period of political and theological liberalism in the college. In 1760 he was appointed librarian of the university, and in 1764 became Knightbridge professor of moral philosophy. He left Cambridge in 1768 on being appointed bishop of Carlisle. A year later he was prompted by the criticism of Locke in an anonymous *Essay on Personal Identity* to write and publish—also anonymously—the work that follows: *A Defence of Mr. Locke's Opinion Concerning Personal Identity. In Answer to the First Part of a late Essay on that Subject* (1769). When in 1777 he published an edition of Locke's *Works* in four volumes, he included his *Defence*, but did not identify himself as its author.[*]

The text that follows is that of the first edition, published by T. & J. Merrill in Cambridge, England, in 1769. The numbers in square brackets are page references to that edition. The italics are Law's own, as are the footnotes, except for those whose text is enclosed in square brackets.

[p1] A DEFENCE OF MR. LOCKE'S OPINION CONCERNING PERSONAL IDENTITY

Edmund Law

THE candid Author of a late Essay upon personal identity[1] cannot justly be offended with any attempt to explain and vindicate Mr. Locke's hypothesis, if it is carried on in the same spirit, though it should be attended with the overthrow of some of his own favourite notions; since he owns that it is of consequence to form right opinions on this point: which was indeed once deemed an important one, how little soever such may be regarded now-a-days. I shall proceed therefore, without farther apology, to settle the terms of this question, and endeavour to state it so as to bring matters to a short and clear determination.

Now the word *Person*, as is well observed by Mr. Locke (the distinguishing [p2] excellence of whose writings consists in sticking close to the point in hand, and striking out all foreign and impertinent considerations) is properly a forensic term, and here to be used in the strict forensic sense, denoting some such quality or modification in man as denominates him a moral agent, or an *accountable* creature; renders him the proper subject of *Laws*, and a true object of Rewards or Punishments. When we apply it to any man, we do not treat of him absolutely, and in gross; but under a particular relation or precision; we do not comprehend or concern ourselves about the several inherent properties which accompany him in real existence, which go to the making up the whole complex notion of an active and intelligent Being; but arbitrarily abstract one single quality or mode from all the rest, and view him under that distinct precision only which points out the idea abovementioned, exclusive of every other idea that may belong to him in any other view, either as substance, quality, or mode. And therefore the consideration of this same [p3] quality or qualification will not be altered by any others of which he may be possessed; but remains the same whatever he shall consist of besides: whether his soul be a material or immaterial substance, or no substance at all, as may appear from examining the import of these pronouns, I, thou, he, &c. (the grammatical meaning of such words generally pointing out the true origin of our ideas primarily annexed to them) which both in their original sense and common acceptation are purely *personal* terms, and as such lead to no farther consideration either of soul or body; nay, sometimes are distinguished from both, as in the following lines,

---

[1] [Law is referring to an *Essay on Personal Identity* that was published anonymously in 1769. Thiel notes that this essay "does not produce any new arguments against Locke ... but repeats those that were by then well known, such as those by Butler and Watts" (Thiel 2011). All notes of the form "Essay, p. ..." are to this essay.]

Linquebant dulces animas, aut aegra trahebant Corpora.[2]

An enquiry after the *identity* of such person will be, whether at different times he is, or how he can be, and know himself to be the same in that respect, or equally subjected to the very same relations and consequent obligations [p4] which he was under formerly, and in which he still perceives himself to be involved whenever he reflects upon himself and them. This we shall find to consist in nothing more, than his becoming sensible at different times of what he had thought or done before; and being as fully convinced that *he* then thought or did it, as he now is of his present thoughts, acts, or existence.

Beyond this we neither can, nor need go for evidence in any thing; this, we shall soon see, is the clear and only medium through which distant things can be discovered and compared together; which at the same time sufficiently ascertains and establishes their several natures and realities respectively; so far as they relate to ourselves and to each other: or if this should not be esteemed sufficient to that end, we shall find, in the last place, that there is nothing else left for it. This distinct consciousness of our past actions, from whence arise all the ideas of merit and demerit, will most undoubtedly be regarded with the greatest exactness *in foro divino*; and indeed has [p5] its due weight *in foro humano*, whenever it can be with certainty determined: wherever this appears to be wanting, all judicial proceedings are at an end. How plain soever any criminal act were, the man would now-a-days be acquitted from guilt in the commission of it, and discharged from the penalties annexed to such fact, could it at the same time be as plainly made out, that he was incapable of knowing what he did, or is now under a like incapacity of recollecting it. And it would be held a sufficient reason for such acquittal, that the punishment or persecution of a creature in these circumstances could not answer the end proposed by society in punishment, viz. the prevention of evil, the only end that I know of, which can justify punishments in any case.[3]

The reason then why such a plea has usually so small regard paid to it in courts of justice, is, I apprehend, either the difficulty of having this incapacity proved with the same clearness that the fact itself is established; or the common maxim that one crime, or criminal indisposition, is not admissible [p6] in excuse for another; as in cases of drunkenness, violent passion, killing or maiming men by mistake when one is engaged in an unlawful pursuit, &c. Or in some of these cases perhaps men are not punished for the murders, &c. because they possibly *may* be conscious of

---

[2] See *Locke* on I *Cor.* xv. 53. [Virgil *Aeneid* book 3, l. 140: "they abandoned their precious souls, or dragged their sick bodies about."]

[3] Here the direct discussion of Locke breaks off, to resume on p. 242.

them, and yet that consciousness not appear; but that such evils may be more effectually prevented by striking at the remoter cause, i.e. exciting a salutary terror of those confessedly evil practices and habits, which are often found to terminate in such fatal effects. A kind of injustice is here indeed committed by society, which we have no reason to suppose will be admitted *in foro divino*, and some worse instances may be seen in our statute books. By the 23 of HEN. 8. a man becoming lunatic after an act of treason shall be liable to be arraigned, tried, and executed. But *Hales*[4] in his P C. C. says, That if a traitor becomes *non compos* before conviction he shall not be arraigned; if after conviction, he shall not be executed: [p7] and Hawkins[5] observes the same concerning those who have committed any capital offences.

In human courts, which cannot always dive into the hearts of men and discover the true springs of action, nor consequently weigh the effects and operations of each in an equal balance; in this state of ignorance and uncertainty, such a notorious indisposition as that of drunkenness, v.g. being generally a great fault in itself, is seldom allowed in extenuation of such others as are committed under its influence; nor indeed does it, I believe, often produce any new, materially different trains of thinking, or totally obliterate the old ones; but where this is really so, the Deity would make just abatement for such defeat or disability, as was at the time both unconquerable and unavoidable; nor can we properly impute actions consequent upon any real disorder of the rational faculties, howsoever that might have been contracted; and therefore all animadversions upon them must be in [p8] vain: nor is a man punishable for any thing beside the bare act of contracting such disorder, or for the original cause of this disability, how great or durable soever; the dangerous consequences of which he did, or might foresee. As is the case in some other confirmed habits, viz. that of swearing, &c. which often operate mechanically and unperceived, and in which therefore all the moral turpitude (or what is so accounted) arising from them, never can reach beyond the fountain head from whence they are derived, and from which all the effects of them naturally, and even necessarily flow.

We must therefore conclude in general, that a person's guilt is estimated according to his past and present consciousness of the offence, and of his having been the author of it. Nor is it merely his having *forgotten*[6] the thing, but his having so far lost the notion of it out of his mind, that

[4] *Hale* P.C. 10.
[5] *Hawk*. PC.C.
[6] Essay, page 23.

how frequently soever or in what forcible manner soever it may be presented to him again, he lies under an utter [p9] incapacity of becoming sensible and satisfied that he was ever privy to it before, which is affirmed to render this thing really none of his, or wholly exculpate him when called to answer for it. Suppose this same consciousness to return, his *accountableness* (call it personality, or what you please) will return along with it: that is, the infliction of evil upon him will now answer some purpose, and therefore they will consider him as now liable to it. Thus some wholly lose the use of their intellectual faculties for a time, and recover them at intervals. In such cases they are considered as punishable by laws, and so declared by juries, in proportion to the probability of their being conscious of the fact. Others lie under a partial deprivation of some one faculty for certain periods, while they continue to enjoy the rest in tolerable perfection. I knew a learned man, who was said to recollect with ease subjects upon which he had written, or any others that had been discussed before the last ten or fifteen years; could reason freely and readily turn to the Authors he [p10] had read upon them; but take him into the latter part of his life, and all was blank; when any late incidents were repeated to him, he would only stare at you, nor could he be made sensible of any one modern occurrence however strongly represented to him. Was this man equally answerable for all transactions within the last period of his life, as for those in the first? Or if he could have been made sensible of the latter part, but had irrecoverably lost the former; could that former part have been in like manner imputed to him?

Surely not. And the reason plainly is, because society could find no advantage from considering him as accountable in either case. Which shews personality [i.e. personal identity] to be solely a creature of society, an abstract consideration of man, necessary for the mutual benefit of him and his fellows; i.e. a mere forensic term; and to enquire after its criterion or constituent, is to enquire in what circumstances societies or civil combinations of men have in *fact* agreed to inflict evil upon individuals, in order to prevent evils to the whole body from any irregular [p11] member.[7] Daily experience shews, that they always make consciousness of the fact a necessary requisite in such punishment, and that all enquiry relates to the probability of such consciousness. The execution of *Divine* Justice must proceed in the same manner. The Deity inflicts evil with a settled view to some end; and no end worthy of him can be answered by inflicting it as a punishment, unless to prevent other evils. Such end may

---

[7] [One doesn't have to endorse Law's account of the justification of punishment in order to see that he is giving a correct account of Locke's conception of personal identity.]

be answered, if the patient is conscious, or can be made conscious of the fact, but not otherwise. And whence then does this difference in anyone's moral capacity arise, but from that plain diversity in his natural one? from his absolute irretrievable want of consciousness in one case, and not in the other. Suppose now that one in the former condition kills a man; that he, or some part of what we call *him*, was never so notoriously the instrument or occasion of that death; yet if he was either then insensible of the fact, or afterwards became so, and so continued: Would he be any more guilty of murder, [p12] than if that death had been occasioned by another person? since at that time he was truly such, or at least is so now, notwithstanding that most people might be apt to judge him still the same, from a sameness in outward circumstances, (which generally supply the best means men have of judging) from his shape, mien, or appearance; tho' these often differ widely from the internal constitution, yet are as often mistaken for it; and this accordingly thought and spoke of with little more philosophical propriety, than when we, in the vulgar phrase, describe a man's condition by saying, We would not be in his *coat*.

Suppose one then in the situation abovementioned; could any pains, think you, inflicted on him suit the idea, or answer the ends of punishment, either with regard to himself or others, farther than mere shew and delusion? Rewards and Punishments are evidently instituted for the benefit of society, for the encouragement of virtue or suppression of vice in the object thus rewarded or punished, and in the rest [p13] of the community; but what tendency to the above purposes can either of these have, if dispensed to one who is *not* so far *himself* as to become conscious of having done any thing to deserve it? What instruction is conveyed to him? What admonition to such others, as are duly acquainted with the whole of the case, and see every circumstance thus grossly misapplied? And as in these cases, laws only can define the circumstances in which a man shall be treated as accountable, they only can create guilt, i.e. guilt also is a forensic term, or a mode of considering any action, which in its essence implies knowledge of a law, offence against that law, and a sense of having offended against it; i.e. an after consciousness of the fact; without which after consciousness, punishment would be of little avail, as it would neither serve to guard the man himself against a like delinquency, nor tend to the warning of others, who by such inflictions would only perceive that they might chance to suffer pain, without being able to assign a reason for it. — Thus may [p14] personality be extended or contracted, and vary in various respects, times, and degrees, and thereby become liable to great confusion in our applying it to various subjects; yet is the ground and foundation of it fixed; and when once discovered, its consequences are no less so, both before God and man.

Abstract, general ideas (of which this is an eminent one) are alone productive of certain, uniform, and universal knowledge: Thus qualities. of a certain kind, when *abstracted*, or taken apart from nature, and set up for common standards, are so far independent as to become absolute, unmixed, or perfect in themselves,[8] however different they may be found in their respective *concretes*. Thus Goodness, Justice, Guilt, Merit, &c. in general are ever the same *Goodness, &c.* all the world over, however imperfectly they may appear in any particular subjects, times, and places. In the same manner as a line, or the abstract consideration of length without thickness or breadth; the [p15] consideration of surface, i.e. length and breadth without thickness, must be the same in all intelligent beings of like faculties with us, tho' the natural substances which suggest them may differ with an endless variety. Let personality answer to a line or surface; let the substances it is predicated of, like the infinite variety of solids in nature, (with their appendages, heat, cold, colour, &c.) in which length and breadth are found, vary as you please, still the abstract ideas of line and surface, and therefore of person, will remain invariable. And thus propositions formed out of these general ideas contain certain truths, that are in one sense eternal and immutable, as depending on no precarious existences whatever. Being merely what we ourselves make them, they must continue the same while the same number of such ideas continue joined together, and appear the same to every intelligent being that contemplates them.[9] They do not stand in need (I say) [p16] of an objective reality, or the existence of any external things in full conformity to them, since we here consider things no farther than as coming up to these original standards, or as capable of being included in such measures as are applied to determine their precise quantity, quality, &c. we are ranking them under a certain species or *sort*, hence called their *essence*, which entitles them to the name descriptive of it, as is sufficiently explained by Mr. *Locke*. They want therefore nothing more to establish their reality, than to be consistently put together, so as may distinguish them from others that are merely chimerical, and qualify them for the admission of any real beings that may occur: Thus, not only the instance of a triangle so frequently used by Mr. *Locke*, but every theorem in *Euclid*, may be ranked among the abstract considerations of quantity, apart from all real existence, which seldom comes up to it: As it may be justly questioned whether any triangle or circle, as defined by him, ever existed in nature, i.e. existed so that all [p17] the lines of the triangle were right ones, or all the lines drawn from the centre to the circumfer-

---

[8] Note 10. to *King's* Origin of Evil. Rem. k.

[9] See the first note to A. B. *King's* Origin of Evil.

ence equal. These ideas *presuppose*[10] no one Being in particular, they *imply* nothing more than a proper subject of enquiry (as was said above) or some such creature as is either actually endowed with, or at least susceptible of these specific qualities, or modes, which furnish matter for the whole tribe of abstractions daily made and preserved by such terms as usually serve to denote them; whether appellatives, in order to distinguish men in their several stations and relations, private or public; to describe their character or conduct, office, &c. as Parent, Patriot, King, &c. or such more general, technical ones, as Paternity, Patriotism, Kingship, &c. the nature, end, and use, of all which abstractions, with their names, are well enough understood, and would not easily be mistaken in affairs of common life, which are happily less liable to such kind of subtle refinements, as have brought metaphysical speculations into that [p18] contempt under which they have long laboured.

In short, of these same abstractions consist all general terms and theorems of every science; and the truth and certainty contained in them, when applied to morals or theology, is no less determinate than in other sciences; it is equally capable of strict demonstration, and equally applicable to full as useful and important purposes: The great general truths, I say, arising out of these general essences, or *entities*, (as they are sometimes called) are all clear, constant, and invariable in themselves, though the names, in which such a collection of ideas should be preserved, are often through the poverty and imperfection of language rendered extremely vague and uncertain in each writer or speaker, and the ideas formed by them in other men's minds (which are their proper archetypes, and a conformity to which alone makes them *right* or *wrong*, truly or untruly applied) thereby become no less frequently confused and indeterminate. Thus, in the case before us, the word *person* is often used to signify the [p19] whole aggregate of a rational Being, including both the very imperfect idea, if it be any idea at all, of *substance*, and its several properties, (as is the common way) or taking all the essential qualities together, (which properly constitute the substance of any thing[11]) with several of their modes. As when speaking of anyone, we include soul, body, station, and other circumstances, and accordingly style him a wise, worthy person, a tall, comely, a rich, great one, &c. where *person* in a lax, popular sense signifies as much as *man*. In which popular sense Mr. Locke manifestly takes the word, when he says, it *stands for a thinking intelligent Being, that has reason and reflection, and can consider itself as itself, the same thinking Being, in different times and places*. B. 2. C. 27. § 9. But when the term is used more

---

[10] Vide Bp. *Butler*'s Diss. on *Pers. Identity.*

[11] See the first note to *King*, and the authors there cited.

accurately and philosophically, it stands for one especial property of that thing or Being, separated from all the rest that do or may attend it in real existence, [p20] and set apart for ranging such Beings into distinct classes, (as hinted above) and considering them under distinct relations and connections, which are no less necessary to be determined in life, and which should therefore have their proper and peculiar denomination. And thus sameness of *person* stands to denote, not what constitutes the same *rational agent*, though it always is predicated of such; but we consider his rationality so far only, as it makes him capable of knowing what he does and suffers, and on what account, and thereby renders him amenable to justice for his behaviour, as above mentioned.

Whatever ingredients therefore of different kinds go to the composition, what other particulars, whether mental or corporeal, contribute to the formation of this intelligent Being, these make no part of our enquiry; which, I beg leave to repeat it again, is not what enters into the natural constitution of a thing, but what renders it so far a *moral* one, and is the *sine qua non* of its being justly chargeable with [p21] any of its past actions, here or hereafter: Or, in other words, it does not affect the reality or the permanency of such intelligent Beings, but only regulates and retains those Beings under such a *moral* relation, as makes them properly accountable to some superior for their course of action. It is an *artificial* distinction, yet founded in the nature, but not the *whole* nature of man, who must have many other essential powers and properties to subsist as man, and even to support this in question; but none other, we say, that can affect, or in any wise alter his condition in the abovenamed respect, and therefore none that come with propriety into the present consideration.

This is all the mystery of the matter, which has puzzled so many ingenious writers, and been so marvellously mistaken by such as are not sufficiently acquainted with the doctrine of *abstractions*, or are misled by terms of art, instead of attending to the precise ideas which these ought to convey, and would always convey if they [p22] were but carefully and steadily applied; for want of which proper application, men of genius and good sense have fallen into such egregious trifling,[12] as serves only to disturb

[12] An extraordinary instance of this kind is to be met with in Bishop *Berkeley*, which he calls a *demonstration* of the point; where the supposed union of A and C, not with the *whole* of B, but with some *different parts* of which B consists, will hardly make them *one* with each other: — But this famous demonstration may be ranked among some others of the same sort, and safely trusted with the reader. 'Let us suppose that a person hath ideas, and is conscious during a certain space of time, which we will divide into three equal parts, whereof the latter terms are marked by the letters A, B, C. In the first part of time the person gets a certain number of ideas, which are retained in A: during the second part of time he retains one half of his old ideas, and loseth the other half, in place of which he acquires as many new ones: so that in B his ideas are half old and half new. And

[p23] this beyond most other parts of science, and has filled the above celebrated question with a multitude of quibbles, which Mr. *Locke's* clear and copious answers to his several opponents might, one would have hoped, have most effectually prevented, but which are subsisting to this very day, to the no small mortification of all sincere lovers of truth, and admirers of that able defender of it. And I have been the larger on this head of general words and notions, which have so close a connection with each other, and with the present question, as the subject is not perhaps sufficiently explained by Mr. *Locke* in any one place of his admirable Essay, though it occurs pretty often; and since the several properties or attributes of these same *abstract ideas* are still so miserably misunderstood, as to have their very *existence* disputed, probably because he has been pleased to set it forth in a manner somewhat paradoxical. Though this word *existence* also is a term often misapplied, as if nothing could really exist which was not an object of the senses: Whereas in these, [p24] and several other ideas, as has been often observed, their *esse* is *percipi*.

Again, we are often misled on the other hand by imagining what things are *in themselves* (as we usually term it) or in their internal essences; instead of considering them as they *appear*, and stand related to *us*; or according to the *ideas* that are obviously suggested by them; which *ideas* only should be the objects of our contemplation, (since we really perceive nothing else) and ought always to regulate our enquiry into things, as these are the sole foundation of all our knowledge concerning them, of all that can with safety direct, or be of service to us.

But to return to our author. That property then, or quality, or whatever he chooses to call it, which, in his own words, renders men *sensible that they are the same*[13] in some respects, is in Mr. *Locke's* sense, in the legal, and in common sense, that which so far makes them such, or brings them into the same relative capacity of being ranked among moral, social creatures, and [p25] of being treated accordingly for several obvious purposes in social life. This consciousness, I say, of being thus far ourselves, is what, in Mr. *Locke's* language, *makes* us so. In this case, as in some other ideal objects, to *be*, and be *perceived*, is really the same, and what this author calls

---

in the third part we suppose him to lose the remainder of the ideas acquired in the first, and to get new ones in their stead, which are retained in C, together with those acquired in the second part of time.—The persons in A and B are the same, being conscious of common ideas by the supposition. The person in B is (for the same reason) one and the same with the person in C. Therefore the person in A, is the same with the person in C, by that undoubted axiom, *quae conveniunt uni tertio conveniunt inter se.* But the person in C hath no idea in common with the person in A. Therefore personal identity doth not consist in consciousness.' *Alciphron*, v. 2. p. 160.

[13] Essay, page 20.

the *sign*[14] coincides with the thing *signified*. Whether any intelligent Being is at present what he is in every respect, wants no proof; of this he has self evident intuitive knowledge,[15] and can go no higher. And whether he now is what he was once before, in this single article of personality, can only be determined by his now being sensible of what he then thought and did, which is equally self evident; and thus again, consciousness at the same time, and by the same means, that it convinces *him* of this, does likewise constitute him such to all ends and purposes whatsoever.

Well then, having examined a little into the nature, and enumerated some few properties of an abstract idea in general, and [p26] shewn that this particular one before us can be nothing more, we may find perhaps that however fluctuating and changeful[16] this account may be judged to render personality; how much soever it may fall short of some sublime systems about purely immaterial substances, and perfectly independent principles of thought, yet there is no help for these changes in the seat of personality, since, in the last place, we know of nothing more stable and permanent in our constitution that has the least pretence to settle and support it. All parts of the *body* are to a certain degree in perpetual flux, nor is anyone of them, that we are acquainted with, concerned in the present case more than another. As to the *mind*, both its cogitative and active powers are suspended (whether they be so or not is a matter of *fact*, in which experience only, and not subtle argumentations drawn from the nature of an unknown, perhaps imaginary, essence ought to decide) during sound sleep: Nay, every drowsy nod (as [p27] Mr. Locke expresses it) must shake their doctrine, who maintain that these powers are incessantly employed. Call then a resuscitation or revival of these powers, when we awake, *another beginning of their existence, a new creation*; and argue against the possibility of any such *interruption* or *annihilation* of them, as long as you please, yet that it is matter of fact, and nightly experience, and capable of as good proof as a negative proposition will admit, is made out sufficiently by the abovenamed excellent writer. This, if properly attended to, and pursued through its genuine consequences, would go a great way towards unfolding the true nature of the human mind, which many thoughtful men seem yet very little acquainted with, and very much afraid to examine.[17] [p28] And while this disposition holds, we can never

[14] Essay, p. 42.

[15] See note 10. To *King*. Rem. a.

[16] Essay, p. 23.

[17] Will not the least hint of this doctrine, say they, give great offence, by appearing to undermine the settled distinction between *soul* and *body*, which is so much countenanced and confirmed in Scripture? —Does not it tend to disturb common apprehensions, and confound both the sense and language of mankind?

expect to come at the original core of all those corruptions that have in-
fected this branch of philosophy, and extended themselves to some other
parts of science; Nor are the several proofs, or, if you please, [p29] prob-
abilities, that I was not thinking all the last night, sufficiently answered by
the old excuse that I may *forget* all such thoughts immediately as soon as
ever I awake: for setting aside the great improbability of this happening so
very constantly, for so long a time, it must appear to any one who understands what he says, that whosoever, or whatsoever, was thus employed,
it could not possibly be *I* who was all this while busily engaged in such
thoughts, since they never bore the least share in my series of consciousness, never were [p30] connected with the chain of my waking thoughts,
nor therefore could any more belong to *me*, than if you suppose them (as
you might full as well, for argument's sake, and to salve an hypothesis) to
be the working of some secret mechanism, or kept up in the watch that
was lying by me. Something like this, I presume, would be the plea, which
all the advocates for this lame system would offer in their own defence,
were anyone so injurious as to charge them with things done or said in
their sleep. The same observation may be urged against that absurd, self

Answ. I. If this doctrine be true, and a truth of some importance, it will surely stand
the test, and ought to be supported, against all such inconclusive argumentations as are
drawn from *consequences* and common prejudices, and can only serve to obstruct all kinds
of improvement in any science whatsoever.

Answ. 2. The *two* great constituents of our frame frequently alluded to in Scripture,
and to which (as to other popular notions and received forms of expression) it usually
accommodates itself, are here no more confounded, than when St. *Paul* introduces a
third as no less essential to the *whole* of our composition; *I pray God your whole spirit, and
soul, and body, be preserved blameless unto the coming of our Lord Jesus Christ.* I *Thess.* v. 23.

So far is either the true sense of Scripture, or the real nature of things, from
being confined to the logical arrangement of them under their established genera or
species; so little concerned either in our physical or metaphysical distinctions of them,
v.g. into animal and vegetable, material and immaterial, substance and property, &c.
nor is its language more confounded, or its authority shaken, by such a new system of
Pneumatology, than it was by the late one of *Copernicus* concerning each of the planetary
motions; which proved, that strictly and philosophically speaking neither does the *sun
rise*, nor the *earth stand upon pillars*, &c. or by *Newton's* Principles of *Gravity* and a *Vacuum*
(for which supposed [p29] innovations his *French* commentators think themselves still
obliged to enter their caveat, and make apology to the church;) or *Locke's* more hardy
doctrine of *no innate Ideas*: all which were once equally dangerous and offensive positions;
but would such surmises, as have been advanced about them, be admitted in any other
case? would even a *Romish*, or any *other* Inquisition now be found weak or wicked enough
to proceed upon them? and if at last an Author shall incur the *Odium Theologicum*, and
be traduced by the name of *Saducee, Socinian*, &c. for his innocent, as he thinks, perhaps
laudable intentions; —if *offence* will be taken, as it often happens, where no just *cause* of
offence is given; he must patiently submit to his hard fate, and only beg leave to enquire
whether there be not some room for suspending our judgment a while, 'till it more fully
appears where the fault of all this chiefly lies, and who is really answerable for it.

repugnant hypothesis of our having been in a *pre-existent state*: for what-soever was done there, it can be nothing to *us*, who had never the least notice or conception of it.

To the difficulties so often objected, of this being *a new creation*,[18] and making the same thing have *two beginnings of existence*;[19]—We may ob-serve, that it would indeed be an absurdity to suppose two beginnings of existence, if the identity of a substance, Being, or man were enquired [p31] into; but when the enquiry is made into the artificial abstract idea of personality, invented for a particular end, to answer which consciousness only is required, beginning and end of existence are quite out of the ques-tion, being foreign to any consideration of the subject.—It may be farther observed, that in fact we meet with something of the same kind every morning after a total *interruption* of thought (and I hope, we may by this time in one sense be allowed to term it so) during sound sleep: nay, if we search the thing narrowly, and may in our turn enter into such *minutiae*, thus much will be implied in the *successive* train of our ideas each hour of the day; that same article of *succession* including some degree of distance between each of them, and consequently at every successive step there is a new production, which may with equal reason be styled an *interruption* of thought, or a new exertion of the thinking power. But enough of these *nugae difficiles*. Such changeable, frail creatures then are we through life, yet safe in the hand of that [p32] unchangeably just, wise, good, and all-powerful Being, who perfectly understands our frame, and will make due allowances for each defect or disorder incident to it; who at first created us out of nothing, and still preserves us through each shifting scene, be the revolutions in it never so frequent and *rapid*,[20] and will at length most assuredly conduct us to immortality. Though in every respect we are here *fleeing as it were a shadow, and never continue in one stay*, and at last suffer a short seeming pause[21] in our existence, which is in Scripture termed the *sleep of death*; yet will he again raise us *out of the dust*; restore us to our-

---

[18] Essay, p. 38.

[19] Essay, p. 55.

[20] Essay, p. 23.

[21] I.e. a pause in the opinion and sight of other sentient Beings existing after our departure, but not a pause strictly so called to the person himself, in which there will be an unbroken thread of consciousness or continued personality; time unperceived being no time, *time absolute* a fiction, and no new idea intervening between the moments of his falling asleep and waking again, these will be to him coincident: which shews, that personality cannot have two beginnings of existence, though the substance in which it is found may be perpetually varied, and though sometimes a greater, and sometimes a less number of facts rise up to his remembrance.

selves, and to our *Friends*;[22] [p33] revive our consciousness of each past act or habit, that may prove of the least moral import; cause the *secrets of all hearts to be laid open*, and either reward or punish everyone according to his *works done in the body*.

Nor does it imply a *plurality of persons* in any man at any given time to charge him with various actions or omissions; since he may become guilty of a plurality of crimes, as often as he is induced or enabled to reflect upon them, though these cannot be crowded into his mind all together, any more than they could have been so committed. Nor therefore need all past actions [p34] become *at once present*[23] to the mind; which is utterly inconsistent with our frame, as it now stands, and perhaps with that of every other created Being: nor is there a necessity for any one idea being *always* actually in view;[24] which is equally so; but only for a capacity of having such brought to mind again, together with a consciousness of their having been there before, (which distinguishes them from entirely new ones,) or a possibility of recognizing them upon occasion, at least whenever we are to account for them, as has been frequently observed. So far as any such recognition reaches, such person is the same; when this faculty varies, that must vary also; and he become the same, or not, at different times and in divers respects, as observed likewise; at least his accountableness must vary in proportion, call this personality, or what you think fit. Nor does it properly lie in a *power of causing* a return of the same idea;[25] but rather in the *capacity of receiving* it, of readmitting the same consciousness concerning any past [p35] thought, action, or perception. Nor is it merely a *present representation*[26] of any such act; but a representation of it as *our own*, which entitles us to it; one person may know or become conscious of the *deeds of another*, but this is not knowing that *he himself was the author* of those deeds, which is a contradiction; and to treat him as such upon that account only, would be inverting all rules of right and wrong; and could not therefore be practised by either God or Man, since no end could possibly be answered by such treatment, as observed above.

---

[22] To one who has not seen and felt the unhappy effects of human prejudice and partial judgment in such cases, it might appear strange that so many wise and able men should still continue *ignorant* of this, after all the fullest information given us in the following express declaration of that great and good Apostle St. *Paul*: I WOULD NOT HAVE YOU TO BE IGNORANT, BRETHREN, CONCERNING THEM WHICH ARE ASLEEP, THAT YE SORROW NOT EVEN AS OTHERS WHICH HAVE NO HOPE. FOR IF WE BELIEVE THAT JESUS DIED AND ROSE AGAIN, EVEN SO THEM ALSO WHICH SLEEP IN JESUS, WILL GOD BRING WITH HIM—WHEREFORE COMFORT ONE ANOTHER, WITH THESE WORDS. I. *Thess.* iv. 13, &c.

[23] Essay, p. 40.

[24] Essay, p. 24.

[25] Essay, p. 31.

[26] Essay, p. 33.

To dwell upon those surprising consequences that might attend the transferring the same consciousness to different Beings, or giving the same Being very different ones, is merely puzzling and perplexing the point, by introducing such confusions as never really existed, and would not alter the true state of the question, if they did.

Such *Fairy* tales and *Arabian* transformations, possible or impossible, can only serve to amuse the fancy, without any solid information to the judgment. These [p36] flights of mere imagination Mr. Locke generally avoids, though he was here tempted to indulge a few such, in playing with the wild suppositions of his adversaries, (v.g. a change of souls between *Socrates* and the mayor of *Queenborough*, &c.) probably to enliven a dry subject, and render it more palatable to the bulk of his readers.

Nor are those cases of a disordered imagination in lunacy, or vapours, where persons are for a time *beside themselves* (as we usually term it) and may believe such chimerical alterations to befall them, any more to the purpose.

But it were endless to unravel all the futile sophisms and false suppositions, that have been introduced into the present question; I have endeavoured to obviate such as appeared most material, and account for them; and at the same time to inculcate a doctrine, which, though common enough, seemed not enough attended to; yet is fundamentally requisite to a right understanding of this intricate subject. And if that which is laid down above be a true state of the case, all the rest of our Author's plan, (of placing [p37] personal identity in a continuation of thought[27]) will drop of course. I trust the Reader will make allowance for some repetitions, which were left to render things as plain as possible, and prevent future subterfuges of the like kind; and if the substance of these few hasty Observations on the first part of this ingenious writer's *Essay*, prove in the least degree satisfactory to himself, or have a tendency to enlarge general knowledge, and guard against popular errors, I must rely upon his candour for excusing the manner in which they are thrown out; and shall take the liberty of closing them in the form of a Syllogism, which is submitted to his consideration:

Quo posito ponitur personae identitas, et quo sublato tollitur, id personalem identitatem constituit:
Sed posita conscientia, &c.
Ergo.[28]

---

[27] Which disposition, could it be made out, would never answer the intent of society, or help to direct us in our duty, the two grand objects which first gave birth to personality; i.e. to a very partial confined consideration of that complex idea, Substance, or Being called Man.

[28] ["Personal identity is constituted by that which is such that the identity of the person is given when it is present, and removed when it is subtracted. But if consciousness is present ... etc."]

[p38] APPENDIX.

A friend, well acquainted with the subject of the foregoing sheets, having communicated to me some observations concerning the use of the word Person, which came too late to be inserted in their proper place, I must take the liberty of annexing them, though they occasion some more redundancies and repetitions, in order to throw as much light as is possible on this very obscure and long controverted question.

AS Mr. Locke's definition of the term *Person*, (Chap. xxvii. § 9) may possibly create some difficulty, it will be proper to examine into the sense which should be put upon this word, whenever we enquire, after the identity of any *man's person*; which may perhaps at once lead us to a just conception of the whole. In the aforementioned section, Mr. Locke says, that *Person* stands for a *thinking intelligent Being, that has* [p39] *reason and reflection*, &c. whereas I should imagine, the expression would have been more just, had he said that the word person stands for an attribute, or quality, or character of a thinking intelligent Being; in the same sense as *Tully* uses it, *Orat.* pro *Syll.* §3.[29] "*Hanc mihi tu si, propter res meas gestas, imponis in omni vita mea personam, Torquate, vehementer erras. Me natura misericordem, patria severum; crudelem nec patria, nec natura esse voluit: denique istam ipsam personam vehementem et acrem, quam mihi tum tempus et respublica imposuit, jam voluntas et natura ipsa detraxit.*"[30] It came at last to be confounded with, and stand for *homo gerens personam*, (*Taylor*, Civ. L. p. 247, 248) and in this sense *Locke* has incautiously defined the word. It is attributed also to more intelligent Beings than one; as by the Jesuits in their declaration prefixed to the third Book of *Newton*, *alienam coacti sumus gerere personam*.[31] The

---

[29] [This should read "pro *Sull.* §8."]

[30] ["If you impute this *persona* [moral character] to my whole life, Torquatus, on account of what I have done, you are gravely mistaken. Nature made me merciful; it was my country that made me severe. But neither nature nor my country required me to be cruel, and nature herself—and my will—have now at last released me from the fierce, strict *persona* imposed on me by the times and matters of state."]

[31] ["We are obliged to adopt an alien or foreign mask or standpoint"—to "wear a different hat." The Franciscans Jacquier and Leseur made this move in their *Elemens Du Calcul Integral* (1768) in order to protect themselves when discussing the motion of the earth—a doctrine deemed false by papal decree. Their move prompted the following comment from Lord John Russell (Bertrand's grandfather) in his lecture "Obstacles which have retarded moral and political progress" (1855): "The best commentary on Newton's Principia is written by Jacquier and LeSeur, two members of the order of St. Francis, called Minimi. This commentary is so simple and complete that it enables a person who has but an imperfect knowledge of mathematics, to comprehend and to master the sublime discoveries of Newton. There was, however, a trifling objection to the publication of this commentary. The Pope had, by his decrees, forbidden any one to

word person then, according to the received sense in all classical authors, standing for a certain guise, character, quality, i.e. being in fact a mixed mode, or relation, [p40] and not a substance; we must next enquire, what particular character or quality it stands for in this place, as the same man may bear many characters and relations at the same, or different times. The answer is, that here it stands for that particular quality or character, under which a man is considered, when he is treated as an intelligent Being subject to government and laws, and accountable for his actions: i.e. not the man himself, but an abstract consideration of him, for such and such particular ends: and to enquire after its identity, is to enquire, not after the identity of a conscious Being, but after the identity of a quality or attribute of such a conscious Being. All difficulties that relate to a man's forgetting some actions, &c. now vanish, when person is considered as a character, and not a substance, or confounded with *homo gerens personam*: and it amounts to no more than saying, a man puts on a mask—continues to wear it for some time—puts off one mask and takes another, i.e. appears to have consciousness—to recollect past [p41] consciousnesses—does not recollect them, &c. The impropriety consists in saying, a *man* is the same *person* with him who did such a fact; which is the same as to say, a man is blackness, guilt, &c. i.e. a mixed mode is predicated of a substance; whereas it ought to be in strict propriety of speech, the person of the man who did such a fact, is the same with the person of him, who now stands before us; or, in plainer terms, the man who now stands before the court is conscious of the former facts, and is therefore the proper object of punishment. It may be observed, that the word personality is really an absurd expression: since person itself stands for the mixed mode or quality; — and personality therefore may be ranked among the old scholastic terms of corporeity, egoity, tableity, &c. or is even yet more harsh; as mixed modes, such as gratitude, murder, and therefore person, cannot be thus remodified without peculiar absurdity.

---

maintain the doctrine of the motion of the earth. The learned Franciscans disposed of the difficulty very easily. They prefixed a notice to this part of the work, declaring that they bowed with implicit submission to the decision of the Pope that the sun moved round the earth, but that they had been incited by curiosity to show what would have been the case, had it been a truth instead of a fiction, that the earth moved round the sun. The world laughed and learnt; the Holy See was satisfied and silent."]

References

Aristotle. c. 340 BCE/1953. *Nicomachean Ethics*. Trans. J.A.K. Thomson. London: Penguin.

Aristotle. c. 340 BCE /1936. *De Anima*. Trans. W. S. Hett. Cambridge, MA: Harvard University Press.

Aristotle. c. 350 BCE /1924. *Metaphysics*. Trans. W. D. Ross. Oxford: Oxford University Press.

Augustine. 397–398/1961. *Confessions*. Trans. R. Pine-Coffin. Harmondsworth: Penguin.

Ayers, M. R. 1991. *Locke*. Vol. 2, *Ontology*. London: Routledge.

Ball, B. W. 2008. *The Soul Sleepers: Christian Mortalism from Wycliffe to Priestley*. Cambridge: James Clarke.

Bayne, T., and Montague, M. 2011. "Introduction," in *Cognitive Phenomenology*. Oxford: Oxford University Press.

Berkeley, G. 1732/2008. *Alciphron: or the Minute Philosopher*, in *Philosophical Writings*. Ed. D. Clarke. Cambridge: Cambridge University Press.

Boethius. c. 510/1918. *De Trinitate*. In *The Theological Tractates and The Consolation of Philosophy*. Trans. H. F. Stewart and E. K. Rand. Cambridge, MA: Harvard University Press.

Butler, J. 1736. First Appendix (*First Dissertation*). In *The Analogy of Religion*. 2nd ed. London: Knapton.

Camus, A. 1956/2008. *La Chute*. Paris: Folio.

Castañeda, H.-N. 1966/1994. "On the Phenomeno-Logic of the I." In *Self-Knowledge*, ed. A.-Q. A. Cassam. Oxford: Oxford University Press.

Caston, V. 2002. "Aristotle on Consciousness." *Mind* 111:751–815.

Clarke, D. 2003. *Descartes's Theory of Mind*. Cambridge: Cambridge University Press.

Clarke, S. 1707. *A Second Defense of an Argument made use of in a Letter to Mr. Dodwell*. London.

Dainton, B. 2008. *The Phenomenal Self.* Oxford: Oxford University Press.

Damasio, A. 1999. *The Feeling of What Happens: Body and Emotion in the Making of Consciousness.* New York: Harcourt Brace.

Damasio, A. 2000. "Interview." *New Scientist* 165:46–49.

Descartes, R. 1641/1985. *Meditations.* In *The Philosophical Writings of Descartes.* Vol. 2. Trans. J. Cottingham et al. Cambridge: Cambridge University Press.

Descartes, R. 1644/1985. *Principles of Philosophy.* In *The Philosophical Writings of Descartes.* Vol. 1. Trans. J. Cottingham et al. Cambridge: Cambridge University Press.

Flew, A. 1951/1968. "Locke and the Problem of Personal Identity." In *Locke and Berkeley*, ed. C. B. Martin and D. M. Armstrong, 155–78. Garden City: Anchor/Doubleday.

Frege, G. 1918/1967. "The Thought: A Logical Inquiry." In *Philosophical Logic*, ed. P. F. Strawson. Oxford: Oxford University Press.

Gallagher, S., and D. Zahavi. 2008. *The Phenomenological Mind: An Introduction to Philosophy of Mind and Cognitive Science.* London: Routledge.

Garrett, D. 2003. "Locke on Personal Identity, Consciousness, and 'Fatal Errors'." *Philosophical Topics* 31:95–125.

Gorky, M. 1913–1923/2001. *Autobiography.* Trans. Isidor Schneider. Amsterdam, The Netherlands: Fredonia Books.

Greene, B. 2004. *The Fabric of the Cosmos.* New York: Knopf.

Gurwitsch, A. 1941. "A Non-egological Conception of Consciousness." *Philosophy and Phenomenological Research* 1:325–38.

Husserl, E. 1921–1928/1973. *Zur Phänomenologie der Intersubjektivität. Texte aus dem Nachlass. Zweiter Teil: 1921–8.* The Hague: Martinus Nijhoff.

James, H. 1864–1915/1999. *Henry James: A Life in Letters*, ed. P. Horne. London: Penguin.

Johnston, M. 2010. *Surviving Death.* Princeton, NJ: Princeton University Press.

Kant, I. 1787/1933. Preface to *Critique of Pure Reason.* 2nd ed. Trans. N. Kemp Smith. London: Macmillan.

Kant, I. 1790/1973. "On a Discovery." In *The Kant-Eberhard Controversy.* Trans. H. Allison. Baltimore, MD: Johns Hopkins University Press.

Kierkegaard, S. 1850/1991. *Practice in Christianity.* Trans. H. V. Hong and E. H. Hong. Princeton, NJ: Princeton University Press.

King, P. 1830. *The Life of John Locke.* 2nd ed. London.

Law, E. 1769/1823. *A Defence of Mr. Locke's Opinion Concerning Personal Identity. In Answer to the First Part of a late Essay on that Subject.* In *The Works of John Locke.* Vol. 3. London: T. Tegg.

Lee, H. 1702/1984. *Anti-Scepticism: Or, Notes upon each Chapter of Mr. Locke's Essay concerning Human Understanding.* New York: Garland.

Leibniz, G. 1686/1988. *Discourse on Metaphysics.* Trans. R. Martin, D. Niall, and S. Brown. Manchester: Manchester University Press.

Leibniz, G. 1687/1967. "Letter to Arnauld, 9 October 1687." In *The Leibniz-Arnauld Correspondence*, ed. and trans. H. T. Mason. Manchester: Manchester University Press.

Leibniz, G. c. 1704/1996. *New Essays on Human Understanding.* Ed. and trans. J. Bennett and P. Remnant. Cambridge: Cambridge University Press.

Locke, J. 1689–1700/1975. *An Essay concerning Human Understanding.* Ed. P. Nidditch. Oxford: Clarendon Press.

Locke, J. 1695/2000. *The Reasonableness of Christianity, as delivered in the Scriptures.* Ed. J. C. Higgins-Biddle. Oxford: Clarendon Press.

Locke, J. 1823. *The Works of John Locke.* 10 vols. London: T. Tegg.

Mackie, J. L. 1976. *Problems from Locke.* Oxford: Clarendon Press.

Martin, R., and J. Barresi. 2006. *The Rise and Fall of Soul and Self: An Intellectual History of Personal Identity.* New York: Columbia University Press.

Mauss, M. 1938/1985. "A Category of the Human Mind: the Notion of Person, the Notion of Self." In *The Category of the Person*, ed. M. Carrithers, S. Collins, and S. Lukes. Cambridge: Cambridge University Press.

Milton, J. 1671/2008. *Paradise Lost: and Paradise Regained.* London: Vintage.

Nuovo, V. 2002. *John Locke, Writings on Religion.* Oxford University Press.

Overton, R. 1644. *Mans Mortalitie.* Amsterdam: John Canne.

Overton, R. 1655. *Man wholly Mortal.* London.

Parfit, D. 1984. *Reasons and Persons.* Oxford: Clarendon Press.

Perry, J., ed. 1975. *Personal Identity.* Berkeley: University of California Press.

Perry, J.J. 1979. "The Problem of the Essential Indexical." In *Self-Knowledge*, ed. A.-Q.A. Cassam. Oxford: Oxford University Press.

Priestley, J. 1777/1818. *Disquisitions Relating to Matter and Spirit.* In *The Theological and Miscellaneous Works of Joseph Priestley.* Vol. 3. Ed. J. T. Rutt. London.

Pufendorf, S. von. 1672. *De jure naturae et gentium.* Lund.

Raine, K. 1975. *The Land Unknown.* New York: George Braziller.

Reid, T. 1764/2000. *An Inquiry into the Human Mind*, ed. D. Brookes. Edinburgh: Edinburgh University Press.

Reid, T. 1785/2002. *Essays on the Intellectual Powers of Man*, ed. D. Brookes. Edinburgh: Edinburgh University Press.

Schechtman, M. 1996. *The Constitution of Selves*. Ithaca, NY: Cornell University Press.

Sherlock, W. 1690. *A Vindication of the Doctrine of the holy and Ever Blessed Trinity*. London.

Shoemaker, S. 1970. "Persons and Their Pasts." *American Philosophical Quarterly* 7:269–85.

South, R. 1693. *Animadversions upon Dr. Sherlock's Book Entituled A Vindication of the Holy and Ever Blessed Trinity*. London.

Stephens, J. 1996. "Edmund Law and his Circle at Cambridge: Some Philosophical Activity of the 1730s." In *The Philosophical Canon in the 17th and 18th Centuries*, ed. G.A.J. Rogers and S. Tomaselli, 163–73. Rochester, NY: University of Rochester Press.

Stokes, P. 2008. "Locke, Kierkegaard and the Phenomenology of Personal Identity." *International Journal of Philosophical Studies* 16: 645–672.

Strawson, G. 1994. *Mental Reality*. Cambridge, MA: MIT Press.

Strawson, G. 1997/1999a. "'The Self.'" In *Models of the Self*, ed. S. Gallagher and J. Shear. Thorverton: Imprint Academic.

Strawson, G. 1999b. "The Self and the Sesmet." *Journal of Consciousness Studies* 6:99–135.

Strawson, G. 1999c. "Self, Body and Experience." *Proceedings of the Aristotelian Society* 103:227–56.

Strawson, G. 2004/2005. "Against Narrativity." In *The Self?* ed. G. Strawson. Oxford: Blackwell.

Strawson, G. 2008. "The Identity of the Categorical and the Dispositional." *Analysis* 68:271–82.

Strawson, G. 2009. *Selves: An Essay in Revisionary Metaphysics*. Oxford: Oxford University Press.

Strawson, G. 2012. "*I* and I: Immunity to Error Through Misidentification of the Subject." In *Immunity to Error Through Misidentification: New Essays*, ed. S. Prosser and F. Recanati. Cambridge: Cambridge University Press.

Taylor, C. 1989. *Sources of the Self*. Cambridge: Cambridge University Press.

Thiel, U. 1998. "Personal Identity." In *The Cambridge History of Seventeenth-Century Philosophy*. Vol 1. Ed. M. R. Ayers and D. Garber. Cambridge: Cambridge University Press.

Thiel, U. 2011. *The Early Modern Subject: Self-Consciousness and Personal Identity in Eighteenth-Century Philosophy*. Oxford: Oxford University Press.

Uzgalis, W. 1990. "Relative Identity and Locke's Principle of Individuation." *History of Philosophy Quarterly* 7:283–97.

Velleman, D. 2006. "The Self as Narrator." *Self to Self*. Cambridge: Cambridge University Press.

Wearing, D. 2005. *Forever Today*. New York: Doubleday.

Yablo, S. 1990. "The Real Distinction Between Mind and Body." *Canadian Journal of Philosophy* 16:149–201.

Yolton, J. 1951. "Locke's Unpublished Marginal Replies to John Sergeant." *Journal of the History of Ideas* 12:528–59.

Zahavi, D. 2006. *Subjectivity and Selfhood: Investigating the First-Person Perspective.* Cambridge, MA: MIT Press.

Index

This index does not cite every occurrence of every listed name, term or topic. Page numbers in bold indicate the place at which an entry is introduced or defined, or the main place at which it is discussed.